The words crawled slowly
across the great electric sign...

.... TRUMAN ANNOUNCES ....
.... JAPANESE SURRENDER ....

And on Times Square, at the crossroads of America, two million cheered, embraced, wept.

They gathered here beneath the landmark sign, bound by a common emotion they would never know again.

And high atop the Hotel Astor one man watched the throng with cold, Teutonic eyes, knowing that in moments he would turn their joy to shrieking chaos.

In one clenched hand he held the black device,
And in his mind he held the hatred...
The memory of Dresden...
The image of a girl who died.

This was the day he had waited for...

August 14, 1945

V-J DAY

V-J DAY

ALAN FIELDS

A DELL BOOK

For The Mate and Crew
of the Unicorn

Published by
Dell Publishing Co., Inc.
1 Dag Hammarskjold Plaza
New York, New York 10017

Copyright © 1978 by Alan Fields

All rights reserved. No part of this book may be reproduced or transmitted in any form or by any means, electronic or mechanical, including photocopying, recording or by any information storage and retrieval system, without the written permission of the Publisher, except where permitted by law.

Dell ® TM 681510, Dell Publishing Co., Inc.

ISBN: 0-440-19250-1

Printed in the United States of America

First printing—August 1978

> "Forgive us our trespasses
> as we forgive those
> who trespass against us..."

PROGLOGUE :::::::::::::::::::

The tall, broad-shouldered man came striding briskly along West Forty-seventh Street toward Times Square. The heels of his heavy work shoes sounded on the nearly deserted pavement and echoed in empty doorways. He wore neatly laundered and pressed work clothes of green cotton twill, and he carried a black metal lunch pail. A baseball cap was set squarely on his head. His hair was light blond and his eyes a pale, washed-out blue.

Despite the simple, unremarkable clothing, there was an almost military air about him. It might have been his gait: strong, carefully measured, vigorous. It could have been the coldness of his eyes. They were exceptional eyes, lacking light. Perhaps it was simply the erectness with which he carried himself, the discipline of his gaze. He was a man who knew just where he was going and why he was going there. He seemed to have no time whatever for the peculiar beauty of Manhattan at dawn, nor for the occasional New Yorkers he met along the street in those magic moments as the sun rose. He didn't scan the buildings and alleys around him, washed with the rosy glow of the dawn. He had no eyes for the city's towers, gilded in the light of a new day.

New York City pleased him only with its impersonality. Here, on Manhattan Island, he was able to be nearly anonymous. It allowed him to draw a kind of magic circle of privacy around himself and his activities. It was a city which permitted him to play the solitary among its millions, bearing his own plans, his own thoughts.

New York gave him a feeling of security. He would not be bothered here. He had become convinced over the past three years that no one would interfere with him . . . especially now that the whole war had ground to a halt.

He became aware of a dirty-gray pigeon struggling on the sidewalk in front of him. The creature seemed to have fallen from a nearby building or from flight, and one of its wings was obviously broken. The tall man stopped for a moment and looked down at the frantic bird. It distressed him to see the wretched creature in such a state. He sighed. Then without hesitation, he raised a booted foot and stepped down hard on the ribcage of the agonized animal. One could hear the crack of bones and cartilage beneath his foot.

He had put the pigeon out of her misery. He saw little value in extended suffering. In his view pain, when it had to be suffered at all, should be terminated in as short a time as possible. For an instant the image of a woman, her hair on fire, blazed brightly in his imagination. Quickly he extinguished the vision. He didn't turn back to look at the dead bird. He knew he had killed it. Within seconds, he had pushed both images from his mind. He was not a man for looking back, and there was only one burden of sentiment he still allowed himself.

A solitary pedestrian, he crossed Sixth Avenue. Though the broad street was nearly empty of traffic, he crossed carefully, waiting for the light to turn green, alert for the sound of approaching cars. It would have made no sense at all to be run down on that particular day, Tuesday, August 14, 1945. He had a destiny to work out which would require his survival just a little bit longer.

He kept his mind blank. It was important for him to use these early morning walks as a means of psychic regeneration as well as physical exercise. It was excellent mental hygiene to scrub the mind as blank as possible, an exercise that enabled him to renew himself for the trying task at hand.

He rounded the corner into Times Square, which was boarded up and still nearly deserted. The Times Square merchants had nailed plywood panels over their windows on the previous Friday, in prudent anticipation of the great, excited, jubilant masses expected to converge on the square to celebrate the end of the war. On Sunday a premature celebration had in fact broken out, and the unpainted plywood sheets had saved most of the area's plate glass and window-displayed merchandise.

Times Square at the moment of dawn was a beautiful place, despite the raw plywood that gave it the unfamiliar aspect of a bullring. The new light of the day was beginning to catch the very tallest buildings, highlighting them while the street level was still touched with indigo shadows. The street, still wet from the passing of the sanitation trucks, had an insistent, damp odor, somehow springlike.

The familiar view of Times Square reminded him of a room decorated for Christmas with everything in place, the tree ornaments turned off. Waiting. The great image of the billboard character who blows smoke rings seemed to be holding his breath. A gigantic replica of the Statue of Liberty, several stories tall, torch temporarily extinguished, loomed like some sleepwalking stranger. The scaffolding on the square's incredible neon signs was ominously beautiful in front of a streaky, pink sky. The statue of Father Duffy stood his regular vigil, staring southward at the Times Tower's illuminated electric sign.

Slowing his pace for an instant, the tall man stopped before a prone figure on the sidewalk, a drunk, lying in a sleepy stupor, vomit on his clothes, a nearly empty bottle of cheap wine clutched in his hand. Disgusting, he thought. He stepped over the drunk. His face remained impassive.

V-J DAY : : 11

As the sun continued to rise, the man approached his place of employment. The Hotel Astor, unlike most of the buildings in New York, interested him greatly. The old structure had a certain style, an air of fascinating dignity.

The Astor, standing tall on the Seventh Avenue side of the square between Forty-fourth and Forty-fifth Streets, was a massive pseudo-Renaissance structure in brick and limestone, with a formidable ornate mansard of green slate and corroded copper. The great hotel loomed like an imperial presence, facing eastward over Times Square.

The broad intersection was beginning to come to life. Men and women emerged blinking from the subways. More of the city's great fleet of taxicabs began to venture through the square. The voices of news vendors could be heard, huckstering the world's woes. The great metropolis was stretching and coming to an excited state of wakefulness, on what could be the long-awaited day of victory. The tall man knew that by seven or eight o'clock in the evening, the crowds would be immense, eager to celebrate.

The electric signboard on the Times Tower, a brilliant banner of moving light high above the street, spoke eloquently of the day just dawned:

AMERICAN B-29 BOMBERS FROM GUAM AGAIN HAMMER THE JAPANESE HOMELAND . . . . PRESSURE MOUNTS FOR SURRENDER . . . .

12 : : V-J DAY

For twenty-five years the great, illuminated sign hung high on the Times Tower had flashed the news of the world to New Yorkers, and to American and other travelers passing through. Little did eleven-year-old Iphigene Bertha Ochs realize in 1904, when she struck the cornerstone for her father's new Times Tower the prescribed three taps with her symbolic silver trowel, that she was placing the first stone of what would ultimately become America's ceremonial front porch. And that building's gleaming girdle of lights—the electric sign—became the centerpiece for that gala place where the nation's attention often focused in times of trial, at moments of joy.

As the tall man stood there, watching the moving letters in light, his mouth became a grim slash across the bottom half of his strong, prominently boned face. Again, American bombs were raining death.

Once again, the electric sign sent a new message flashing around the Times Tower.

ANTICIPATION GROWS NATIONWIDE FOR WORD OF JAPANESE SURRENDER . . . . EXPECTED TO BE MERE HOURS AWAY . . . .

The tall man smiled grimly.

CHAPTER ONE

The dream startled her awake. She sat bolt upright in the unfamiliar hotel bed. It wasn't precisely a nightmare, but Diana Remington had been jolted to consciousness by its vividness.

She had been witnessing a struggle in which the violent details had been so strong and realistic that the Astor suite around her seemed a pale, insipid imitation of reality. She couldn't tell whether the wild dream had been a subconscious replay of one of Dan Baron's movies, or some mysterious insight into the real-life war experiences Dan had been undergoing in Europe. Whatever the dream had been, Dan had inspired it with that same star quality which made him a box-office hero and so exciting a man.

In the dream, she could remember, there was a group of German officers in what seemed to be a ruined farmhouse. There was an elderly man lying on a sagging bedspring, with his arms trussed behind him. In a strange way he looked like the director, John Ford, for whom both she and Dan had often worked. Even more disturbing, though, was a girl, bound to a chair, who looked distressingly like Dan's dead wife, Barbara.

"We aren't going to tell you anything," the woman had shouted. "You can do what you want with me."

The German officer nearest the chair to which the woman was tied struck her across the face. Diana could see the welt on her cheek. There was a tiny trickle of blood at the corner of the girl's mouth.

Then Diana had caught a glimpse of Dan's tough, determined face at the window. It was like a movie close-up. There were gunshots and the Nazi officer collapsed, blood spurting from a hideous wound in his throat.

Dan, dressed in fatigues, a tommy gun held out in front of him, catapulted through the wrecked window frame, followed by a half-dozen American soldiers, faces smeared with black makeup. More entered through the door. There was gunfire. Diana remembered flinching, for fear that Dan would be hit.

His face was so fierce, his blue eyes so coldly contemptuous of the cowering Germans and his fallen foe, that in the dream he had frightened her. He was a study in concentrated fury, and she had cowered from him, from that terrible intensity. Then, suddenly, he had become again the Dan Baron she knew.

"Don't be afraid," he said in a low, calm voice in the dream, standing over the still-bleeding corpse of the officer he'd shot. "Everything's gonna be all right." He had a way of making people believe things like that.

He had grinned that strangely appealing grin of his and said, "Let's get outa here."

But he had not been speaking to her. Diana had felt a pang of jealousy that it wasn't Diana Remington playing the part of the rescued girl in the dream film. The ghost of Barbara Baron had competed with her long enough.

The clock on the hotel night table said 7:03.

It was an ungodly hour for her to be awake. She was a night person. But there'd be no sleeping now. Dan was coming home today. She was tingling with excitement, nerves, anticipation. She got up and moved over to the windows looking down on Times Square. She couldn't remember having seen it at this time of day before.

She smiled ruefully. Life had changed in so many ways since she first lost her heart to Dan Baron. She looked back at the clock on the table and wondered how long it would be till he'd be knocking at the door.

Damn! Let it be soon!

As if terrorized by the sun's abrupt ascent out of the sea, the black gelding broke into a wild gallop down the beach. Clinging desperately to everything he could grab, leaning forward in the saddle, already wincing from the pain of the hard landing he knew he'd take, Seaman Claude Libby, United States Coast Guard, shouted madly in panic, though there was no one to hear him on the lonely, deserted beach near Long Island's Orient Point.

The horse veered unaccountably from the hard-packed wet sand nearest the surf onto the dry sand farther up the beach. The sudden deceleration betrayed the youthful beach patrolman, and Libby, with singular grace for so wretched a rider, flew out over the horse's right front quarter to land face first in the sand. The horse kept running for a short distance up the beach and then slowed, made a half-circle, and seemed to glance gleefully back at its vanquished rider.

For a few seconds Libby lay still, too angry and exasperated to move. His pride stung even more than the flesh of his face and hands. He had torn through his pants at both knees.

"Son of a bitch," he muttered into the sand, a good bit of which was in his mouth. He spat it out and wiped his mouth against his sleeve.

Finally, he moved each of his limbs experimentally. He was intact, though every muscle ached from the shock of the hard landing. With difficulty he rose to his feet. Addressing the beast who now stood some two hundred feet away, in a deceptively pastoral pose, he spoke with misleading calmness.

"All right, you devil! You won another battle. But if it takes me the last day o' my life, I'm gonna win the war—*our* war!"

For Claude Libby, this was a long, threatening speech, a full-scale diatribe. He was known both at home Down East and in the U.S. Coast Guard as a man of few words. Lately a good proportion of those words were addressed to Tom Collins, the gelding of dubious value he had been assigned. It wasn't difficult to see why someone had found it no sacrifice to contribute Tom Collins to an unsuspecting government. It was difficult only to see why the helpful Coast Guard deserved to be given so flawed a gift.

Libby, a lobsterman back home in Damariscotta, Maine, had joined the Coast Guard because he was a man of the sea, an experienced handler of small boats. Then some brilliant admiral had conceived the farfetched notion of mounting Coast Guard beach patrolmen on horseback so they could cover more ground in less time. To Libby's chagrin, he'd found himself struggling without success at becoming a cavalryman.

As he turned to survey the place of his sudden downfall, Libby became aware of something strange. In the long skid he'd made in the sand, he'd involuntarily unearthed something. Painfully, he walked over to investigate.

"What the hell?" he said aloud. He went down on his skinned knees, ignoring the pain, and began scraping the sand away with his hands. It seemed to be a big plastic bag buried in the sand. The deeper he dug, the more he unearthed. There were several bags. Once he'd dug out the first one and opened it, he knew exactly what he'd come up with. The bag contained a set of German navy fatigues and a German inflatable life preserver. There were three more packages and buried beneath them, an inflatable boat and two sets of collapsible oars.

What a find!

Libby was excited. How did they get here? It must have been from a U-boat, he concluded. How long has this stuff been here? Even though the Germans have surrendered, could they be smuggling war criminals ashore? Rudolf Hess had parachuted into England. What if Goering or Hitler himself had landed here? Then too, there might have been more saboteurs than we suspected in 1942. Two teams had been captured, and imprisoned or executed, three years back—eight men in all. Maybe there had been more. Or could this have something to do with all the German prisoners transferred to Long Island last week? Hundreds had been sent to Suffolk County from Pine Camp in upstate New York to help the potato farmers. Maybe all this material was buried here for some sort of escape attempt.

He didn't know the answers to any of the questions that raced through his mind, but he knew one thing for sure: Uncle Sam was going to get his money's worth out of Claude Ephraim Libby. That's the way it should read on the citation. Claude Ephraim Libby III. It may be late in the war, he conceded, but what the hell! It was never too late to be a hero.

Having noticed the name tag PLANCK sewn onto the pair of coveralls he'd opened up, Libby mouthed a warning to the fatigues' owner wherever he might be. "We're gonna get you, Herr

Planck. We're gonna catch up with you no matter how hard you wiggle."

That said, Libby, carrying one bag of fatigues along with him as evidence, limped off in pursuit of the decoration he'd long dreamed of bringing back to Damariscotta. Tom Collins, the horse, followed at a discreet distance.

The cop was sick to his stomach. He didn't lose his breakfast, but he came so close to doing so that twice a cold sweat had broken out on his forehead. He was surprised at himself for feeling that way. He was no dumb rookie. In twenty-seven years as a cop, both in the city and now here in Nassau County, he'd seen it all. He had gathered up the dead after bloody auto accidents. He'd surveyed the horrors left in the wake of murder—grotesque relics of man's cruelest inhumanities to his fellow man. But somehow here in the antiseptic confines of the hospital, against clean white sheets, the sight of so cruel a caricature of a living human being struggling to speak had sent him twice into the corridor to compose himself.

"Are you all right now, officer?" the nurse, a young nun, asked him. She was ready to lend him smelling salts again.

"Think I'm doing okay now, sister," he replied, disliking the idea of admitting his distress to this young, good-looking girl, even if she did wear the uniform of the church. She seemed to be handling herself so well.

20 : : *V-J DAY*

"She's still trying to say the same thing. She's been saying it over and over again."

The cop shook his head despairingly. "It seems there's no way we're gonna figure it out, sister. There's no way in the world we're gonna understand her."

So severe was the fire's damage, there was no possibility for recovery. The critically burned woman could not speak normally. Nor was there any way for her to write out whatever it was she wanted so badly to say. Both hands were charred off at the wrist.

Again, the unnerving sound came from the seared throat. "Unnnnnnchay . . . Unnnnnnchay . . . eyrrrr!"

The fire at Drummond Air's Plant Six had been a general-alarm nightmare. By the time the first companies had arrived, the whole place was a maelstrom of flame shooting nearly a hundred feet in the air. Many of the workers never had a chance. They were literally incinerated at their work benches. The woman, Loretta Grenon, thirty-eight, unmarried, winner of several production E's, was the only person pulled alive from the area in which the original fireball had burst.

"Unnnnnnchay . . . Unnnnmnchay . . . Unnnnnnchay . . . eyrrrrr . . . oh, eyrrrrr!"

"We're trying hard to understand you, miss," the cop said gently. He wondered whether she could even make out what he was saying to her. God knows, the pain must have been unbearable. Had it been his wife or one of his daughters lying there, he would have taken out his service revolver, no question about it.

"Unnnnnnchay!"

He wished to hell she'd stop trying. He wished with all his heart the poor woman would die. There was no way she'd survive as she was. There was no way she'd function again as a whole person. And there was no way they'd get information out of her. Why couldn't they just let the poor thing die in peace? Let the crime lab boys do their thing in the ashes of the plant. Let the FBI hotshots earn their money. But for God's sake, let this poor woman alone.

"Has she had the priest, sister?"

The nun didn't seem to hear him. It was as though she were very carefully considering some deep line of thought.

"Sister?"

"I'm sorry," the nun said, slightly embarrassed. "I was thinking about what she's been trying to tell us."

"I asked if the priest had been by to see her."

"Oh yes," the sister assured him. "She's been given the last rites."

"Maybe I ought to leave, sister. There's nothing to be gained by tormenting her like this. There's little likelihood she'll be able to tell us anything at all."

"Could she be trying to say 'lunch pail'?" the nun ventured.

"Lunch pail? Why would she say something like that? *Lunch pail?*"

"With those burns on her mouth, there are certain sounds she simply can't make. I've been sitting here trying to make substitutions," the young sister explained. "It sounds to me like that's what she's trying to say . . . 'lunch pail, fire'."

"Maybe," the cop allowed, trying to sound neither skeptical nor condescending. "Maybe she's worried about her lunch pail. Sometimes, when I used to work on the ambulance, accident victims would ask me to go back and pick up the darndest things for them—things they left behind at the scene."

"It was just an idea," the nun admitted.

The cop walked back over, close to the bed. "It's all right, miss," he said gently. "We'll see if we can find it for you."

"Eyrrrrr!"

Loretta Grenon's agony was rendered even more unbearable by the knowledge that she'd come so close to being understood and still failed to convey her meaning. Betrayed by the very man she'd learned to love. Killed by a horrible, devastating fire. Unable to tell anyone what had happened. If she could only tell them about the lunch pail. He had packed her lunch for her before he left to go back to the city. It was out of that old lunch pail that the fire had burst. If she could only manage to tell them!

She knew death was close. She knew also that dying was the only thing left to her. She could sense the degree of her disfigurement. She could see it on the policeman's face. Loretta Grenon had never been a good-looking woman, but she did manage to have male friends.

She didn't, however, think of those men now—not even Richard. Instead she thought of her sailor brother, Jerry, due home any day now from the war. She hadn't heard from him for a long time. How would he manage without her? He was so vulnerable.

And then she could think no longer. It was happening to her. There was so much light. Not fire, but light. She was bathed in it, absorbed in it. It was so cool.

"She's gone," the nun whispered.

"Thank God," said the thick-bodied, middle-aged cop. "Thank God it's all over."

The nun bowed her head to pray as the cop left.

CHAPTER TWO

"Would you just take a good look at that goddamn Jap waltzin' outa here?" asked the night clerk of the cashier. "You'd think the little bastard owned New York."

"How come he's wearin' *our* uniform?" the cashier asked. She knew very little about things of a military nature—the war.

"Guess they'll do anything for money, those Jap people."

"But they're treacherous, ain't they?"

"*Real* treacherous," the night clerk said. "Look at Pearl Harbor. See what they done there?"

"Kinda makes you sick, don't it? An American uniform on a little yellow Jap."

"Wouldn't have let him in here 'cept I thought he might be a Chink. Then when he signed the register 'Nakamura' I could tell he was pure Japanese. But by then it was too late to do anything about it."

"Whose side they on?"

"Who?"

"The Chinks."

"Guess they're on ours," the clerk said, still watching the Japanese soldier through the window. "Least they didn't bomb Pearl Harbor."

The object of their discussion stood outside, on the curb, trying to get his bearings. Sergeant George W. Nakamura, wearing the red, white, and blue Liberty Torch patch of the 442nd Regimental Combat Team, U.S. Army, which was made up entirely of American soldiers of Japanese extraction, had spent the night in the Piccadilly Hotel. He was wide awake and ready for the adventures morning would offer.

The humid weather of the last several days hadn't made itself felt yet on the city. It was still quite cool in the street. But he didn't give a particular damn about the weather. Nakamura was exultant just about being back in the good old U.S.A., and he felt great because this week he had a chance to see New York, something he'd dreamed about since he was a kid.

His father, in one of his frequent letters from the resettlement camp in Idaho, had urged the young soldier to stay out of New York City. His father seemed to feel that he'd be risking a great deal in an already dangerous environment. "You are Japanese, George. No matter how American you may feel, in point of fact, the eye sees you and identifies you as Japanese."

George knew what his father meant, but on the other hand, he was not the man to hide away like a criminal. A man who had survived the battle at Monte Cassino, he told his father in a carefully worded reply, could surely survive six days of rest and recreation in Manhattan.

Of course, Nakamura hadn't survived Monte Cassino all that well. He was functioning at the moment on a single kidney and he'd wear a back brace for the rest of his life. A piece of German shrapnel had done terrible things to Nakamura's lower back.

Now here he was in the world's most exciting city. He was here to enjoy himself. He wasn't about to tie himself down as a civilian without having done the big town at least once.

"Hurry home to me," Helen Toshira had said in every letter from the camp. She and her whole family were living in the same wooden barracks with Nakamura's parents and sisters. "I can hardly wait to see you again," she had written.

"Of course, I'll hurry," George had written back. And he fully intended to get back to the coast to marry Helen—even in the damned resettlement camp if he had to. But there was time. He felt he'd earned a few days of rest and recreation in the Big Apple. A little burlesque. Some good booze and fancy food. Then he'd try to get theater tickets. Maybe he could get in to see *Harvey* or *Oklahoma!* Back at Bakersfield High, he'd always been interested in dramatics. Here was a chance to see it all big time. He'd also take in a couple of ball games. The Giants and the Dodgers were both playing home stands.

George Nakamura, holder of the Purple Heart

and the Silver Star, walked up Shubert Alley, engrossed in his own plans and dreams, unaware he was under hostile observation.

"Look at that little bastard," a tall, heavyset man said thickly to his buddies. He was drunk. It wasn't one of those modest "excuse me" drunks when someone accidentally takes a couple too many. He and his shipmates had been on a bender for the last three days and he was sick, sour-breathed, mean drunk—spoiling for a good fight. The four men with him were not in much better shape. "Look at them slanty eyes."

"Good day for it," another agreed. "It's a good day to put it to a stinkin' Jap!"

All five of them were merchant sailors. Three had survived torpedoings. All five had lost shipmates, relatives. All five hated Japs and Krauts—especially Japs.

"I'm gonna tear that little prick's ears off," said a third sailor.

"Why not, for Crissakes?" another of them said. He was too far gone to throw effective punches, but he was sober enough to goad his fellows on. "Let's go get the Jap bastard!"

Nakamura turned at the sound of their voices. Angry sounds. He should have read their intentions. They made no secret of what they were up to. But on the other hand, there was no reason to suspect trouble. He wore the uniform of his country. He was *in* his own country for the first time in over two years. He kept walking.

"Hey, Tojo!" one of the sailors yelled at him, just as he emerged from Shubert Alley onto Forty-fourth Street.

Nakamura didn't answer.

"Hey, you, playing soldier in the wrong suit! Pull your head outa your ass, Jap!" another sailor jeered. "Can't you understand English?"

The only intelligent thing to do was to ignore them. That's what people had always said about drunks. Maybe they'd get tired of it and get lost.

They were on him fast. There was no bullshit either about making it a fair fight. They wanted his ass and Nakamura made up his mind right then that he'd make them work for it.

The first assailant piled on the sergeant's back, grabbing the much smaller man in a bear hug, while the other four jockeyed for position in front, eager to land their own blows. Fortunately for Nakamura, the first sailor held onto him too high, almost around the shoulders. The combat veteran threw the larger man headfirst over him, where he hit the pavement with a jarring thud.

Another sailor stuck the palm of his hand on Nakamura's chest and pushed him up against the building, pinning him there with his right hand while cocking the left fist back to the shoulder. But before he could throw the punch, Nakamura had snapped his wrist and kicked him in the jaw with a perfectly executed judo move. He went down like a sack of grain.

Despite Nakamura's courage, it didn't last. There were five of them and they were very strong.

The next thing the soldier knew, he was being slammed from three different directions and fireworks were going off inside his head. He stood up and fought as long and as hard as he could, managing to drop another man with a sharp kick to the groin. He knew that none of them got off easy. He'd put marks on every one of them.

He went down and they worked him over thoroughly, kicking him. He was aware of spitting out several teeth. He was aware too of gagging on a mouthful of his own blood. Then he blacked out.

A police whistle shrilled from the corner of Seventh Avenue. A flashbulb popped. The photographer was a small, dark man who had just come out of the Astor. A tall blond man with a lunch pail stood watching the whole scene with a peculiar grimace, almost a smile, on his face.

The five sailors took off. At least two of them looked injured. One was clutching his side and limping.

"What the hell happened here?" the cop demanded.

"What's it look like?" asked the photographer. "They just beat the crap out of this soldier. Looks like he's out cold."

The witness with the lunch pail started to leave, but a second policeman grabbed him by the shoulder.

"Where you think you're going?"

For a second there was a grim look in the man's eyes—a look of desperation and fear.

"To work," he said.

"I need your name. You're a witness."

The fearful look disappeared.

The police officer took the man's name and the photographer's and wrote them down after taking a quick look at the victim. Nakamura was semiconscious now.

"Don't you think you'd better get an ambulance?" the photographer asked.

"He ain't goin' anywhere," the first cop said, looking at the bloodied sergeant on the pavement. "He'll keep."

The photographer said nothing. He just took a picture of the policeman, the victim, the witness with the lunch pail. As he snapped the shutter, the blond man's hand went up to shield his face.

"What the hell you doin'?" a cop asked.

"Want to be in *Life* magazine?" The photographer was wearing a grim smile.

"Sure," the officer said. He adjusted his uniform blouse.

"*After* you call the ambulance," said the photographer.

The cop went to call assistance while the other squatted next to the moaning victim.

A small crowd began to gather—those who would have heedlessly passed just moments before.

"How did the night go?" asked the commissioner.

"Almost routine," said the chief inspector. "A few too many drunken GIs, but nothing flashy."

"You set for today?"

"Valentine, you know we're *always* set down here."

"Don't give me that. *He's* already out poking around." The commissioner was, of course, talking about His Honor the mayor.

"It's not seven o'clock yet," the line officer objected.

Commissioner Valentine's chuckle came clearly through the telephone. "Since when does that stop our beloved Fiorello? Whenever trouble threatens, a problem erupts, our Little Flower blooms."

"We're ready for anything, sir."

"All right. I'll take your word for it. What about the crowds?"

"They're gonna be record breakers. And they'll be on the streets all night long, if this turns out to be the big day. Times Square's gonna be a real madhouse."

"How many? Can you estimate it?"

"Not yet. But I'll bet you, sir, off the cuff, it'll reach a million easy."

"A million?" The commissioner chuckled again. "Well, you called that LaMotta fight pretty good."

"That I did, sir," said the chief inspector. "That guy Pescora was a bum."

"You got ambulances on Times Square?"

"Broadway and Fifty-sixth and Broadway and Forty-third. Uptown for Roosevelt Hospital, downtown for Bellevue."

"Good, John."

"Everything's gonna be under control. The mayor's gonna be satisfied."

"I hope so. And I trust you to do everything first class."

"Thank you, sir."

Police Commissioner Lewis J. Valentine put down the phone and raised his second cup of coffee to his lips. There was a lot on his mind. On the other end of the line, Chief Inspector John O'Donnell got back to bracing New York's Finest for what promised to be one hell of a day.

Bill "Red" Bickford worked for the *New York Times* as an electrician. He was one of the three veteran employees who operated the big electric sign on Times Square. Although he wasn't due to go on duty until noon, he was an early riser, who liked lingering over his coffee in the morning, playing around with his shortwave radio. Even though he couldn't understand most of the outlandish tongues that came from the speaker, he loved moving from station to station, from one meter band to another, listening to all those languages, the codes, the jargons, all those millions of words set free in the air.

The Bickfords sat in the cluttered kitchen of their MacDougal Street apartment. "Red," a paunchy man of forty-eight, sat leaning forward at the table, sweat already staining the clean shirt he'd put on for work. Lucy Bickford, an overweight woman with brassy blonde hair, was still in her nightgown.

"Why don't you invite him over here sometime?"

Lucy asked her husband. "You ashamed to introduce me to your friends?"

"He's not the social type. Keeps to himself."

"Maybe it's because nobody asks him."

Bickford said nothing. He was trying to adjust his radio to pick up a very weak signal.

"We could have him over to dinner and invite Polly."

"Listen," he said, getting hold of a very weak, broken transmission. "Doesn't that sound like German to you?"

"You're not paying attention to me," she complained.

"Sounds like somebody's broadcastin' in German. What you think it could be?"

"Maybe he'd like Polly."

Bickford lost the signal. "Damn! I think I was getting Germany. It's amazing they got any stations left on the air."

"I was talkin' about your friend, Peck," she said, refusing to be distracted. "He may never get invited out."

"He gets around," Bickford said, snapping off the radio. "Never see him in New York on weekends. Think he's got some girl stashed outa town."

"I still think it'd be nice havin' him here," Lucy said. Lucy was a pouty person. Never seemed willing to accept anything but her own way. She could crab for hours on end. And, of course, there was always the matter of Polly, her kid sister. She'd never quit trying to hook a new man for Polly.

Polly's husband had died in the first days of the war. Polly wasn't something to excite every man to come along, but Bickford had to admit she'd probably make somebody a good wife again. Somehow, though, he couldn't see her with his friend Richard Peck. Peck had a lot of class.

"You know what?" he asked, trying to get the subject away from Peck and Polly. "I think it'll be today."

"What will?"

"The peace announcement. I have a feeling I'm gonna set the letters for that announcement that the Japs have surrendered. Fred got the German announcement." Red Bickford and his two fellow workers in the fourth-floor sign room enjoyed a friendly competition over major news stories.

For twenty-five years, Bickford had been one of the three electricians assigned to the Times Tower's electric sign. Along with the responsibility for keeping the big sign operating, it was their chore to set the news bulletins, sent over from the editorial offices, into 7½-by-3-inch metal-backed letters, mount them on the endless belt, and then run them over the thirty-nine thousand electric brushes that set off the sign's twenty-two million flashes per hour.

The last couple of big ones Bickford had gotten were bad news: FDR's death back in April and, two Saturdays ago, the story about the B-25 that crashed into the Empire State Building. It was time for some good news.

"Think it'll really come today?" Lucy asked.

"They're on the ropes, Lucy. They're really on the ropes since we dropped them bombs."

"I hope you'll get your wish."

"You comin' down?"

"Where?"

"The square. Don't you want to see it?"

"Not especially."

"What are you gonna do? This is gonna be a historic day!"

Lucy shrugged. "I'm gonna do what I always do."

Bickford stood up and took his lunch bag from the refrigerator.

"I'm gonna get some ironing done and then I'm gonna listen to my programs."

Bickford shook his head despairingly. History was going to be made in the streets today and Lucy was gonna listen to "Stella Dallas" and "Just Plain Bill." How could he have married such a woman?

Henry Mettich wasn't especially proud of his profession, but he was proud of the fact he was so good at it. He had been able to make a decent living for the eight full years since he last got out of jail. He had a few bucks put away. He'd never get rich but he was comfortable. He worked five or six days a week, and almost never got less than a hundred and fifty bucks. He paid no taxes. He could even consider getting married one of these days, soon as he found a nice, honest girl.

The war had been good for him. There were

plenty of working women around who carried money in their handbags. There'd been plenty of drunk GIs too. They were easy to pick. And he was as good at picking pockets as he was at snatching purses. The draft wasn't interested in a convicted felon even if he'd already done his time.

Mettich was a very ordinary-looking man. He blended readily into a crowd. His hair was medium brown and getting a little thin. He had big, innocent-looking eyes and nondescript features. He was slender, with only a slight thickening around the middle to show that he was pushing forty. Most of the time when his victim found his wallet lifted, Mettich was mistaken for an innocent bystander. His glance never wavered. His story never lacked the ring of conviction.

The middle-aged woman he was following at the moment looked like a good prospect. She was an independent working woman by the look of her. Mettich smelled greenbacks. The ideal victim was always carrying an amount worth stealing, but not so much as to be especially vigilant about it. If they had too much, they weren't so easily surprised or overpowered. There'd be quite a few bucks in the bag, and, judging by the way she carried it, it'd be a quick, clean snatch.

He started to make his move, speeding up his pace so as to be just a step or two behind her. Then with a deft grab, he snatched the bag. He ran. He could run very fast. He had run the 440 in track back at Christopher Columbus High.

The woman let out an indignant yell, but made

no serious move to pursue him. She just stood there yelling for help, her eyes darting frantically around her. But there were no would-be rescuers around. Mettich had checked that out before he made his move.

Mettich broke around the corner. No one was in pursuit, so he crossed the street and cut back to a quick jog, until he reached the relative shelter of a subway entrance two blocks down. On the first landing, he reached into the bag and he took out the wallet and change purse, discarding the handbag itself in a wire-mesh trash container. A V-mail letter fell out and blew away.

This was his first hit of the day and it was a healthy one—seventy-six dollars in folding money, two dollars and thirty-three cents in the change purse. A damn fine way to begin the day. He had a peculiar hunch that this would be a very special day for him.

The BMT express pulled into the station and he got on. Still no pursuit. He was away clean. With the stolen wallet secure in an inside jacket pocket, he sat down on a side-facing seat and checked out the people in the car. Mettich was a careful and enthusiastic observer of his fellow human beings.

A group of young girls, high schoolers by their giggles and saddle shoes, came aboard. Several of them were very pretty. He enjoyed looking at their slim, young legs in bobby socks and saddle shoes. One of the girls was especially attractive. There was something about her full lips, the enticing little shadows beneath her eyes. The loose man's white shirt she was wearing failed to hide the proud thrust of her young breasts.

Wouldn't I like to hold that one in my arms and fondle those breasts, Mettich asked himself impatiently. Goddamn! Mettich felt the ache in his loins. Wouldn't this be a day to be young again with the sap rising!

CHAPTER :::::::::::::::::::
::::::::::::::::: THREE

Hundreds of khaki-clad figures lined the rail. Some had been standing there throughout the long night. Others had joined the vigil at three or four in the morning. They were quiet. There was little conversation. Instead, they were peering through the haze, trying their damnedest to make out anything that spoke to them of home. They were coming back among the living. Home was just out there, somewhere in the shadowy haze.

There was a brief murmur of conversation when the Ambrose lightship came rising up out of the sea, and then even more animated reactions as Coney Island appeared in the light of a new day.

Then Sandy Hook was off the port quarter, with other vessels silhouetted in the gray blue beyond. The magnificent playthings of Coney Island's great amusement park off to starboard were stippled rose and gold. Then the ordered ranks of Brooklyn's homes began to pass swiftly abeam. Staten Island loomed cool and green to the west and a kind of excitement began to build. Still they were quiet.

40 : : *V-J DAY*

Suddenly, the shouting began:

"There she is! There she is! Will you look at her standing there, big tits and all!" The paratrooper was waving his arms and jumping up and down.

"Lady goddamn Liberty! There she is! Look at her all green and beautiful risin' outa that mist!"

She was beautiful in her way, so tall and graceful—her green the color of hope, promising new opportunity, renewed and revitalized life. A goddess of a new and brighter day for all of them.

A crazy, joyous scene exploded on the drab steel decks of the U.S.S. *Governor Tawes*. But there were men standing silent and thoughtful too, men with salt tears running down their cheeks, no less moved than those shouting their joy. A young sailor who didn't join in the jubilation on deck seemed just as deeply touched as any man there. One could tell from the rapt expression on his face.

"So there you are," he said softly, as if to himself.

A captain from an airborne unit who was standing near him seemed startled by his words and turned to look briefly at him.

"It's damn fine to see you again," the kid in the navy jumper said, speaking aloud again.

"What?"

The sailor was surprised when the officer challenged him. He was unaware that he had spoken aloud.

"What's that, sir?"

"Just thought you were saying something."

"I guess I was talking to . . ." He was going to say "talking to myself," but he decided to be honest. "I was talking to . . . to . . . to her."

"Oh."

Both men lapsed back into silence, carefully searching their own thoughts.

"She's quite a girl, isn't she, sir?"

"Yes," the officer responded. Perhaps he was a little disappointed to have this very special moment interrupted by the conversation of someone else. But he didn't want to be rough on the kid or seem uninterested.

"She certainly is," he responded to the sailor's evident enthusiasm for the great statue.

"That's my honey," the youngster said with a smile.

"Willin' to share her?"

"Absolutely, sir. There's plenty there for all of us."

The officer marveled at how easy it was to express love for the huge patriotic symbol on this day of return—nothing ridiculous or mawkish about it. Would it always be so?

Now it was easy to see her standing there in the Upper Bay. The slight haze had drifted away. Everything looked clear and very near.

"Ever climb up inside, sir?"

"Never been this close," the captain admitted.

"Not from New York?"

"Hartford, Connecticut."

"Went all the way to the top when I was in junior high school. Damn near died of exertion.

Didn't want to take the elevator. Must be at least a million steps in there. I might have got my name in the paper or even a headline. Thirteen-year-old dies of a coronary in Lady Liberty's belly."

"First page of the *Daily News*."

"Wouldn't make the *Times*."

"Sure it would. The electric sign."

"Hot damn!" said the young sailor. "Would have liked that."

Somehow it pleased Captain Timothy Stait to talk with the youthful sailor. He already missed the kids in his own company. This boy was much the same: the same grin, the same easy enthusiasm.

"Got a girl waiting for you?" the captain asked. If there was one thing the kids in his company had liked talking about, it was the girl friend back home.

"No, sir. Just my sister. She's more like a mother to me."

"No girl friend?"

"Just never had too much to do with them. Sis used to think I was a little too young."

"No girl back in the ETO?"

"Too busy swimmin'."

"What?"

"Lost two ships."

The captain didn't follow up the business of the sinkings. It was something a man'll talk about if he has to—or wants to.

"Maybe you were better off."

"Sir?"

"Without a girl."
"Oh."
"Women can be very fickle."
"What about you, sir?"

The captain was slow to answer. How did he want to put it? Did he want to rave and rant about betrayal or call her names? No. The hell with it. It was time to get on with life, to put all that misery behind him.

"My woman is now someone else's woman," he said flatly.

"A 'Dear John'?"
"On scented stationery."
"That's tough, sir. That's really tough."

"Tough," the kid had said. Stait wondered if the youngster could understand just how tough it really was. He pictured the wind blowing through her dark hair, the way he'd seen her the last time, standing near the window of their room; he could see her small lovely breasts, those wonderful long legs she'd wrap around him. Son of a bitch! He missed her more every time he thought about her. And coming into New York. It wasn't fair. It was as though the magnetism grew stronger the closer he came to her.

"There ought to be . . . to be . . ." the sailor started to say.

"What?"

"I don't know. Maybe a law or something like that. It's just that it seems to be so rotten when you're so far away."

"Contrary to what they say," the captain said, "absence doesn't make the heart grow fonder. Take it from an expert."

What was he giving advice to this kid for? Jesus, he thought with some sadness, we really do take babies out to die in our wars, don't we?

"Your sister meeting you?" he asked the kid.

"No. She works on the Island. Makes parts for fighter planes. She ain't got time to meet me. Hell, she doesn't even know I'm comin' home today."

"You gonna call her?"

"Bet your ass . . . sorry, sir."

"That's okay."

"What about you, sir? You bein' met?"

"I'll call my father."

"He live here in the city?"

"Temporarily."

"What's he do, sir?"

"Puts the heat on factory owners who don't do enough for the war. Helps track down scarce materials. That kind of stuff."

"You must be proud of him."

Captain Tim Stait didn't say anything to that.

"He must be a patriot," the young sailor said. "Like my sister."

"No. Not really."

Stait was more than a little disappointed with himself because he didn't feel like bragging about his father. But how could he call the man a patriot? He knew his father well enough to know that the man doled selflessness out in very small goddamn doses. His father was in it—whatever he was in—for whatever he could get out of it.

He loved him. He understood him. He was an egotistical, lecherous, glory-hungry old bastard.

"You slated to get out, sir?"

"Shit, no. They've already cut my orders for the Pacific theater."

"That's tough, sir."

That was the second time the sailor had told him it was tough. But what the hell! He was a sad goddamn case after all. Where was Kathleen? With whom? Maybe they were both better off.

The magic towers of Manhattan had risen out of the morning haze. The welcome boat with a WAAC band aboard came alongside. The sound of a Glenn Miller arrangement of "Sentimental Journey" overtook Stait's thoughts. He wasn't at all sure it was good to be back. New York could be a cold town, a lonely town. What good was the triumphal homecoming when you return to an empty room? To hell with "Sentimental Journeys."

An ambulance was wailing way down below on Forty-fourth Street. Bobby Noel stuck his head out as far as he dared from the eighth-floor hotel room, but he couldn't manage to see what was happening in the street hundreds of feet below him. He was still in his pajamas and his roommate was still snoring, but he'd already decided that New York was truly the most exciting place in the whole world.

Courtesy of the Manchester *Gazette* of Manchester, New Hampshire, and three other papers located in Philadelphia, Baton Rouge, and Fresno, Bobby Noel and three other newspaper-route carriers had won a fabulous "cultural-educational" week in New York City, the highlight of which would be the presentation of a fifty-dollar war bond to each boy by movie star Diana Remington. Accompanied by an associate editor of the Worcester, Massachusetts, *Star Banner*, the four boys had arrived Monday night at the Hotel Astor.

"Somebody must have got hurt down there in the street," Bobby said to his still-sleeping roommate. "Can't see him from here, but he must be hurt bad." There was no response from the sleeping kid from Philadelphia. Bobby couldn't even remember his name.

Bobby wanted badly to talk to someone. He really wanted to go down to the street where all the excitement was. He wanted to start exploring now. After all, they'd been in New York City nearly thirteen hours and the only thing they'd done besides checking into the hotel was buy some cheap souvenirs at the Hotel Astor drugstore.

Of course, they *had* caught a glimpse of Joe Louis, the heavyweight boxing champion of the whole world, in his soldier uniform. And they'd seen Mr. Fredric March in the lobby. Bobby had gotten his autograph for Miss Gardner, his English teacher. Miss Gardner had once been an actress in summer stock and knew all there was to know about the theater. She had told them about Fredric March and *A Bell for Adano*, the Broadway show he was playing in right then. She seemed to think that Mr. March was even more important and exciting than Diana Remington. But then she was an English teacher—and a woman.

"When can we go out and look around?" Bobby threw back over his shoulder. "You think Mr. Keefe would get sore if we just went down and walked around the neighborhood for a while?"

Still there was no response from the kid from Philadelphia. He wondered if the dumb guy was going to sleep away the whole trip. Bobby had found getting to sleep last night really tough. His mind had been so full of things. And this morning he was so full of anticipation of all the things they were going to see that there'd been no way he could stay in bed. Once he'd heard that siren down below, he was up for good.

Maybe he should go into the next room to see if Keefe was already up. Maybe he was all ready to let them go out or to take them somewhere, but afraid they were still asleep. They only had six days and there were so many things to see. There was a list a mile long!

The party of newspaper-route carriers and their chaperon had three rooms in a row on the eighth floor. The boys were in doubles on either end, with Keefe in a single room in the middle. Bobby Noel went to the door of the adjoining room, prepared to knock. Then he decided it might be better to quietly open the door to see if Keefe was still asleep. There was no sense getting him sore by waking him up.

Quietly, he eased the door open. He was stunned by what he saw. For a second or two, it simply didn't register. Fat old Keefe, all his clothes off, was on his hands and knees bumping up and down on top of a naked woman. Keefe had coarse black hair, matted all over his back and rear end, that made him look like some kind of fat monkey. As Bobby Noel stood there, mouth hanging open, trying to digest what his eyes were telling him, the woman—really a beautiful young girl—moaned loudly in something that sounded halfway between laughter and a shriek of pain. What was happening there on the rumpled bed disturbed Bobby Noel a great deal.

Just then, the girl turned her head and saw the boy standing in the doorway.

"Jesus Christ," she screamed, straightening up so fast that she nearly threw Keefe onto the floor. "I didn't know you had a kid here!"

Keefe looked over at Bobby Noel, confusion rapidly being replaced by anger.

"What do you want?" Keefe shouted.

"I . . . I . . . I came in to . . . to . . ." Bobby could barely manage to get the words out. He was too flustered. His face burned. He knew what they were doing from descriptions he'd overheard at school. He knew all the names for it too, but he'd never seen people actually *doing* it.

"Hey, get the hell out of here," Keefe yelled at him.

By now, the girl was trying in vain to cover herself with a pillow that was too small. Had the boy been less embarrassed, he might have laughed at her losing battle. But he didn't. He simply closed the connecting door as quickly as he could. It closed harder than he intended it to and it woke up the kid from Philly.

"What?" the other boy said, sitting up startled.

Bobby didn't answer him. He just retreated to the open window, the farthest point in the room from the door to Keefe's quarters. He felt kind of sick, somehow betrayed.

"I'm gonna get dressed," he said.

"What's the matter?" the other kid asked. "You look like you seen a ghost."

"I want to go out." Bobby grabbed his clean clothes and went into the bathroom, locking the door behind him.

He dressed hastily, hardly bothering to clean up. He wouldn't wait for Keefe to give him permission to leave the room. He didn't want to see the man at all.

When he came out of the bathroom, the other boy was waiting with his own clothes to go in.

"Hey, what's your name?" the kid from Philly asked. "I didn't get it last night."

"Noel. Bobby Noel." He was glad the other kid had missed his name too.

"I'm Ciccone. Tony."

"Hi."

"You act like there's something bothering you. Is there?"

"I don't want to talk about it now."

Ciccone shrugged and went into the bathroom. Bobby heard him singing in the shower. He didn't recognize the tune. But Bobby didn't feel much like singing. He was too . . . too disgusted. It was disgusting and yet he wanted to see it too. He didn't like all the contradictory feelings it got going inside of him.

So far, he had only one good thing to show from his long-awaited trip to New York City. He picked it up. It was an inexpensive metal reproduction of the Statue of Liberty. He felt like throwing it out the window. Keefe had bought them each a souvenir the night before. Somehow, Bobby Noel didn't want the thing now.

Again, he leaned out of the window. The ambulance was gone, but there were still a lot of people in the street. If he threw the statue out, it'd land on one of the setbacks below him.

"Hey!" Ciccone yelled at him, coming out of the bathroom. "Don't throw that out!"

"Why not?"

"You stupid or somethin'? You could kill somebody."

"With this?"

"Sure. Even a penny from way up here could kill somebody. Cut right through their head like butter."

"Really?"

"And besides, if you don't want it, I'd like it. He gave me a stinkin' New York Giants pennant. You can have that if you want."

V-J DAY : : 51

"I don't want the pennant. I'm a Boston Braves fan."

"Look, I'll buy it from you. What do you want for the statue?"

"You can have it."

Bobby didn't want to talk about what he'd seen. If he talked about it and expressed his dismay, the other guy would probably laugh at him.

"You want to go exploring the hotel?" he asked the other kid.

"Why not?" Ciccone said, grinning. He had real dark skin and black eyes. He looked like a pirate.

"I'll bet there's plenty of neat things right here in the hotel."

Before Keefe emerged from the next room, they had gone to search the hotel—to explore.

Fireman Luke Tarrantino had his nose buried in the rotogravure color comics. He hadn't gotten to them Sunday and here it was Tuesday already. But if he missed the color funnies on the weekend, he would wonder for days how his favorite characters were doing—Tracy, Palooka, all of them. As a result, the guys on the other shift would always save them for him. He was grateful.

He sat in the firehouse now, feet up on the table, mug of steaming coffee on the floor next to his chair. He had the funnies spread wide in front of him.

"Ten—shun!" came the order from the lieutenant in the next room.

What's all the military crap? he wondered.

"Chickenshit!" he muttered aloud from behind the funnies. The lieutenant was a good guy, but now and then he got chickenshit with petty things, as though they were in the goddamn army or something.

Tarrantino heard footsteps. He lowered his paper and to his dismay he was eyeball to eyeball not only with Lieutenant Frank Mullarkey but with Fire Commissioner Walsh, and, if his eyes weren't playing tricks on him, the Little Flower himself, Mayor La Guardia.

He leaped to his feet, nearly breaking a leg in the process. The coffee mug went over.

"Sorry, sir."

He had only seen La Guardia a couple times before. Both times he'd been working and only glimpsed the mayor from a distance, a little guy in a white chief's helmet. Now he was here in the flesh. Tarrantino was amazed how short the mayor was. Yet there was no mistaking La Guardia's power and personal magnetism. The man seemed to be surrounded by an aura of personal force, like some saint wearing a halo. Tarrantino had never met anyone so overpowering before—so altogether electric.

"What's your name, son?" the mayor demanded.

"T—T—Tarrantino, sir. L—L—Luke Tarrantino."

"I'm La Guardia, City Hall."

"Yessir," the fireman said awkwardly. "Recognize you."

"You like the funny papers?" the mayor asked, noticing the color comics on the table. Tarrantino asked himself, what was he up to? Chew his ass for reading comics on the city's time? It couldn't be a firing offense, could it?

"Yessir. I follow the comics pretty close."

La Guardia walked over and picked up the funnies from the table. He glanced through them quickly while the lieutenant and the commissioner stood there watching like he was doing something very important.

"Ever look at the Little King?"

"Yessir. All the time."

The other officers didn't seem to know what was going on. Mullarkey looked stricken, but the commissioner wasn't as easy to read. At one point, Tarrantino thought the man was going to laugh.

"There's a lot of homely wisdom in the comics," the mayor said with great seriousness. "Ever think of that, Tarrantino?"

Tarrantino considered for a moment. He couldn't really come up with a sensible answer. "Not that much, sir," he said. "Just read 'em for the hell of it."

"Got any kids?" the mayor asked.

"Three, and one on the way."

"Good," said the mayor. "You're going to be busy today, Tarrantino."

"Expect so, sir."

"Be careful now," Mr. La Guardia cautioned. "Those kids need their father alive and well."

The next thing the fireman knew, the inspecting party was gone. But Luke Tarrantino still thought about the mayor. Imagine a guy like that having time to read the funnies. The mayor of the whole damn city.

The sad-ass, beat-up C-47 began its approach for a landing. Major Dan Baron had hoped that when they made their final approach to Mitchell Field at Hempstead, Long Island, it would be clear enough to see the Manhattan skyline. As a kid growing up in Jersey City across the Hudson, those same incredible towers had lifted his heart and fired his imagination.

But the weather on this particular Tuesday wasn't that good. The only part of the urban scene Baron caught through the plane's ports on this trip was the sight of the endless ranks of development houses. Like barracks, he thought. It surely wasn't the American dream he'd been risking his neck for during the past two years.

Baron looked away. Then, without warning, terrifying images too well remembered were invading his mind again, the same images he'd been fighting off for the last five years. Now he was seeing it all again—the three strangers, the cliff-top house in Malibu. They'd been skinny-dipping, he and Barbara, in the new pool, on that ill-fated day in 1940.

"What the hell do you guys want?" he'd demanded, startled at the way the three of them just walked in through the pool gate he'd thought was locked. They were rough-looking characters, badly dressed.

"Truck broke down," the tallest of them said.

V-J DAY : : 55

He had a pockmarked face and a beak like a bird. His prominent Adam's apple bobbed up and down when he talked. "Son of a bitch won't turn over."

"You got a phone?" the swarthy one demanded. He hadn't asked. He had demanded. Dan had never lost a single detail of the scene. He remembered the bastard had been sweating profusely. He could see the beads of perspiration on his lip and on his forehead.

"Look," Dan said angrily. "I don't give a goddamn what you want—"

That was as far as he got. The third man must have gotten around behind him. Suddenly, he felt as though the top of his skull had been driven down through his neck. The last thing he remembered as the blackness engulfed him was Barbara calling from the pool, her voice choked with terror.

With a shake of his head, Baron tried to put the rest of the nightmarish memory out of his mind, and claw his way back to the present; he was landing on Long Island now, Tuesday, August 14, 1945. But something inside was driving him through the old terrors again.

She had been calling his name when consciousness returned. They'd lashed his arms behind him and tied him firmly to one of the wrought-iron pillars that supported the roof of the cabana.

"Jesus, Dan! Make them stop! Oh Christ, make them stop!" There was blood on her thighs even then.

They had spread-eagled her on the tiles and the

tall one was standing over her, penis swollen and ready. The swarthy man held a knife against her throat.

Dan roared like a wild beast and strained. He could feel the iron pilaster bend with him, but he couldn't manage to tear himself free.

"Thinks he's in the goddamn movies," sneered the third man, short and powerfully built with close-cropped red hair. "Thinks he's a fuckin' hero." Dan would never lose the memory of that face, those feral eyes, that hateful, contemptuous sneer.

"Why shouldn't we get some of this choice Hollywood ass?" the swarthy one asked as his taller companion pumped savagely on Barbara's prone body. Dan could see her distorted, terrified face, the mass of wet black ringlets against the blue and white tiles, and the way the cords in her tanned neck were tensed with her effort to resist.

She screamed again, her voice hoarse and raw. *"Dan, for Christ's sake!"* It was a plea that had gone ringing through his mind endlessly in the years since.

Then they were dragging her up onto her knees and the red-haired bastard was undoing his fly. Dan leaped once more against his bonds and he felt something give way where the wrought-iron support joined the roof. Barbara cried out again, a choking scream. Then it was the red-haired man screaming as he clutched frantically at his groin, thick blood spurting out between his fingers.

"Cut her," he screamed hysterically at the top of his lungs. *"Cut her!"*

Dan saw the knife blade press Barbara's arched throat and then it sliced her open and the blood—her blood—came and came . . .

"Major!" Someone was shouting at him, shaking his shoulder vigorously. The C-47 was landing at Mitchell. "You all right?"

Baron nodded dumbly.

"You look like you're gonna pass out."

"Airsick," Baron lied.

The weather had been rough most of the way over and to his immense disgust, he'd been miserably sick a couple of times. Further, few military aircraft were built to accommodate Baron's six-foot five-inch heroic frame. He felt uncomfortable in the uniform, still unworthy of it. The memory of the horror at Malibu was still too vivid, too fresh.

Finally he managed to drag his thoughts back to the present. He was coming home. Diana would be waiting for him. All of the other was light years away now, behind him—Barbara, the funeral, the trial, the screaming headlines:

> SCREEN HERO FAILS HIS WIFE IN HER HOUR OF
> NEED BARBARA MADDOCKS RAPED AND MURDERED
> WHILE MATE DAN BARON LOOKS ON HELPLESS

For nearly two years now, he had been overseas, as far away from Malibu as he could get. But no matter how he tried to force it all away from him once and for all, it kept coming back, the nightmare images, the overpowering sense of guilt.

"Dan, there was nothing you could do! There was no way you could help her," friends had told him.

But the excuses they made weren't good enough. He had to try mending the gaping wound in his own conscience.

The prescription would be action. Finally making up his mind to do something about it, since 1943 he'd worn the nondescript clothes of a sailing-ship master in the Adriatic for General "Wild Bill" Donovan and the Office of Strategic Services. Running guns to Yugoslav partisàns on behalf of the American government, he'd worn sailor clothes and a piratical moustache. They didn't seem to go with the OD blouse and the officer-pink trousers of the U.S. Army he found himself in now. He looked like a swashbuckling buccaneer masquerading unconvincingly as an officer and a gentleman.

Dan checked his wristwatch. He had set it to New York time even before he'd left Italy on his first hop. He'd been on New York time a day and a half later when he finally reached Diana by phone in Boston from London.

In less than an hour he'd be in Manhattan, surrounded again by the good life. He'd seen enough for a while of a world at war. He was fed up with the taste of boiled octopus and the smell of fear. It's time now, he told himself, for a radical change in the bill of fare—bright lights, laughter, gourmet food, fluffy bath towels, clean, white sheets, and elegantly coiffed, sophisticated ladies with long, lovely legs.

There was an even keener anticipation. In less than an hour, Diana would be in his arms. She was the greatest of all the eagerly awaited joys, the brightest ornament in that constellation of dreams called home. If the Creator hadn't turned out the exquisite Diana Remington in the first place, to long for and to love, Dan Baron would have found it altogether necessary to create her as an ideal against which to measure all other women. And if the public thought Diana was the answer to a dream, bursting forth from billboards and movie screens, magazine covers and calendars, it was nothing compared to the intense excitement of knowing her, having her to love. Diana had picked him up when he was altogether down.

The C-47 was over the end of the runway now, and Baron felt the downward pull with a momentary clutching in his stomach, a combination of exhilaration and fear.

He'd undergone his share of close ones in the war. The whole mission had been bizarre . . . out-and-out insane, as a matter of fact. Who but Donovan and his OSS brain trust would have put a highly recognizable movie actor like himself in charge of an extremely visible clandestine mission? Twice he'd been challenged by Germans who thought they'd recognized him. Both times he'd used the same way out. He accepted their observations that he looked like Dan Baron as a compliment. Then, with suitable gusto and gruff seaman's Greek, he told them how receptive the resemblance had made the girls in Piraeus to his amorous advances. He and the deluded Germans had a hearty laugh about how easy it is to deceive a woman.

The gunrunning operation was dangerous enough. There was always the possibility of discovery, of being challenged or sunk by German E-boats. There was peril even in the factionalism of the Yugoslavs. Both the Chetniks and the Partisans, the major rival groups, were trigger-happy. There could always be a slug out there with Baron written on it.

But even this danger hadn't been enough to lay his ghost. He could handle the day-to-day tensions of fooling the enemy, of pulling his whole operation off just behind the Germans' backs. But Dan longed for the hunt. He dreamed of the situation where it would be his wits, his presence of mind, his own personal courage that would put the foe away. It had to be more than just acting.

Perhaps the closest he came to it was in the port town of Dubrovnik on the Montenegrin coast. There had been an informer, one of the Partisans. Two of Dan's men had been jumped by a German patrol boat as they sought to land a shipment of fifty-caliber machine guns from a rubber raft. As a result of the leak, Baron's adjutant and friend, a young captain from Massachusetts, had been killed.

Baron knew who the traitor was. They all did. Baron decided it was up to him to hunt the man down.

After four days of tense, nerve-shattering stalking, he'd cornered his prey in a mountaineer's cabin, a good fifty miles inland, only to find the informer hanging from the rafters, his tongue lolling ludicrously from his mouth, as though mocking the man who had set out to track him down. The self-imposed mission had come perilously close to a disastrous end several times on his way back to the sea and his waiting command.

It was all over now, he reassured himself. No more hiding. In mere seconds, he'd be on solid American ground, in his own native land. No longer saboteur and agent, but actor; no longer Greek-Italian skipper from Piraeus, but Greek-Irish American actor from Jersey City. From now on, he promised himself, the only place he'd use firearms would be on a movie sound stage.

The C-47 had landed and was taxiing to the flight line. As it came to a stop, Baron gathered his flight bag and his chute and moved toward the exit. There was supposed to be a staff car waiting to drive him into the city.

"I'm Major Baron," he announced to a slender, dark-haired sergeant in the operations room. The sergeant didn't look up; he was busily writing something in longhand. The guy had a whole chestful of fruit salad—obviously he'd been damn near everywhere in the war.

"So?"

"Supposed to be a staff car waiting for me here."

The sergeant put down the pen, folded his hands in front of him, and gave Baron a withering once-over.

"And what else would you like us to do for you, colonel? A manicure? A bottle of cognac? A hot shower? A broad?"

"Major. It's major, not colonel."

The sergeant had obviously seen too many people coming through, looking for special consideration.

"There are no staff cars available," he announced. "We got a six-by-six loading up for New York City right now. You better hustle if you want to catch it."

"You sure you haven't got something for me? Dr. Krebbitsch in General Donovan's office was supposed to arrange it."

"Listen, major," the sergeant said, foregoing sarcasm. "Thousands of guys from four-star general to buck-ass private fly through here every day. There's guys gettin' off every plane. This here is no fuckin' Traveler's Aid station."

Noncom smart ass! Baron resisted the urge to climb all over him. What was the use? If he was going to turn himself back into Mr. Peace Loving Citizen, it was no time to be playing big shot. A lousy major sporting a moustache and wearing no unit shoulder patch wasn't going to make too many waves at Mitchell Field. If there was a truck going into Manhattan, who the hell was he to think himself too important to ride in it?

"Okay, sarge. Where's the truck?"

"Out that door," the sergeant said. He waved Baron in the right direction with an imperious gesture.

Baron grinned and picked up his flight bag.

"Hey, major," the smart-ass sergeant called after him. "This your chute on the floor?"

"Belongs to my rich uncle," Dan called back.

"You can't leave it here, for Crissakes!"

"Won't need it. I trust your truck driver."

"What am I supposed to do with it?" the sergeant yelled.

"Stick it in your ear, sarge. Stick it in your ear."

Dan Baron rode into New York City in the back of a six-by-six.

CHAPTER FOUR

The great Gothic pile of Saint Patrick's Cathedral on the northeast corner of Fifth Avenue and Fiftieth Street was unusually crowded with worshipers thanking God for the great gift of victory. It had been especially crowded now for several days, as America eagerly awaited official word of the Japanese surrender. There were the usual sightseers shuffling through, trying to identify all the statues on the side altars, gaping up at the red hats of the deceased cardinals of New York suspended from the ceiling of the nave, high above the sanctuary.

But most had come into the great church for prayer. In the pews, beside the regulars, were hundreds of additional worshipers. Among them were also the footsore who had come in for a rest. Some were praying. Others were just thinking about the war and wondering what its aftermath would bring. The room hung heavy with prayer. There were countless thousands of them going up like sparks in a chimney: prayers for returning servicemen, prayers for those who wouldn't be returning.

Americans everywhere were beginning to realize and be thankful that the long nightmare was over.

At the main altar in the central nave, Monsignor Joseph P. Flannelly was saying a votive mass of thanksgiving. Later in the day, if the official announcement came, he was to conduct a solemn Te Deum. One of the several intentions for his eight o'clock mass this morning was to ask God to protect his superior, Francis Cardinal Spellman, on his way by plane to the Pacific theater of operations to be with "his boys." The cardinal was Vicar for the Armed Forces of the United States, in effect the GIs' bishop. Monsignor Flannelly asked God to keep the tiny, lion-hearted prelate safe in the palm of His hand.

Among the many hundreds of people kneeling in the pews, Mary Grasso, a widowed Gold Star Mother, knelt, rosary in hand, at her favorite place in one of the back pews of the south transept, in front of the Altar of the Blessed Sacrament. She had attended mass every day since receiving the cruel telegram three years ago that told her Anthony was dead.

This morning, as usual, Mary ran through her shopping list of petitions to be placed before the Lord. First, she asked his continued protection for Greg, her eldest. "He's all I've got left now, Lord," she prayed silently. "Please don't let Greg be one of the last boys killed." In every war, even after everybody's made up his mind to stop shooting and go home, someone dies. It was Mary's greatest fear that Greg would be the victim of the very last bullet fired. It was a recurring nightmare. That would be typical of her luck, she said to herself. Mary, for all her piety, had always been somewhat resentful of the hand God had dealt her.

Then, she asked God to take a special interest in her Anthony—her baby. "Keep Anthony by Your side, Oh Lord," she implored. "Now that You've taken him to be with You, look out for him. You're in the best possible position to know what a good boy he really is." She was still a little afraid that Anthony might be languishing in Purgatory, still being punished for whatever sins he may have committed. As if the terrible march from Bataan hadn't been more than enough punishment to wipe away the few sins a boy like that could have managed to accumulate in only twenty-two years of life.

She was also asking God to keep her financially solvent, to keep her arthritis from hurting so much, to help her sister Gloria's girl Debbie find a good husband, to get her brother Louis a job, and to send someone along who'd want to rent her late husband's barbershop. Of course, she would have liked being better looking so she could shed her widow's weeds. But there were some things that were simply too much to ask.

Mary Grasso was wise enough in her dealings with God to know He demanded thanks as well as requests for favors. And she realized she had a lot to thank Him for, troubles or no troubles. Despite the arthritis, she enjoyed reasonably good health.

She thanked God for that. She thanked Him also for the insurance check she got regularly. Frank had left her decently provided for. With the insurance, the Social Security, and the boys' allotments, she'd been able to live adequately. But she'd taken in a boarder. Even there, she had a lot to be grateful for.

The boarder had been a tremendous help. She needed someone to fret about, to take care of. He was a fine man, a clean-cut gentleman who paid his rent promptly and was often out of town on weekends. She thanked God for him as well.

As she knelt, examining in her mind all the things she had reason to be thankful for, Mr. Peck, her tenant, came more and more into her mind. He would always put out the rubbish for her. He'd repaired the hinges on the cellar and fixed the locks on the vacant barbershop. He never played his radio loud or smoked in the house. He would eat whatever was placed in front of him and he'd always thank her for it and tell her what an excellent cook she was.

Sometimes, she wondered about Mr. Peck. She wondered about the fact that he seemed to have no friends. She wondered about all the weekend trips. Perhaps he had a sweetheart somewhere. But he was not the sort of man she could ask about that. He was far too private a person.

"Thank You, dear Lord, for all these benefits!"

It may have been the fact she was counting her blessings at that particular moment that caused her to glance back over her shoulder at her purse on the seat. A man was just picking it up and getting ready to walk off with it.

"That's mine," she said.

He made no sign he was going to stop. He kept moving away from her, almost smiling. He was a thief.

"Wait!" she called aloud, forgetting for a moment where she was.

The man whirled and hurried away from her. Several people looked over, trying to see what was going on.

"He's got my purse!"

She stood up in the pew, intending to chase him, but she stumbled on the kneeler and nearly fell down. Two men and a boy started in pursuit of the thief, but there was no way of telling whether he was still in the church. There were simply too many people in the building.

"Where's he gone?" one of the men asked.

"I don't know," she admitted.

"We don't know where he went," the other man explained.

"He may still be in here," added the boy.

People were turning around in the front pews, trying to hush them in the back.

Mary thanked her would-be helpers and sank down on the pew. What was that Saint Teresa had said about God having so few friends because He treated the ones He had so badly? Yes, that was it.

"How come?" Mary Grasso asked God. "How come You treat me this way?"

V-J DAY : : 69

* * *

"What the hell you think you're doing, Pop?" the news vendor in Times Square called out.

A wizened man in the uniform of the American Expeditionary Force of 1917 was setting up a small tripod table on the sidewalk next to his newsstand.

"This ain't your corner."

"Tell it to the chaplain," muttered the old soldier. He was a bald-headed old bird, much in need of a shave and a bath.

"There ain't no such thing as a chaplain 'round here, Pop. So get lost!"

The old man, wearing an overseas cap and a horse blanket overcoat, with his skinny calves wrapped mummylike in olive drab puttees, was arranging poppies on the table.

"You can't sell your poppies here, Mac. Poppies is for Easter and it's the middle of August already."

"Memorial Day, you danged fool."

"This ain't Memorial Day!"

"I was in Flanders Field."

"I don't give a goddamn if you was in the Polo Grounds. Have a heart and get lost."

The newsdealer was in an ornery mood and it was only 8:30 A.M. He knew damned well it was gonna be a hell of a day. He didn't need extra aggravation. A lot of the boys had decided they were gonna shutter their stands. There'd be too many people in Times Square. With all the drunken sailors and marines around, there'd be no telling what was gonna happen. And if he was gonna stay open, he didn't need some damn poppy seller to drive away the action.

The old man was muttering, but he was packing up his gear. The news vendor watched him go. In a way, he felt annoyed at himself for having chased him, but life was a matter of every man for himself. And besides, he thought, taking comfort in skepticism, how do I know he's real? How do I know he fought in any war at all?

"Getcha paper," he called. "Getcha mornin' paper? End of the war comin' up. Surrender on the way. Getcha papers here!"

"You have such a nerve, Dan Baron," Diana Remington said aloud, still lying in bed, green eyes wide with excitement. "You are so goddamn arrogant!"

How many times had she said that in the past five years and here she was waiting for him again.

He'd grin at her. That damn, disarming little-boy grin of his. It was like magic. It always won her no matter how seethingly angry she was at the moment.

"I suppose he grinned at you," Max Pictou, the studio press rep had said Saturday afternoon when Dan's call had reached her in Boston.

"Over the phone?" she asked, laughing at him.

"Yes, over the phone. Listen, I been workin' with that big son of a bitch since you was just a gleam in Sam Goldwyn's eye. He acts like a complete bastard, walks all over everybody; he grins and it's all right."

Diana had laughed. "All right, Max. He grinned."

"I told you."

Diana started for the elevator to get to her room. She had things to pack. She was taking the next train to New York to wait for him.

"Where you goin'?" Max demanded.

"To pack."

"You got a schedule to keep, lady," Pictou said. "He'll have to catch up to us."

"Not on your life, Max. I'm going to him."

"I'm your press rep, Diana. I call the shots on this tour."

"The tour is over," Diana had snapped.

"You gonna call Hollywood?" Pictou demanded. Diana raked him with her eyes. He was a desiccated little man in a baggy tweed suit. They called him the "Gray Eunuch" in the film business. With his colorless face, the drab clothes he wore, it seemed to fit. As a matter of fact, the only color to be found on Max were the stains on the fingers of his right hand and the bottom of his aquiline nose, yellowed from the strong French Gauloises he chain-smoked.

"Crissakes, *Mr.* Pictou," Diana said as nastily as she could, "you aren't my father or my keeper. You are just the studio watchdog. I have a right to a private life of my own."

"Don't you believe it," Max said. "You belong to the studio, kiddo." He studied the schedule on his clipboard.

"So long, Max," she said.

"You ain't goin' nowhere."

"You want to put money on that?"

Pictou pushed his battered Panama back to scratch at his temple. "You've got appearances booked for the next three weeks. Like I said, Dan will have to pick up the tour."

Diana had looked around the lobby. There was a Boston cop no more than thirty feet away.

"Officer," Diana said. "This old man just made an immoral suggestion."

Pictou's face had been a study. The cop came right over.

"She's lying," Max had insisted.

The cop gave him a funny look. "Of course she's lying, Pop. You were just giving her the weather report, weren't you?" He took the press agent firmly by the arm.

It still made Diana laugh four days later. Poor Max. The people in Hollywood would have to give her someone a little speedier than Max if they wanted to keep a leash on her.

Whether anyone liked it or not, the magical day was finally here. For seven hundred and thirty-one days she'd anticipated it, hardly daring to dream it'd ever happen.

It had been two years—two long, arid years— since Dan had gone off to indulge what he called his patriotic inclinations. It was more than that, though. Dan had something to prove to himself. He could have gotten involved in bond drives, recruitment, pushing the war effort, that sort of thing. He could have done USO shows like a number of their movie and theater friends. It'd been two years since she'd lain in his arms. It had been so incredibly bleak and lonely a time.

Diana kicked off the sheet covering her and rolled upright on the edge of the bed. She raised her arms and stretched. She wondered if Dan would still find her beautiful. She wondered what he'd look like, how he might have changed. Would he be drawn and undernourished like some pathetic war victim? Or would he come back purged of the devils that Barbara's death had loosed on him? Saturday's crazy, confused call from London had been too frantic for questions.

Diana stood up and went in to take her shower. She was a striking, auburn-haired beauty, tall, full breasted, and with the eyes of a jungle predator. She exulted in her beauty. It had been her lifelong license to hunt down any man she wanted. There was, however, only one man she wanted. She'd made up her mind to have him when she was a teen-ager and had seen him in an early John Ford western.

The phone rang.

It was probably the damned studio.

But what if it was Dan? She wasn't going to take any chances.

"Hello?"

"I have a call for you, Miss Remington," came the nasal voice of the hotel operator.

"Where is it from?"

"Long distance."

"From where?" demanded Diana angrily.

She heard the operator asking the long-distance operator.

"Hollywood," came the answer.

"Tell the bastards to get off my back," Diana said loudly, hoping they'd hear it in California. She could hear the shock in the hotel operator's voice before she slammed down the receiver.

A lot of people were afraid of Diana Remington and she shocked them with her frankness. There was too much intelligence, too much spirit, too much independent female for most people to put up with. Diana couldn't be dominated, possessed by any man created on a mere mortal scale. That was the logic of it. But the wild, ungovernable passion she felt for Dan Baron blew all logic away.

Diana picked up the phone again. Eager for what the day would bring, refreshed by a good minor tantrum, wide-awake, she called room service and ordered a hearty breakfast—eggs, sausage, toast—a real peacetime meal. She'd need all the strength and vitality she could get when Dan arrived. She'd need fortitude.

Then she had an idea—a thoroughly wonderful idea.

"Oysters? Do you have oysters?"

There was silence for a few seconds on the other end of the line. "Oysters?"

"Yes," she said sarcastically. "Surely you've heard of them?"

"We don't ordinarily serve them with breakfast, Miss Remington. That's not our normal—"

"Never mind what's normal," she interrupted.

"Can you get me a half-dozen on the half shell?"

"Yes, Miss Remington," the voice said with a gulp of resignation.

"Then I'll have them."

She hung up the phone and giggled. Oysters for breakfast? Fantastic! As if she needed them!

CHAPTER :::::::::::::::::::
::::::::::::::: FIVE

"Exploring" was a tremendously exciting thing for Bobby Noel. One of the best things about the activity was that it made him feel ever so slightly like a crook or some sort of bad guy. It was a thrill to challenge official-looking signs that said NO ADMITTANCE or HOTEL STAFF ONLY, to thumb his nose at NO TRESPASSING warnings. Of course, there was always the chance of getting caught and yelled at, chased out of the place.

But who cared? Name-calling and yelling didn't truly hurt, especially if it was a total stranger doing it.

Even though Bobby was twelve, at least a year younger than Tony Ciccone, his new roommate, he assumed the leadership of the pair. He found the kid from Philly a little hard to move. Obviously, the guy was afraid of breaking rules, worried about getting grabbed by the cops or somebody else in charge. That made him a lot different from the kids Bobby hung around with back in New Hampshire. They'd take off for "exploring" or "scouting" at the drop of a hat—'specially after suppertime when it was dark. They'd climb on people's garages and shed roofs, move through backyards, reconnoiter deserted shacks and outbuildings. It was always a little dangerous. Mrs. Kaminiewski had a shotgun loaded with rock salt. It was unnerving to know there were people around like her. Periodically, someone would call the cops or the boys would miscalculate and stumble across a nasty watchdog they had overlooked on the last expedition.

"Come on, Tony," Bobby kept saying, urging his companion into the mood for exploration. Buildings were neat anyway. Back stairways, fire escapes, rooftops, underground tunnels, and airshafts all seemed to have a romance of their own. And they had discovered a new feature here—sub-basements. Where Bobby Noel came from, the modest buildings and the rocky New Hampshire soil made it virtually impossible to find anything deeper than a regular old cellar. Cellars, of course, were fascinating in themselves. There was even something about the run-of-the-mill everyday cellar that tugged at your insides and stoked up your imagination.

Once the boys found the regular basement of the hotel, they were intrigued by the fact the stairway kept going down. That was exciting. It was hard to tell at first how far.

"What if it just keeps on going down into the guts of the earth?"

Ciccone looked at him strangely. Probably Ciccone thought he was some kind of a nut. Then it became obvious from the look on the other kid's face that it scared him merely to think about it. Ciccone wasn't very brave. Bobby would have to humor him a lot.

So far the highlight of the morning's exploration had been the kitchen where they'd been able to weasel out a couple pieces of pie and a single small carton of milk. But the appearance of more than one basement was exciting—especially to Bobby Noel.

"You sure about this?" Ciccone asked him for at least the fifth time. "You sure we won't get arrested?"

"You sure do a lot of worrying, don't you?"

Ciccone looked a little hurt. "No," he said. "What makes you think that?"

"You're always askin' if we should be in here or not."

"So?"

"So maybe we're not supposed to be in here," little round-faced Bobby said. "But if we were supposed to be here, what fun would it be?"

"Never thought of that." They had come to a long corridor in the second basement level.

"Hey, look," Bobby said excitedly, opening another door. "This looks like some kind of mine shaft."

"Don't go in there," Ciccone begged. "What if we get lost?"

"Come on, chicken. I got a perfect sense of direction." It was true that Bobby gave every sign of knowing just where they were. It was as though he had a sixth sense, so adept was he at figuring out what connected with what. In this passage, he had even found a kind of grillwork hatchway that opened into a subway tunnel. They both got a delicious scare when a subway train roared deafeningly by, just inches from their noses.

"Can you imagine what would happen if we'd been on the other side of that screen?" Tony asked the New Englander.

"Sure," Bobby said brightly. He pushed his palms together expressively. "Squish!"

Ciccone made a face.

"Did you ever see somebody killed?" Bobby asked. "I mean *really* squished."

"No," Tony confessed.

"Well, I saw a guy get his leg cut off by a train. Never saw so much blood in my whole life. It was sickening. He musta bled six or seven buckets full. They were practically scoopin' it up off the railroad tracks."

"Really?"

"Sure," Bobby said. "But do you know what the strangest, weirdest thing was?"

"What?"

"The guy didn't die."

"How come?" Ciccone was skeptical.

"They put some blood back into him."

"What if it had been Jap blood?"

Now it was Bobby who made the disgusted face.

"That'd be real neat, wouldn't it?" Ciccone went on. "Imagine how you'd feel wakin' up full of Jap blood. Wonder if your eyes would go slanty and you'd get all yellow?"

"That'd be repulsive," Bobby said. He was tired of conversation now. "Let's see where this hall leads?"

"Okay." Ciccone was reluctant, but he didn't like being called "chicken."

Within ten minutes, to their delight and amazement, they found they'd emerged diagonally across the street, in the New York Times Tower.

"It's all connected by tunnels," Bobby Noel declared. "The whole city of New York must be like Swiss cheese, all full of holes."

Ciccone laughed. "My old man says it's full of rats too."

"Hey, look!" Bobby announced, as they crossed crowded Seventh Avenue to make their way back to the hotel. "Gene Krupa!"

"Where?"

"On the sign in front of the hotel. It says that Krupa and his orchestra are playing on the Astor Roof tonight. He's supposed to be a good drummer, a regular wild man. Let's sneak up tonight and hear him."

Ciccone thought Noel talked funny: "Astah" Hotel, "drummah," "heah" instead of hear.

"If I was Lamont Cranston, the Shadow, I could go right up there, eat up all the food, kiss all the good-looking girls, and maybe pull a tablecloth out from under the dishes. I always wanted to do that. Nobody could see me."

"That'd be neat," said the boy from Philly.

"Damn right," Bobby said, his imagination working. "We could really get to see all kinds of stuff then. I bet a lot goes on in this city that people don't talk about or even know about."

"Like what?"

"Spies. Crooks."

"Screwin'," added Ciccone.

"Yeah," Bobby admitted, blushing. "That too." Way down deep, he wanted to tell Tony about Keefe, about what he'd seen in the other room, but he really didn't dare. Maybe later on.

"Let's find the way to the Astor Roof," said Ciccone out of nowhere.

"Sure," Bobby said. At least the kid from Pennsylvania seemed to be getting a little braver.

CHAPTER SIX

The great hospital was experiencing a normal day.

The Andrews Sisters were warning in song, "Don't Sit Under the Apple Tree with Anyone Else but Me." The song and its advice didn't please the young nurse sitting at the nurses' station. She reached out and turned the radio off.

Who am I going to sit under the apple tree with? Anna Sangillo asked herself bitterly. Vince was dead, his body somewhere in the Pacific Ocean. She tried hard not to think of him, but it was so difficult. She kept hearing his voice. She kept seeing his intense, darkly tanned face in her mind, that look of determination, that strong jaw. How could he be dead?

Sure, it had gotten easier to handle it over the past months, but he wasn't altogether out of her mind. He never would be. She should have married him before he'd gone off to war. Maybe then she would have had a child, a miniature Vince to love and to cherish.

Anna was a realist. She knew that someday the

pain would fade; eventually it would be gone. There would be someone else. She was healthy. She'd find someone else to love. She'd have her children and her home. But when and where would that be? There was another song around that spoke to that very question—"They're Either Too Young or Too Old." She certainly didn't need an off-the-record romance with some oversexed old doctor. The only intern she knew well was a woman.

"Miss Sangillo, we have another patient for you up here." The voice of the chief floor nurse broke into her thoughts and she looked up to see an orderly pushing an occupied gurney down the corridor toward her.

Anna was glad for the interruption. Being busy kept her from dwelling on Vince and the injustice of losing him. The prospect of peace was bringing up too many mournful memories.

"We've got a double room right down here," Anna said.

"All right," the senior nurse said to the orderly, "put the sergeant in there."

As Anna helped to move the patient from the gurney to the bed, she saw, to her surprise, that he was Japanese. He had the same Japanese face she'd seen in the movies recently, staring out from the war posters.

"All right, fellow," the older nurse said, "just a little bit more and we'll have you all tucked in."

"Thank you," the young Japanese man said politely, seeming somewhat embarrassed to have to

84 : : *V-J DAY*

be assisted by women. George Nakamura didn't like being flat on his back. He didn't like being dependent on anyone at all. He had always put a high value on self-reliance.

The two nurses stepped just outside the door and the older nurse went over Nakamura's chart with Anna, speaking briskly. "He's strapped up with three broken ribs. He's got a severe concussion. There's a double fracture of the right forearm, some dental injuries, cuts, and lacerations."

"What happened to him?"

"A beating. On the street just off Times Square."

Anna was shocked at her own lack of sympathy for the injured man. But that Japanese face! How could she ignore that?

"He's a soldier?"

"That's right."

"Whose?" Anna asked bitterly. It just slipped out before she had a chance to think.

"One of yours. I'm an American soldier," Nakamura spoke up from his bed, having overheard.

Anna looked at the man's battered features. Weren't his people the slant-eyed killers who knocked her Vince out of the sky? Of course, Anna knew she was being more than a little unfair. She chastised herself. Wasn't she herself Italian-American? Italian soldiers had killed a lot of Americans too. His face was badly swollen. He was injured—in pain. How could she blame him for the war, for what happened to her fiancé?

"I'm sorry," Anna said. She was, after all, a

nurse. She had dedicated herself to serve the sick and the injured. "I shouldn't have said that."

The soldier said nothing.

"I'm really sorry," Anna said again as she readjusted Nakamura's bed to try to make him more comfortable. She wanted to do something to make up for what she'd said. "What happened to you?"

"Bunch of merchant sailors. They didn't like my face and they tried to rearrange it."

"Did they get away with it?" asked the older nurse from the doorway.

"If a sailor with a hangover and a broken wrist comes into the emergency ward of this hospital," the patient said, "you better not send him into this room. I think I may have broken his jaw too."

"What about the police?" Anna asked.

"Forget it," he said. "Like you said, I look like a Jap."

"We'll remember not to send him up," the nurse at the doorway said. "Now take care of him, Sangillo."

"I will," Anna said. She would too. She was good at nursing—dedicated to its ideals. A good nurse, she told herself firmly, puts prejudices aside and cares for her patients in the best traditions of the profession, with the best of her abilities. She got Nakamura settled in as comfortably as she could and then she returned to her station.

Anna was lonelier than hell.

Commodore Vincent Astor glanced up at the giant electric sign on the Times Tower.

86 : : V-J DAY

. . . . MOSTLY CLOUDY TODAY WITH SHOWERS AND THUNDERSHOWERS . . . . TODAY'S HIGH TEMPERATURE 85 . . . . FAIR WEATHER TOMORROW . . . .

It was a good-day already as far as the commodore was concerned. He was deeply moved that the U.S. Navy was recognizing him today for his work with the Submarine Watch. It had been a good project for some of his fellow yachtsmen and he'd done it for the war effort. After all, it was a man's patriotic duty to do the best he could for his country. He glanced back up at the great sign.

. . . KODAK UP 4.39 PER SHARE . . . . CHRYSLER 3.98 PER SHARE . . . .

Absently, the commodore wondered if he still had those Chrysler shares. It was, despite the weatherman's predictions, not a bad day at all. He walked on.

The young man with the blond, almost white, hair ducked into an end phone booth, one of a line of several. Out of a long-cultivated habit of caution, he had stood back and watched for a time when no one was using any of the booths. Adroitly, he put a paper sign he had just improvised saying "out of order" in the booth next to the one he occupied. With a quick glance around, he dialed a number.

"Hotel Astor."

"Mr. Peck, please," he said gruffly, as if trying to disguise the sound of his voice.

"Is he a guest?"

"No. Staff."

"Thank you."

He waited nervously, drumming on the dirty glass with his slightly pudgy hands. Had it not been for his stubby hands and feet, George Beaton would have been a fair caricature of an aristocrat. His finely cut features were perfectly complemented by the silvery blond hair. His eyes were a penetrating blue and he looked intelligent and most pleasant. Only the hands and feet betrayed his peasant origins.

"Hello. This is Peck here," came the voice over the telephone. It was the same Richard he had last seen and talked with nearly two years ago. Or was it? There was the same metallic edge to the voice. The same impatient tone.

"Peck speaking," the voice on the other end of the line repeated impatiently.

"This is a friend of Andrew Weber," Beaton said, using the elaborate spoken challenge code they had worked out back in 1942 to cover just such phone conversations. "I was told that you could direct me to someone who could manufacture a good cuckoo clock . . . something handmade."

There was a long pause. Then, a sigh. "I know such a man," came Peck's cold, perfectly controlled voice. "I know such a man who could meet you at your convenience."

The man in the phone booth was mildly amused

at the subtle way the otherwise well-guarded Peck revealed his state of mind—at least a portion of it—with the sigh.

"I would like to see him."

"Why?" Peck demanded, jumping abruptly out of the formalistic recognition, information-passing dialogue.

"To reassure me," Beaton said. "I have become very upset in the past several weeks."

"As a result of what?" Peck insisted. There was no doubt left that he disliked being contacted. It was gradually becoming evident in his tone of voice. Despite all the emphasis he used to put on personal discipline, it was apparent his own emotions were slipping into his tone of voice. He must have been stretched pretty taut, Beaton reflected.

"Newspaper stories. There is so much needless, aimless violence going on in the world. The war is over and yet it seems to continue."

"It is an *evil* world. Moral authority has eroded. Godlessness has taken over. Perhaps the corrupted society that encourages this should be punished with such occurrences."

"I do not agree with you, sir." To be truthful, the blond man who called himself Beaton knew he wasn't pleading for morality. He was speaking in support of prudence. He had surrounded his new life with a cloak of careful circumspection, abandoning all the compromising pursuits that could make one subject to public observation. He had even taken a job running trains underground.

This was the course he had expected Peck to adopt also.

"So?"

"I want a meeting to discuss . . . the clock."

"Yes."

Beaton could almost hear the cogs and wheels turning rapidly inside Peck's head.

"The park?" Peck suggested.

"No." He no longer trusted Peck. In a park, screened from surveillance, one might be very vulnerable. Beaton was enjoying his new life too much, drawing too much pleasure and consolation from it, to expose himself needlessly.

"The Little Hideaway," Beaton said.

"Where?" Peck asked as if to indicate he didn't know the place.

"Just off Sixth Avenue. Surely you remember." How could Peck forget? It had been three days after Keating, the ardent political enthusiast, had blown himself out of existence; caution and good sense had been fatally overwhelmed by zeal. Brown was still with them then, and the three survivors had sat there in a small, dark booth, setting up a strategy for their survival.

"I remember it."

"And?"

"I will be there at one o'clock."

"Very good."

"You'd better have a good reason."

"I have."

For a moment, Beaton was tempted to add *auf*

wiedersehen, but he knew he'd be setting himself up for an emotional explosion when the two men met. Why aggravate Peck? There was no sense in it. He hung up.

CHAPTER :::::::::::::::::::
::::::::::::::: SEVEN

"What the hell do you mean, you'll see what you can do? That's a load o' horseshit!" The veins on J. Walter Stait's thick neck bulged, and his wide, beefy face turned red. "You'll get the goddamn table for me. That's what you'll do and that's all there is to it. You got that absolutely clear?"

"Yes," came a chastened male voice over the telephone receiver.

"Any questions?"

"No."

"Good."

J. Walter Stait didn't merely converse on the telephone, he bludgeoned people with it. As he understood the nature of the instrument, it was a device created by Western Electric as the natural and proper weapon for people like himself—people who have the right and the responsibility to bring others around to their point of view without endless wrangling and face-to-face negotiation. He knew how to intimidate. He used the skill. It was, as he saw it, a legitimate device for making weak, easily cowed persons accomplish fantastic things. There were damned few men around who could do this sort of thing better than J. Walter Stait. If I tell somebody he's going to walk on water, he was fond of saying, he might just as well start unlacing his shoes.

"It's not as though I want to go to the grand opera. I want a table for a party of seven at the Cotton Club," he said to his unseen listener. "Why can't you boot some dumb night fighter outa there to make room for me and my friends?"

"That just isn't done," the other man protested, horrified by Stait's insensitivity. "It isn't right."

"Don't give me *that*. You know who I am. That's J. Walter Stait of the War Production Board. Hear me?"

"That's not the point, J. W."

"Allocations of raw materials," Stait said. "*Your* allocations. *That's* the point."

There was a long pause. Stait sat back surveying his elegant hotel suite, in no hurry to break the silence.

He preferred the Astor to his office downtown as a base of operations. The government was picking up the tab. He liked the surroundings. They went nicely with his self-image. He was a good-looking, big man who gave the lie to the old notion that men in their fifties lose vigor. He was nearly overloaded with it, a man constantly on the move, larger than life. Under a crop of rich, healthy hair, still auburn, his eyes were bright and challenging. He had more than the usual number of lines and shadows on his face. They didn't, however, suggest age as much as they implied he was a man of intense emotion, given to extreme highs and lows. His face was flexible. He could win prizes for his smile one minute and then blaze with a frightening anger the next. He looked like a professional athlete slightly past his prime.

"You want me to call you when I get the table?" the other man asked finally.

"Hell, no! I'll show up at nine o'clock. If there's no table, it's your ass!"

He hung up the phone and chuckled with pleasure. He really derived a lot of good feeling out of bulldozing lightweights. To hell with them. It's the stupid and weak who seem to breed with the most enthusiasm. If someone didn't kick them around, knock a few of them off from time to time, they'd end up outnumbering the strong and the wise.

Stait felt tip-top. Wasn't his boy coming home today? He checked his watch. The *Governor Tawes* would be docking soon with Tim aboard. Stait was almost as pleased with the information, obtained by some serious string-pulling, as he was with the fact. And even though the war was all but over and his chore with the War Production Board just about done, he had managed to convert his own plants well ahead of schedule. He was ready to flood the market with new civilian products the public was simply dying to get hold of.

Tonight and for the next several days, he'd show his son the top of the mountain—the dizzying heights where he'd been living all these years. He

had to get the young buck out of the rut that the
war and a cheating bitch of a wife had likely put
him in. Tim took after his mother in several ways—
mostly bad. For one thing, he was too much of a
soft-headed idealist. It was about time to get the
horseshit idea of a career in the army out of his
head. Tim had too much class to get himself hung
up in that particular sling. He'd done his bit. Now
it was time to join his father and skim a little of
life's cream off the top.

Stait walked over to the window and stared
down into Times Square, twelve stories below him.
He felt strong and sure of himself, looking down
on all the little people who had begun to throng
the street. Jammed already. He wondered if anyone in the whole goddamn country was working
today except cops, bartenders, politicians, and
whores. It was beginning to look like one gigantic
holiday—a noisy picnic.

Well, why the hell not? Maybe the peasants
down there had a right to their celebration, to
blow off a little steam. Let 'em holler and dance
and raise general hell. Americans *had* done a fantastic job with the war effort. He thought of a few
of the numbers he'd used in his Bridgeport speech
the other night. The raw numbers produced in the
war effort were mind boggling. Forty-one and a
half billion rounds of small arms ammunition, almost six million bombs, two and a half million
trucks, and seventy-one thousand ships. God, what
an accomplishment! It wasn't simple courage or

the intervention of an interested God that had won the war. It was American production.

There was a soft tapping at the door. He could tell by its timidity that it was Laura, his secretary. He threw the chain bolt and let her in.

"Morning, Laura."

"Good morning, Mr. Stait." She looked a bit more disheveled and flustered than usual.

"How are you?" he asked, wondering what was bothering the poor girl now. She was a tense, nervous person anyway. "Anything wrong?"

"Sorry I'm late, sir. There were too many people in the streets and . . ."

"That's all right," he said generously, impelled to be forgiving by virtue of the fact that he felt so good himself. "That's perfectly okay, Laura. Nobody's going to get much work done today. Think nothing of it."

The secretary gave a sigh of relief. She was so scared of him.

"Look at 'em all," he said to her, giving her time to catch her breath. He pulled the heavy flowered drape aside so she could see better.

"They're all kissing crazy," she complained.

"Kissing crazy?"

"I must have been grabbed and kissed at least a dozen times."

He just laughed.

Laura approached the window timidly and stood near him looking down at the growing crowd twelve stories below.

"Look at 'em," he said. "They're all facing the same direction like a bunch of Arabs, looking at the electric sign on the Times building, waiting for official word from the White House. They're like little kids. The poor little critters never felt so American before."

"They look like tiny little dolls."

Stait didn't want to say it aloud, but in his view, they *were* tiny little dolls, pygmy creatures. They were like Laura here, worrying whether her slip was showing, fretting over the pharmacist she was screwing while her tank-driver husband was in Europe, caring more about painting her seams straight when she put on her bottled stockings than about the future of the postwar world. Little people! They were all so goddamn unimportant until you joined them all together. Then, they were a production force, a market, the voting public, the masses that kept everything running.

"Have you seen this morning's *Times*, sir?"

"No. I'll read the mail first," he said. She had brought it up from the office with her.

"I bought *The New York Times*."

"No," he said impatiently. "Give me the mail first."

She didn't respond. For a flash he was angry as she stood there just looking at him. Stupid goddamn cow! "What's the matter with you, Laura?"

"There's something in the paper. Something you have to see."

"Show it to me." It was obvious that Laura wouldn't leave him alone until he'd let her tell the full story, show him the goddamn newspaper. Maybe it was time to get a new girl in to secretary for him.

"It's about Senator Commer."

"He died?"

"No," she said.

"Too bad. He's a pain in the ass. What's he up to?"

"He has a news conference scheduled for later this afternoon at the Algonquin Hotel."

"What for?"

"You better read it yourself," she said, handing him the newspaper, carefully folded open to the proper place.

"New York, August 14," he began reading aloud "... announced he will host a press conference at four o'clock at the Hotel Algonquin and so on and so on ... the sordid story of influence peddling and corruption ... making scarce war-important materials available. Commer promises that evidence will be supplied and names will be named."

Stait threw the paper on the desk. Commer didn't like him. He didn't like Commer. Their paths had crossed a few unpleasant times. But then Commer didn't like anyone. He was forever making threats. The list of people Commer had threatened was long. Naming names? Whose names? What was the sanctimonious old fart after?

"It hasn't got anything to do with us, has it?" Laura asked.

She was so naive, this woman. But then, that

had been the kind of secretary he always looked for, no questions, no challenges. As long as she could spell, type, and take dictation.

"Were you aware of anyone snooping around?" Stait asked her.

"No, sir."

"Did any of the people at the office say anything about investigators?"

"No. Not that I heard."

"Did you ever talk to anyone unusual, someone who might have come from Commer's office? A stranger?"

"Never."

"He's a bastard you know. He's a sneaky old bastard. Get that straight."

"It's not us, is it?"

"Of course not," he said gruffly.

Commer might have the bluest blood on the whole North American continent, but it was the big green that would have the final say. He'd have to buy the goddamn bloodsucker off.

Stait saw himself as having nothing to feel guilty about. Even though he had done well for himself, he'd done well for the country too. He'd kept the factories in his area producing. He'd expedited the flow of needed raw materials. There was no justification whatever for Commer's allegations. Was the senator actually living on his Senate salary? The major difference between a patriot and a thief is whether the man does, in truth, serve the public nobly and well. Stait was confident of that. Didn't today's rejoicing prove it?

So why was he so goddamn sick to his stomach?

"Aren't you feeling well?" the secretary asked him.

"I'm feeling fine."

"You look pale, sir."

"Get your damned book and get ready to take dictation," he said crossly. He would have to get another secretary. Laura had clearly outlived her usefulness.

CHAPTER :::::::::::::::::
::::::::::::::: EIGHT

Major Dan Baron jumped down from the back end of the army six-by-six at a traffic light on Forty-eighth Street and Madison Avenue. Another GI tossed Baron his flight bag.

"Give her one for us, major," one of the dogfaces yelled, "whoever she is."

"Damn right I will," Dan yelled back.

The other men in the truck shouted their approval and stamped their feet on the steel truck floor as the big vehicle pulled away toward the armory on Lexington Avenue.

The sidewalks were choked with humanity. No one seemed in a hurry to get anywhere. It wouldn't have done them much good. But Dan was determined he was going to travel crosstown on foot. He wanted to mingle with his countrymen, to speak English, to wear his nationality openly. He'd been forced to hide it for too long.

A young girl handed him a flower. He took it and without a second's hesitation, he kissed her full on the mouth. She kissed him back enthusiastically. Several passersby applauded.

V-J DAY : : 101

There was a heady excitement in the streets, something that went even beyond his own very strong feelings at being home again. Everyone was infected with it. There was such an *up* quality about people today. They were cocky. They were proud. They had done it—beaten the whole Axis. It was everybody's victory just as it had been everybody's war.

There was a terrific sense of relief and release in people's eyes that offered insight into their involvement with the war. No, they hadn't been bombed and they hadn't been starved, but they'd been at war nonetheless. It was their team out there, their ball game. They'd seen too many hermetically sealed boxes shipped home, too many ambitious young men return in wheelchairs. There had been too many gold stars in too many windows.

"Can I shake your hand?" asked a middle-aged woman, walking up to him.

Baron was startled, but he stuck out his right hand.

"Thanks for winning the war," she said. She gave no signs of being either a nut or an autograph hound.

"I didn't win it," he said. After all, he had never really been in a combat situation as he defined it. It was one thing to run a clandestine operation, disguised, and another thing to get involved in the real dirty work. But how could he explain it to her? "I had a lot of help," he added so as not to disappoint her.

"I'm thanking all of them through you," she said, eyes misty. "You kept my sons from having to go by getting it all over now."

At first he thought the lady had simply recognized him from the movies or the magazines. But she'd given no sign of it. She didn't come at him with the obligatory scrap of paper and pencil stub thrust out. She didn't giggle or act foolish the way the fans did. No. She'd seen the uniform. That was good. The uniform, the luxuriant moustache, the weight loss, all of them screened Dan Baron. Maybe he wasn't as easily recognized as he thought.

But he wasn't going to be ignored. No one in uniform would be today. In the next block he was kissed twice, his hand was shaken four times. It was delightful. Could this be coldhearted New York?

Baron tried to think of the hundreds of times he'd tramped these very streets as an unemployed actor, hoping to hell that someone—anyone—would give him a job, a little encouragement, even a smile. There was nobody there then to shake his hand. Not a soul would have stopped to give him a kiss or so much as the time of day. Those had been lean times indeed.

Then there were the weeks after Barbara had been killed. Even those who recognized him would say hurting things or ostentatiously look away. All except one person . . .

"So you're Dan Baron," she said, looking him up and down in a look of honest appraisal. It had been about three months after the murder. They were on the set of *Apache Mountain*, a film he hadn't been ready to make at the time, and he was standing outside the chuck wagon trailer, his tray in his hand. It was the first day of shooting. She stood directly in front of him, hands on hips, checking him out.

"What the hell is that supposed to be?" he asked. "A greeting of some kind?"

"I've just never seen you in the flesh before." Most women would have become flustered or blushed. She didn't. She was tall, with a luxurious mane of red hair. "Saw you in the movies when I was a kid," she was saying now. "Remember *Overland*? Saw it twelve times."

"Well?"

She stared at him with huge green eyes that reminded him of a big cat.

"Satisfied?"

"So far. With everything but your manners," she said.

He grinned. "Kind of spunky, aren't you?"

"You think I should get all shy and embarrassed meeting a star."

"Most girls do."

She laughed at him. "I'm not most girls, Dan Baron. You'll find that out."

"Who the hell are you?"

"A coal miner's daughter from Wilkes-Barre, Pennsylvania," was her answer. She moved off toward the director's trailer. She had a long, loping stride that made her hips swing provocatively.

"Jesus," Dan had marveled. "What an incredible case of self-confidence!"

Twenty minutes later he found out that the sassy young woman was Diana Remington and she was going to play opposite him. She was the new talent director Ford had just pulled out of nowhere. He called her his new Desert Rose. If Diana Remington was a flower, she'd have to be a rose. She had the thorns to prove it.

"It's a great day, major," someone called out to him, dragging him back to the present.

"I'll drink to that," he replied.

There was a tug at his sleeve.

It was a genuine New York City street kid who looked up at him with a wide grin. "Wanna put the whammy on Tojo?" the kid asked. Three of his friends crowded behind him. They had set up a little booth on the sidewalk made out of old cardboard boxes. A sizable crowd had gathered all around.

"Whatcha mean?" Dan asked.

"Right here, general." The kid indicated a plywood panel on which a savage portrayal of the Japanese warlord had been drawn. "Win a Kewpie doll."

"How much?" Dan asked, digging into his pocket.

"Nuttin' for you," the street kid said. "You're special. You're gonna baptize things, compliments of the management. We just started."

"Terrific," Dan said, putting his flight bag down.

Another kid handed Dan some darts. "Stick 'em good."

Dan took careful aim. If they had chosen him to dedicate their sidewalk enterprise, the least he could do was give them a winner.

He wound up and hurled the dart. It hit Tojo on the tip of the nose and stuck firmly.

"A regular Robin Hood," said the first kid.

Dan threw again.

This time he got Tojo in the eye.

There was a round of cheers and applause from the kid entrepreneurs and the knot of bystanders. The applause felt terrific.

Baron's final toss caught Tojo in the cheek. It was a winning toss.

Dan tried hard to refuse the cheap Kewpie doll. He didn't want to deplete the kids' limited stock, but they insisted on it. They had their pride. Dan understood that. Once, he'd been a Jersey City version of these kids. How long ago it seemed.

"Give it to yer girl friend," the kids told him.

He picked up his battered flight bag and the Kewpie doll and moved along. He passed the Forty-eighth Street Theater. The marquee announced a show called *Harvey*. From the lineup at the ticket window it must be a hit. He resolved to take Diana to see the play. He could use a little laughter now that the damned war had wound down. There was a hell of a lot of negativism to be gotten rid of.

The crowds in the streets were swelling. It was

getting tougher to walk. He rounded the corner on Forty-eighth Street and Seventh Avenue into Times Square. He was startled by the message on the electric sign.

. . . . GERMANS IN POTSDAM RECEIVE DEATH SENTENCES FOR SLAYING AMERICAN AIRMEN . . . . MORE DEATHS IN YESTERDAY'S BURNING OF DRUMMOND PLANT NEAR SMITHTOWN ON LONG ISLAND. DEATH TOLL STANDS NOW AT THIRTEEN . . . . HIROSHIMA DEATH COUNT MOUNTS FURTHER IN AFTERMATH OF A-BOMB DROP . . . .

People were still being killed. Bombs were still falling on parts of the world. People were still worrying about revenge and retribution. He knew better than most that revenge is a kind of illusion. It promises a peace it can't deliver.

It was tough to believe, standing in the middle of a jubilant throng, that there was still grief and suffering elsewhere. The sign bannered death and devastation, but the crowd seemed barely to register it. They were wild, excited, bursting with anticipation. They were looking up at the board of lights only to check the next line of copy; no one wanted to miss the big announcement, the one they'd come to scream for.

Dan squared his shoulders and pushed on. The multitude of would-be merrymakers was spilling over into the streets already and it wasn't yet

10:00 A.M. There simply wasn't room on the sidewalks to accommodate them all. Although the police plan had been to leave Broadway and Seventh Avenue from Forty-second Street up into the Fifties running free until noon, one by one the blocks surrounding Times Square were becoming impassable for vehicular traffic. It was as though the world was congregating at Forty-second Street and Broadway.

Finally, Major Dan Baron made it to the main entrance of the Hotel Astor. He had nearly lost his flight bag three or four times in the crush. He *had* lost the Kewpie doll prize. He had also experienced trouble in retrieving his officer's cap from a happily drunken woman who had insisted on trying it on, only to try walking away with it seconds later.

Once inside the crowded lobby, Dan was briefly tempted to stop for a drink at the Astor Bar. But, good as a standup shot might have tasted to cut the dust of the road, there was no way he wanted his reunion with Diana to be deferred even seconds longer. His excitement mounted as the elevator rose to the seventh floor.

Baron forced himself to walk at a deliberate pace down the long carpeted hallway to the deluxe suite in which they'd spend a week before heading back to Hollywood. He raised his fist and rapped on the door.

It didn't take Diana long to open it. She knew it was Dan. There he stood, tall and tanned with an intense and hungry look on his face.

She had rehearsed this moment in her mind for days, imagining every detail of it, seeing herself hurtling into his arms, kissing him, caressing him, feeling the hard, muscular body, his warmth. Now he was here, and she hadn't moved, hadn't spoken. She could only stare.

"How does a man make up for two years of emptiness?" Dan asked, voice choked with emotion.

"Very tenderly," she advised. Her eyes were soft and filled with wonderment. It was as though she had never really seen him before. She searched every line and crevice of his face with her eyes. But it wasn't enough. Slowly, she raised her right hand and carefully traced the outline of his strong features with her fingertip. He covered her hand with his own and held it lightly to her cheek, his eyes never wavering from hers.

"Oh, Dan," she said. "It's been so terribly long."

"You're a million times more beautiful than I remembered you in all those dreams."

"As long as you think so."

It was only then that Dan reentered Diana's world, the world in which he wanted to be, by stepping into the Astor suite.

He kicked his worn flight bag into the room, closed the door firmly behind him, and finally took her in his arms and kissed her. It was a long, deep, hungry kiss.

"No violins," she apologized, finally stepping back to look at him again.

"I've got all the music I need," he whispered,

grinning the most tender version of the famous Baron grin she had ever seen.

"And no candlelight."

"You provide more than enough yourself, lady," he assured her. He took her now by the hand and started to lead her to the sofa.

"No," she said. "The bedroom." Suddenly, she was being swept up in his arms and carried toward the doorway.

Seconds later, she was deposited on cool, white sheets and Dan was leaning over her, caressing her with his look, his touch as he undressed her. Then the clothing was gone and they lay naked, Dan poised above her, kissing her breasts, his tongue enticing the stiffened nipples one after the other. She moaned with pleasure. Her arms went around him, stroking his back. Suddenly, she stopped. There was a scar on his side, one that hadn't been there before. She sat up quickly. "Oh my God, Dan." She bent to kiss it and he pushed her gently back down on the bed. She opened herself to him then, body arched to his, her arms locking around him in a fierce embrace.

"Come to me," she murmured, her tongue thick with her mounting passion. "Fill me up and make me live again."

He entered her, gently at first, then faster, harder, and she pressed her body to his, rising to meet his rhythm. It was wild and free and almost violent. There was no need for words. It was total, unconditional surrender of self, a complete, loving immolation.

For a few moments, the only sound in the room was their exhausted breathing.

"The war's over, kid," he said softly after a time.

"I know it now," she said, wiping the perspiration from his still damp brow with a corner of the sheet. "Rest now. Be peaceful."

He rested his large, warm hand on her bare abdomen. It was a big, square hand, roughened now with callouses. She didn't know how he'd gotten them. She did know it was a good hand and she wanted it there always. Being held, being touched lovingly by this man was more than enough for her.

"Good boy," she said in a quiet, loving way, well remembered by both of them. She always liked calling him her good boy, afterwards.

Please, God, she prayed, on the gamble that there was a listening deity somewhere, don't let me have to love another man. Don't even allow me to lie with anyone else—ever. This is all the man I need or want. But then this was how she'd always felt, wasn't it?

Then Dan turned to look at her again. He smiled a long, self-satisfied smile.

"Smug, aren't you?"

"Right."

They were both only slightly surprised at how little time it took for passions banked for such a long time to be rekindled.

This time their loving was more lighthearted than before—rough play, almost giddy and improvisational—and yet it was as deeply satisfying. There was a lot of laughter too.

"We're going to wear each other out," she said finally.

"We'll go in for spare parts," he said. "If they can't patch us up, it will have been a hell of a fine way to go."

"Oh, you think so?"

"I do, lady. I do."

Abruptly, he rolled forward, up and out of bed, and stood there stark naked next to the bed. "Now we get out of here for a while and go out into the streets."

"Like that?"

"Why not? Who'd notice?"

"You're insane," she giggled.

"No, come on." He was scooping her into his arms. "We're going to put our clothes back on, however reluctantly, and go out there. This is a day history is being made. It's a day we're going to live to tell our kids about."

She wanted to ask, "What kids?" She didn't. Someday she did want to have Dan's child. But there were always phantoms getting in their way. There was always the image of Barbara, his wife, and his own extraordinary and unmerited guilt.

Diana got dressed quickly. She wasn't about to let him out of her sight. Diana was going to declare war on all ghosts!

CHAPTER :::::::::::::::::
::::::::::::::: NINE

Seaman Libby, still smarting from his fall on the beach, was tired of waiting. He was sore outside and the inside was beginning to sting a little too. He didn't appreciate cooling his heels one little bit. What the hell was going on around here? He'd certainly made it clear what he turned up on the beach. It had been a genuine find, a stroke of good fortune, and, as he admitted to himself in all due modesty, a case of alert observation paying off.

"All right, Libby, whatcha got?"

Startled, Libby leaped to his feet. These young ensigns were really chickenshit. If anybody was going to chew your ass for minor lapses in military courtesy, it was one of these guys.

"Right here, sir. German fatigues. There's three more sets along with a rubber dory."

The young officer looked startled. "This better not be a joke, Libby."

"Look at 'em, Mr. Carter." He handed the plastic bag to the ensign. Libby had told the goddamn yeoman what he'd found when he'd first come in. Why hadn't the yeoman told Carter?

The ensign took out the fatigues and held them up. "They're German navy fatigues all right. They weren't even bright enough to rip the labels off."

"And there's a name on each set, sir. Planck, Boetticher, Kohler, and Braun."

"Too bad you didn't find them six months ago," Carter said.

"We're still going to report it, aren't we, sir?" If Carter didn't want to report the find, his decoration would go straight out the window.

"We'll report it," the young officer said without any great enthusiasm. "But with Germany out of the war, it won't mean as much."

"Well, it means a lot to me, sir."

"Why's that, Libby?"

Mr. Carter grinned malevolently. He wanted to hear the little fisherman say it. It wasn't too hard to figure out what he'd say.

"Maybe it'll get me out of the goddamn cavalry."

Carter shook his head gravely. "Hell no, Libby. You got it all wrong. This amazing discovery of yours proves beyond any doubt that you're a first-rate mounted beach patrolman. And you're an essential part of a first-rate team."

As Libby sat there shaking his head miserably from side to side, the ensign went on, enjoying himself hugely. "I'd be willing to lay odds on the fact that when the Commandant hears about what you've done, he'll order you and Tom Collins to stick together till one of you drops."

Seaman Libby buried his face in his hands and groaned.

The man who sat in the chair, which was placed in front of the wall mirror, was patrician to the core—handsome, white maned, a cruelly intelligent face with an imposing aquiline nose. There was something very keen about his appearance—altogether focused. He was like an eagle. He gave the impression he would be ready for anything, on the alert, ready to move in, resources already measured out.

The barber, on the other hand, was faceless in his white coat—as anonymous looking as barbers are paid to be.

"How's this, senator?" He held up another mirror so that Senator Marc Commer of Connecticut could look at the back of his own imposing head.

"It's all right," Commer said impatiently. He actually didn't have time for the haircut, but he did think it important to look his best for the press conference. There'd be newsreel cameras there, no doubt about it. The way the world was shrinking, with the coming of photojournalism and with television very much on the way, he was convinced that appearances weighed heavily in the way people cast their votes. Now with the continuing independence of women, most of them registered to vote, there was no telling what or where . . .

The phone rang.

Don Flanagan, his new executive assistant, fresh out of Fletcher at Tufts University, picked it up.

"Senator Commer's suite."

The aide listened politely as the other party spoke his piece. Commer watched, listening carefully while the barber finished.

"The senator is unavailable at the moment. He's in conference. Who . . . ? Yes . . . Yes . . . but I really can't say . . . Let me check that out for you, sir."

Young Flanagan held his hand over the telephone mouthpiece and looked across at Commer. He said, "It's Stait. He insists on talking to you."

"I won't be in until after the press conference."

Apparently, Stait had read the papers and was looking for a deal.

"You don't want to speak to him at all?"

"That's what I said."

"Why, Marc?" asked the other aide, Fredericks, Commer's most senior adviser and oldest crony. "You might enjoy yourself with your head in the old lion's mouth."

Commer smiled. It was a bleak smile. "Maybe it would be worthwhile just to hear Stait wiggling around, trying to find a way out of having his dirty laundry aired." Stait was the kind he could enjoy sticking pins into. He was so cocky. He had strutted so long. It would be a pleasing diversion bringing him to heel.

"All right," Commer said. "Tell him to hold. I'll be with him in a few minutes." He spoke to the barber. "Almost done?"

"Done right now, sir," the man said, whipping the barber's apron off with a flourish.

"Very good," Commer said, paying the man. It was a good haircut. Despite his frequent protestations to the contrary, Commer was a vain man, much taken with his own appearance. He always fancied people were looking at him. Most often he was right.

He stood and stared off into space while the barber gave him a last whisk of the brush and gathered up his tools. Commer made no move until the tradesman had closed the door behind him. Then, taking his time, he walked across the room and picked up the phone.

"Hello, Stait."

"Good morning, senator," said a very unruffled-sounding Stait. "And it *is* a beautiful morning too."

"Does it seem all that beautiful to you?" Commer asked.

"The war is almost over. All that's lacking is the news from D.C. It's not raining at the moment. What could be better?"

"I would have to think you might be somewhat ambivalent about the end of the war," Commer said. "After all, the war has been good to you, Stait. You've grown fat on it. And as for today, there are dire predictions for stormy weather this afternoon. Or haven't you read the papers?"

"The war has been indirectly helpful to me," Stait continued without dropping his cheery tone of voice. "It has given me an opportunity to serve my country. But it is, like they say, a two-way street, senator. I have served the war effort and the public interest. To say nothing of the contributions of my family—my son, my nephews, one of whom was seriously wounded at Rabaul."

There was a long pause as Commer considered. This man Stait was certainly a cool customer—and arrogant.

"All right, Stait," Commer said in a low, unpleasant tone of voice. "Let's get down to cases. Why did you call me? We're hardly friends. Let's have it right out in the open."

"No other way, Senator. No other way than open. I just called to tell you how much I approve of what you plan to do. It's damned important that you people from the legislative branch take an interest in those of us who work close to the executive. It's important to have your constructive criticism." A pause. Then: "I'm sure my lawyers and I are going to read only criticisms that are constructive."

For a moment, Commer was rendered speechless. The incredible nerve of the man! "Did I hear you correctly?"

"Depends on how well you listened to me."

"It's *you* I'm after, Stait. You and other vermin like you. Doesn't it sink in? You're the culprit. You're the man who's abused the office, who's appropriated scarce materials for use in his own plants, who's used threats and bribes to gain favor for yourself and your family enterprises. I intend to blow you clean out of the water this afternoon!"

"I'm sorry you feel that you've got to take that tack with me, Senator." Stait hadn't abandoned his calm, cheerful tone of voice. He was still in absolute control and it made Commer mad. "Of course you can damn well *try* to blow me out of the water."

"I'll do more than that. I'll do a hell of a lot more than try," Commer said harshly. "You don't stand a chance, Stait. I've got absolutely solid evidence."

"Well," Stait said, giving the impression of a man who'd never lose his composure, "be that as it may. I have something else on my mind."

"And that is?" Commer asked warily.

"I've heard a rumor about you."

"You can't slander me!" Commer was sure of his moral ground. There was absolutely nothing to drag out to use against him, no scandals, no indiscretions. Nothing!

"That's not what I'm talking about, Senator," Stait went on. "I heard you've got a big dream, a dream many other dedicated, talented public servants have had. You want to run for a higher spot. The top spot!"

"What does that have to do with you?"

"I think you'd make a hell of a president."

"I suppose you think I ought to thank you for that?"

"You're better fitted for the job than Truman."

Commer just laughed at him.

"It's not a joke, Senator. I mean it."

"It's not that easy, Stait."

"Think about it."

Commer laughed again and replaced the phone in its cradle. His laugh was a cruel one, not especially mirthful. His aides both looked curiously at him.

"Did he squirm?" asked Fredericks.

"Like a bloodworm on a hook."

"He want to make a deal?"

"Of course."

The younger aide jumped into the discussion. "He could be a big help to us. I've seen him operate. He *does* have influence. He's got money and he's got access to money. And we're going to need a hell of a lot of it to get you to the other end of Pennsylvania Avenue."

Commer smiled grimly. "He *will* be a big help to us. This afternoon and when the papers come out tomorrow, he's going to help us in a big way. He's going to make me a star. A first-class reformer—one that's not afraid to put things right, to knock down the thieves and hypocrites no matter who they are. Money won't buy an image like that."

Flanagan was still troubled. "Was he actually so bad?"

"You should know," Fredericks commented. "You and those smart characters you recruited were the guys who nailed him."

"He's corrupt all right," Flanagan admitted. "But he's also done the job FDR put him in there to do. There's no way we can deny that."

"We won't deny it," Commer said. "We're simply not going to talk about it."

"I think we're making a mistake," Flanagan said.

"We crucify him," Commer said softly. "We need J. Walter Stait right where he is."

"You're giving him nowhere to go, no position he can retreat to."

"There's always the federal pen." Fredericks was smiling.

"Isn't that a little drastic?"

"A public crucifixion," Commer repeated. There was something about the way he said it that sent a chill down Flanagan's spine. No graduate course in political science could ever quite prepare you for the homicidal determination in the eyes of an ambitious politician. When he's out for blood, it's time to step out of the way. Fast.

Was Commer, for all his much talked-about virtue, better than the man he was about to gore? Flanagan shook his head and looked away.

CHAPTER TEN

"To have stayed at the Astor is to have *lived* in New York." Since its original construction in 1904 on the foreclosed farm tract of one Medcef Eden, the Hotel Astor had led a distinguished and very full life. A massive pseudo-Renaissance structure, with its formidable mansard of green slate and copper, the Hotel Astor loomed like an imperial presence over Times Square. Five thousand hungry people could be served dinner simultaneously in its public rooms. It was an especially favored watering hole for West Pointers—both Eisenhower and Douglas MacArthur called it home when staying in New York City. It was at the Astor that the New York City Police Department's Holy Name Society held its annual communion breakfast. "Meet me at the Astor" had become a watchword with many of the nation's most distinguished citizens. There at "The Crossroads of the World," the Astor had known the great and the gifted, the infamous and the gilded.

Now, unknown to management and patrons alike, the grand old hotel, a New York City institution, was in serious and almost immediate jeopardy.

Building engineer Richard Peck moved through his routine chores that Tuesday morning with a peculiar sense of ritual. He performed all his regular morning checks and inspections on the complicated machines that kept the great hotel's life blood flowing: water, steam, refrigeration. He smiled and greeted all the regulars: the cashiers, the reservation clerks, kitchen personnel, office staff, the bell captain. Peck had become a popular man at the Astor. He had little to say, but was consistently obliging. He was always willing and able to repair whatever needed repair. When asked for such a favor, he'd flash his quick, metered kind of a smile, and turn his attention to the chore. If the device had run in the first place, Peck could manage to make it run again.

Despite his popularity with the staff, no one at the Astor could claim he or she truly knew Richard Peck. At one time or other, most of the female employees had been enamored of Peck's good looks, his neatness, his educated, slightly foreign speech, the apparent calmness and steadiness of his character. He gave none of them the slightest encouragement toward the establishment of a romantic attachment. He would fix their typewriters or rehang their doors—whatever. He would not, however, return their flirtations.

After checking his gauges and dials, after writing a routine report for the management in his strong, vertical hand, Peck left his small cubbyhole office in the subbasement and moved systematically through every floor of the huge hotel. He believed firmly in constant vigilance. It was important to him that he keep reviewing a job until the final moment came. Then, if one had been thorough enough, there would be no last-minute surprises. Peck detested surprises.

On this particular inspection tour on this singular day, Peck carried a reduced set of building drawings with him. He did all his checking on the Seventh Avenue side of the building, that part of the structure overlooking Times Square. He checked off each location on the building drawings as he inspected it.

There was electric wiring to examine, the product of nearly seven months' labor, during lunch hours, extra time in the morning before work, or at night after his shift was over. All the wiring was carefully concealed under rugs, inside partitions, in various much-neglected parts of the building, next to ducting, in slop sink closets, and in the special niches built into the walls to house emergency fire-fighting equipment.

It had to be done just right. He'd made thousands of calculations, worked and reworked load factors, weight distribution of the building—the whole business. It had been built like a fortress. He had the original architects' renderings and blueprints from the firm of Clinton & Russell, and it was clear from them that the demolition contractors would experience tremendous difficulty if the time ever came to raze it.

124 : : V-J DAY

Peck had taken all this into consideration and he knew just what he needed. There were only a few preparations left to be made. Soon, very soon . . .

Lest these exultant, self-righteous Americans continue to think God has ordained them to pare away and cauterize any civilization of which they disapprove, let him come face-to-face with Panikos, god of fear. This was the real objective of his operation.

On each of the floors, Peck opened up the slop sink closets, looked into fire-equipment niches, peered into each and every hiding place, searching for signs that anyone else on the hotel's maintenance staff might have stumbled on his painstaking preparations.

After spending more than an hour checking out all his circuits, Peck returned to his small office deep under the hotel. Some men would have despised having to spend so much of their time in a damp basement away from the sun. For Peck, however, it had been acceptable—almost pleasing. He wanted no strong reminders of vital New York life moving on about him. He wanted to dissociate himself, as much as possible, from Americans. He cherished his solitude. It gave him strength.

The tiny cubicle offered him the opportunity to think things out. He spread the drawings of the building across his desk. He looked them over carefully for the final time, evaluating, as if daring himself to discover an oversight. At this stage, he would have been surprised, shocked, disgusted with himself, had he found one. But there was no need. He had made his plans well and carried them out without a flaw. He knew that.

Satisfied, he took the cardboard box in which he'd placed the five unused detonators and the last of the bell wire, and set it down on the floor near the door so he'd remember to take it out and dispose of it. He didn't want to leave his office cluttered and untidy. He was not that sort of man. He didn't want to be considered disorderly.

Now he sat back and allowed the recurring fantasy of the girl with the burning hair to materialize in his mind's eye once again. Since he'd been given the terrible news, the vision had come to him over and over. To fuel his own resolve, he had encouraged it.

There was something about her great luminous blue eyes he could never forget. Every time he had looked at her, they astounded him with their size and the softness that dwelled in them. Having been brought up in a home where discipline and self-control had been held up as the highest of all virtues, the gentleness of Tereska's eyes had been a revelation. She had offered him something altogether new, a dimension never present in his life before or now, after her.

"Richard," she had said so often to him, "it's important—maybe more important than anything else—to be loving. All things have a right to be cherished."

Back then, he had listened. He had begun to feel that way himself. It was difficult to escape from his own Calvinistic ways, his passion for justice, his innate need for orderliness. But with Tereska, he grew and developed new feelings, new insights into life. These were among the many precious gifts she brought to him.

Now the taste had turned bitter. She had loved the world until February 1945, when it had fallen in on her. The bombs, raining down on their beautiful city, had burned that golden hair, extinguished the light in those loving eyes.

He closed his eyes, summoning Tereska's face again. This time he forced himself to witness the horror of the fire destroying her beauty, turning her into a charred abomination. But this time he became aware of something that seemed even worse than the terrible transformation, something even more frightening. Tereska's face had faded. He was having difficulty re-creating her features with the kind of urgency and accuracy his visions used to have for him. It was as though the other ghosts—Louise, Vivian, Loretta—others who had died in a similar way, were crowding in front of his beloved Tereska, cutting him off from her. It was ironic because their deaths meant nothing to him. They were just accidental victims in his master plan.

Abruptly, he brought his mind back to the present, to the call he had had that morning. What of Boetticher—Beaton, as he now called himself? How much did he know? Would he actually try to stop him? Was the young man actually bright enough, tough enough, indeed, desperate enough?

He recalled that Beaton had been a very determined man in training. He had a tenacity that could now justify alarm. Peck decided that if Beaton became a serious threat, he would have to do something.

Peck unlocked the upper right-hand drawer in his desk and took out the small automatic. He held it in the palm of his hand. It gleamed with a dull sheen. It was a beautiful thing—and deadly. Beaton could not, under any circumstances, be allowed to get in the way.

Poor Beaton. He had allowed peace to break out in his heart.

It was nearly noon.

The Brighton Beach express screamed shrilly and hurled itself through the pitch-black tunnel, its headlamps cutting a narrow swath of light through the damp, deep gloom. Beaton stood at the controls, staring intently into the darkness.

The personal freedom and fulfillment he had achieved in New York was far too precious a thing to surrender without a fight. He had bought a house with his share of the funds they had brought across. He was going to marry Gisela Bauer. He had a decent job and was well thought of.

Somehow, he would have to convince Peck to stop his nonsense. The war was over. There was no reason to extend it. It was utterly without sense. Each new operation raised the probability of a new investigation. What if Peck should suddenly become repentant or frightened and follow in the footsteps of Dasch and Burger, two of the earlier saboteurs who had turned themselves and their companions in the FBI? Here in America, such an admission of guilt would mean a death sentence. Beaton could see that clearly. The American courts could be most vindictive if they chose to be.

Six other members of the two earlier teams had found that out for themselves. Quirin, Haupt, Neubauer, Heink, Kerling, and Thiel all went to their deaths. Their lives were snuffed out on August 8, 1942, in the Washington, D.C., jail, as they sat strapped into the electric chair. Ask them, if you know in which corner of hell they're lodged.

At first, the industrial fires and explosions had seemed spontaneous to Beaton when he read about them in the newspapers. Even to his skilled evaluation, they seemed true accidents and he suspected nothing. There were always processes in manufacturing that rendered factory buildings and personnel vulnerable. Beaton knew that much of the construction and electrical wiring in factories and other commercial establishments did not measure up to current code standards, even where such codes existed. Of course with war materials, there was even greater danger. That was part of the war game. The skillful saboteur learns these weak points in the production process and then exploits them. He knew that Peck, with his advanced training and his sharp intelligence, was a master of that sort of thing.

But when the accidents began to form a pattern, when they seemed to repeat themselves again and again, all in the area within commuting distance of New York City, Beaton's worst suspicions seemed to be confirmed. The hallmarks were all there: the sudden burst of flames, the absence of any meaningful clues, with the trouble originating in a working area where small parts were being fabricated at benches by woman employees. All of it suggested Richard's fine hand. Now, months after the final immolation of the Reich, it seemed that Peck was still risking himself—and thus jeopardizing Beaton—with his persistent incendiary violence. What was he seeking to gain for himself beyond an ignominious death?

There was an element in all this that made no sense at all to Beaton. In the months of careful preparation for the mission, it had always seemed that Peck was the least ideological, the least politically involved of the whole group. Periodically, he'd say sarcastic things, the kinds of remarks that court disaster. He'd make subtle—even not-so-subtle—jokes at the expense of people like Goebbels and Goering. At least once he had obliquely ridiculed the Führer himself. Now why should such a man, so little concerned with the party and with German leadership, seek to continue the war on his own?

But it *had* to be Peck. Theirs had been the third

and last team dispatched by the Abwehr as Operation Pastorius. Brown, the other surviving member of the team, was probably still hiding somewhere in western Canada, no doubt shitting in his pants in some isolated town close to the Arctic Circle. The notion of hiding out in the midst of millions was the kind of scheme that would go right over Brown's head.

Actually, it had been Richard Peck who had in early 1943 picked the locale for both of them to blend into the scenery.

"Where better but in this huge, impersonal city can we find the kind of anonymity required for our survival until we can get home again? Who, seeking conspirators, would think to look in New York's neighborhoods? If we are quiet, we will not be noticed."

That was the line to remember: *"If we are quiet, we will not be noticed."*

"You mean relinquish our mission?" Beaton had asked then, horrified at the prospect of what looked like, on the face of it, treason.

"With Keating dead, Brown terrified, the other two teams apprehended, we shouldn't stick our heads in the lion's mouth," Peck had said. "Perhaps later when things cool down."

But the time for renewed activity had never come.

There had been one hundred eleven thousand dollars in American currency. Beaton had never seen so much money in his whole life. They had split it three ways. He had managed to hang on to most of it. Even the house he had just bought for himself and Gisela had left him an amazing sum. It was a good life, courtesy of the Abwehr's operating accounts.

It was getting close to noon. In a few minutes he'd be off shift, finished with the BMT for today. He had a great deal to accomplish. He would first meet with Peck to see if he could talk him out of his foolish and dangerous course. That failing, he had other chores. He would put up with no sabotage. He had to make Richard see the wisdom of that choice—especially now. He would choose prudence, safety, and circumspection. They are perhaps the homelier sisters in the sorority of virtues, Beaton thought, but they have a warmth and goodness all their own. In one way or another, Beaton promised himself, I will remain secure.

The train thundered on beneath the vast city.

CHAPTER ELEVEN

It was five minutes to noon.

The troop transport *Governor Hiram Tawes* was making her final approach to the berth next to the West Side Highway. Virtually every one of the military passengers aboard was lined up at the rail as the clumsy craft was eased into place by the attending tugs. Even the ship itself seemed small in the looming shadow of the great city's towers.

Captain Timothy Stait was trying to keep Kathleen off his mind. The knowledge she was somewhere here in New York made him even angrier. She was probably with "the really wonderful guy" she'd alluded to on the V-mail letter form. "He loves me and I love him too," her words had gone, making his stomach turn and his heart pound. He had done his share of footlocker kicking and he'd tied on a phenomenal load one night and made a damn fool of himself.

His anger made him feel it would be better if Kathleen and her new man were somewhere miles away instead of here in the city to which he was being returned.

Or would it?

"What if you bump into her?" he asked himself. "With him?"

That was a picture. He could see it. He'd have a blonde on his arm. He would wave casually at her and the son of a bitch whatever-his-name-was. Then he would tell her to go to hell. And he'd mean it. There was an all WAC military band on the "Welcome Boat" playing "Coming in on a Wing and a Prayer." They sounded fine. He tried to get himself into the mood of rejoicing to match the band. It was tough going. He tried to feel cheerful by reminding himself that in a matter of minutes he'd be home. The trouble was, there was no one special to come home to.

Down on the dock, almost directly below him, a WAC lieutenant was waving and blowing kisses. The boxy lines of the Oveta Culp Hobby uniform she wore fought a losing battle to camouflage a fabulous body—the kind every lonely soldier dreamed about.

"Take your hat off," an airborne corporal shouted down in his best parade-ground voice. "Take it off, honey, sir."

"Take it off," the other soldiers yelled, not having her hat in mind.

The WAC officer just looked up and laughed. Then with a flourish, she whipped off her high-crowned, visored pillbox and set free a beautiful mane of golden hair.

There were whistles and cheers all along the side of the transport.

"There's your blonde," Tim Stait thought. "All you've got to do is go down there and put in your claim."

The band had stopped playing.

"Welcome home, fellas," the WAC lieutenant called up to them.

The troops roared back. It wasn't surprising that the WAC was getting a bigger response than Lady Liberty. She was live, luscious flesh, every inch a woman.

"I got something for the first guy ashore," she yelled up to them, blowing a big promissory kiss.

Stait was a man of action. Without a moment's hesitation he jumped up on the ship's rail, crouched in a sitting position, a good twenty feet above the macadam dock; he only looked down once before he jumped.

As he landed hard, with the cheers and whistles of his comrades ringing in his ears, he felt something give in his left ankle. He had rolled with the impact but, even before he tried the ankle, he knew for certain he wouldn't be using it again for a while.

"Stand up and claim your prize," the WAC shavetail told him. She was a beauty.

"You'll have to come down here, Lieutenant," he said. "Think I busted my ankle."

"Oh, my God." She suddenly looked guilt-stricken. "It's my fault."

"You okay?" a Port of Embarkation noncom called, hustling over.

"Not very," Stait answered. "But I'm in the lieutenant's very capable hands." The noncom shrugged, rolled his eyes, and strolled back toward where the gangway was being set.

Actually, Tim felt pretty ridiculous. He'd managed to go through the whole European theater from goddamn Normandy all the way to the stinking Rhine River without picking up so much as a scratch and now here he was busting himself up the minute he landed in New York.

The girl squatted down next to him. "What are you laughing at? Doesn't it hurt?"

"Jesus Christ, Lieutenant. You're beautiful," he said. "You know you're worth breaking both ankles and an arm for."

"You sure you broke it?" she asked, showing considerable concern. She was also showing a lovely knee and an inviting expanse of thigh.

"Yeah. Look at it swell."

"My God," she said guiltily.

"Slip the shoe off?" he asked.

She looked at him disbelievingly. "Won't it hurt?"

"Sure it will. Do it anyway."

Carefully she unlaced his shoe and eased it off his foot.

"Kiss me so the pain will go away."

She did so while the whole company at the rail of the transport above them erupted with cheers and shouts of encouragement. The lady really knew how to kiss.

"Bonus for an injury sustained in the line of duty?" he asked when they finally came out of the clinch.

She smiled widely and kissed him again. He couldn't help feeling the girl was enjoying herself quite as much as he was. Only now the pain was really beginning to pierce the numbness.

"How about dinner tonight?"

She seemed startled. "Won't you be flat on your back in a hospital if it is broken?"

"No, ma'am," he said. "There's no way they're gonna hold me in some crummy hospital if you're willing to have dinner with me. And in view of the fact you incited me to jump in the first place, you owe me at least one date, maybe more."

She grinned an impudent grin. "You're too much, Captain."

"So are you, Lieutenant. That's why I can't resist you."

"You better tell me your name."

"Tim."

"I'm Lil."

"Now you better call the ambulance so they can slap a cast on me."

"All right," she agreed, getting up. "All right, on both counts. Guess I do owe you." She didn't seem at all displeased about the prospect of going out with him.

Tim reflected admiringly that a girl put together like Lil could be arrested for carrying around dangerous weapons. The ankle was hurting more by the minute, but his morale was making a speedy recovery. She had helped take his mind off Kathleen's betrayal. Maybe the headlong leap off the transport had a positive value, even if he *had* broken something. Maybe by the time he got all patched up again, the war would be over. He wouldn't mind celebrating with Lil.

"You all right, sir?"

It was the young sailor he'd been with on deck that morning when they'd seen the Statue of Liberty.

"Thought you might need this, sir." He had Stait's duffel bag.

"Thanks a lot. What's your name again, sailor?"

"Grenon, sir. Jerry Grenon."

"He seems to have broken his ankle," the woman officer said to the sailor. "I'm going to get an ambulance."

"The hell you are," said Stait. He didn't want her to go away. "I've got a better idea. The two of you are going to get me to a cab."

"Carry you?" Lil asked dubiously.

"One holding me up on either side and I'll hop."

"That's silly."

"Lillian, dear," Stait said firmly. "It's my pride at stake. As silly as it may look to see a grown man hopping, nobody's carrying me out of this war. If I can't make it on my own two feet, then I'll hop out on one."

"Okay, Tim," she said with a smile. Tim appreciated the smile. It seemed to say, I understand how you feel and I admire you for it. He liked that. He also liked the little greenish brown flecks in her hazel eyes.

The WAC took the cab with him. Tim was happy about that too. He didn't want to let her get away. She took his breath away. She was so fresh looking and unspoiled with her freckled, Irish-looking face and her turned-up nose.

Since Tim had married Kathleen, he'd never been with—never had—another woman. He'd been too anxious to get back to her. Now it didn't seem to matter. Maybe he owed it to himself to get involved. Hell, he hadn't felt so good since he'd gotten that rotten letter.

Meanwhile, the sailor who'd helped get Stait into the taxicab was working on his own prospects in an entirely different way.

Jerry Grenon didn't want to surprise his sister. He wanted to call up first to advise her he was back. Maybe she could take the train in from Mineola and meet him in town. They could take in the Statue of Liberty, a round trip on the Staten Island ferry, and then go to dinner. He knew of a terrific steak house, Shine's, just a few doors north of Penn Station.

He dialed his home number. No. He tried again and let it ring. Still no one picked up the phone. Maybe they'd switched her shift. She probably wouldn't be working today anyway, with surrender in the air, going to happen any time. It looked like most people were off.

For the life of him, he couldn't remember the

name of the outfit she worked for. All he remembered was that it made parts for navy fighter aircraft on Long Island. She was very proud of that. He knew it was important to his sister to be doing something that would, at least to some degree, support and protect him. She was a hell of a woman, that sister of his. He could hardly wait to see her face when she saw him.

He pushed his gob hat back and scratched his head in puzzlement. Who else could he call? His mind simply didn't register. Didn't she have a new boy friend? She'd mentioned some guy in one of her letters. A guy named Richard. But she hadn't given him a last name or anything else to go on.

Maybe he'd better hang around Manhattan and try calling again later. Maybe she'd be in if he let a couple of hours go by. There'd still be time for a fancy feed even if they couldn't do the boat ride this time. Maybe it was just as well he didn't get Sis yet. He'd enjoy wandering around the city on his own before getting on the Long Island Rail Road for home. There was a lot to see and feel and there are times—even happy ones—when it's good to be alone.

He especially wanted to go aboard the Statue of Liberty. He headed for the subway. He'd make his first stop Bedloe's Island. That was an old promise to himself. He was going to keep it.

CHAPTER TWELVE

It was probably some subtle sort of racial guilt that brought him there, but he was there nonetheless. He didn't like hospitals or being around people who were sick or injured, but here he was, climbing out of a cab on Fifty-ninth Street in front of Roosevelt Hospital.

He went inside.

"I'm looking for a young army sergeant who was brought in here this morning. His name is Nakamura."

"Nakamura?" the girl at the desk spoke the name like a challenge.

"That's right. N-a-k-a-m—"

"I know how to spell it," she said curtly. "That's Japanese." She said it as though she was about to tell him that he'd have to look for Sergeant Nakamura on another continent.

"I believe it is," he said, catching himself almost deliberately mumbling, a habit he fell into whenever he met someone who was hostile.

She gave him the room number and he went up, looking for the soldier he had photographed just hours before. He hoped the poor guy was doing all right.

A nurse, not very old, with black hair and big dark eyes looked up from her charts as he reached the nursing station. There was something so genuine, so wonderfully vital and alive about her, he thought as he inquired about Nakamura. She wasn't beautiful in a conventional way, but she had so strong, so positive a face that he couldn't take his eyes from her.

"Are you family?" she asked.

Without thinking, he raised his hand and pulled one eye back into a slant. "Only on my mother's side."

She blushed.

"He's right down here," she said. He made a mental note that even girls with olive complexions can blush becomingly.

"Is it okay to talk to him?"

"Sure," she said, relieved to discover he had not been offended.

The photographer walked down to the room she had indicated.

"Sergeant Nakamura?"

The patient looked up. His face was so badly swollen you could barely see his eyes. The photographer was aware that the man in the hospital bed didn't know who his visitor was.

"There's not much reason you should know me," he said, trying to reassure the soldier. "I don't want you to think you're coming down with amnesia."

"Glad you told me," Nakamura said, trying lamely to smile despite his sore mouth.

"I was on Forty-fourth Street this morning and I took your picture. I work for Time-Life."

"Must have been a hell of a picture."

"I won't say much for its absolute, aesthetic beauty, but it's got plenty of action."

"Sit down," the patient said.

The photographer did so, perching on the arm of the chair next to the bed.

"The reason I came here," he explained to the soldier, "is because I did get that picture."

"Don't tell me now," Nakamura said sarcastically. "You won a prize with it and you want me to sign a model's release, right?"

"No. I wanted you to know I got good likenesses of the guys who did it, four of 'em anyway. I want you to have the picture."

"What the hell for?"

"I don't know how you feel about it, but I'd like to see those guys get pinched."

"Shit."

"Don't you?"

The sergeant looked like hell warmed over. His eyes were practically closed—probably couldn't see much. There were cuts and bruises all over. Most of his face was a deep, angry red tinged with purple. He was in traction and his arm was splinted. There were sutures on his jawline.

"Hurts, doesn't it?"

"Sometimes more than others. They got me doped up."

"Inside too?" the photographer asked. He was sensitive enough to know that often the worst hurts are inside.

"Guess so."

"Sorry."

"What have you got to be sorry for?"

"Because I'm an occidental."

"I don't go for that kind of crap," said Nakamura. "It's five specific sons of bitches I'm after."

"I want to see them get pinched."

"Don't hold your breath."

"Why not?"

"I'm the enemy." He grimaced. "Can I see the picture?"

"Yeah," the photographer said, handing a print to him.

"Jesus," Nakamura said, trying hard to make out the photograph.

"You're from the 442nd," the photographer said.

"How you know that?"

"Your patch. I saw you guys at Monte Cassino."

"You were there?"

"Were you?"

"I wish to hell I hadn't been." Nakamura gave evidence of being happy to have somebody to talk to. "442nd or not, there's no way the cops are gonna go after those guys. Even if they'd been colored, no cop's gonna run them in for beating up a Jap. More likely they'll pin a medal on 'em. 'Specially today."

"I accuse you of being cynical."

"I come by it honestly," Nakamura said.

"I guess you do."

"But you're the guy who's supposed to be cynical, right? Goes with the job? Professional journalist and all? You stand takin' pictures and writing it down while we throw shit at each other."

"We catch it too."

"Maybe," the soldier said, sounding unconvinced.

"I hope the picture helps," the photographer said, groping for something to say. He could see Nakamura trying painfully to sit up in bed. He wanted to unburden himself.

"I do want to get those bastards, believe me," he said. "But I'd really like to get them myself, one at a goddamn time. I'd beat the livin' shit out of them, not just for me, but for my father and my mother, for my girl, for the rest of my family and for a good bunch of buddies I left behind in Italy—guys with eyes just like mine." Nakamura finished, eyes blazing, just as the little floor nurse with the dark hair appeared in the doorway, relieving the awkward moment.

"Time to check you over," she said cheerfully. "You don't have to leave." She waved the photographer back to his chair as he got up to go. "I'll be done in a jiffy."

"No, that's all right," he said. "I really have to go."

"Hey, look," the Japanese-American soldier said. "It was damn good of you."

"It's just I don't want to see bastards like that get away clean."

"They won't," the soldier said.

The young nurse, treating the little noncom who wore the enemy's face, would have made a terrific picture herself at his bedside. But the photographer had no desire to take the shot. So lovely a girl would have her picture taken again and again, so that someday her kids' kids could marvel and see what a good-looking lady their grandma really was.

He left, feeling somewhat melancholy.

CHAPTER THIRTEEN

Keefe was nursing a hangover, and the thought of chaperoning four boisterous newsboys all over the city didn't help his aching head. They could just amuse themselves however they wanted until the reception and awards ceremony at three thirty that afternoon. By then, a couple of bloody marys might have worked a cure.

"Where we goin' for lunch?" the eldest of the kids asked the editor, as Keefe doled out meal money for the day.

"Anywhere you want," Keefe replied. "Outside most eating places, they'll post a menu. You can look it over before you decide whether to go in. It'll tell you what they serve and whether you can afford it."

"Ain't you eating, Mr. Keefe?" Ciccone asked.

"Not hungry." He hoped they wouldn't say too much about food. He didn't even like thinking about it the way his stomach and head felt now.

"What about Childs?" another kid asked. "My ma told me it's a very nice place. She's been to New York before."

"Sure," Keefe said agreeably. "If your mother says it's a good place to eat, who am I to argue with her?" He tried to grin. He didn't give a damn if they all jumped off the goddamn building. "You'll have enough money with what I just gave you to have a good lunch and go to the Empire State Building as well. Just be sure you're back downstairs before three thirty."

The kids agreed and Keefe, walking gingerly in deference to his throbbing head, returned to his room.

"I think he's got a girl in there," Bobby whispered to Ciccone as the door closed behind the man.

"You're nuts."

"I think I saw her when he opened the door," Bobby insisted, unaware that the whore had already left.

"No girl would be in there," Ciccone whispered with disgust. "Not with a jerk like that."

"He really is a jerk," Bobby agreed. He didn't want to press it further and tell what he'd seen earlier.

Moments later, the four boys stepped out the glass front doors of the hotel. They paused for a moment at the top of the steps under the marquee announcing that Gene Krupa and his orchestra would play that night on the Astor Roof.

They were almost frightened. They'd never, any of them, seen a mob like this before. As huge and high-spirited as the crowds had seemed an hour ago, they were nothing compared to what the boys saw in front of them now. The people packed the streets; auto and bus traffic were halted altogether. The noise was deafening—music, voices, traffic from other streets in the vicinity, the rumble of subway trains underfoot, the cries of street vendors, and over it all, the shuffle of thousands and thousands of feet, the roar of chatter from a half million sets of lips.

"Never saw so many people," one of the kids marveled.

"What?"

"*Never saw so many people!*"

Bobby nodded agreement. There was little point in trying to make himself heard over the din.

"Where we gonna eat?" Ciccone shouted in Bobby's ear. "Never heard of Childs Restaurant. Sounds stupid to me."

Bobby, standing next to him, was the only one who managed to hear what he was saying. "I don't know," he yelled back.

The other kids were already moving down the steps and into the crowd. Tony and Bobby exchanged looks. Should they try keeping up with the two older boys or would they be better off on their own? Each of them carried his own money. That wasn't the problem. It was just that the others were sixteen; they'd probably be interested in other things.

One of the older guys looked back as if to say "Come on." Bobby gestured for them to go ahead, never mind them. The older boys didn't need to be told twice.

"To heck with them," Tony said.

They managed to communicate reasonably well now by reading each other's lips and by a lot of guessing.

"Let's walk around before we eat. It's early," said Bobby. It was shortly after twelve.

Ciccone nodded in agreement.

Can it always be like this? Bobby asked himself. Or is this all just because the war's almost over? If New York City *is* like this all the time, he marveled, how can people stand it? How can they put up with all the shoving and the noise and the smells? New Yorkers must really be tough.

For Bobby Noel Times Square seemed like a piece of candy someone had dropped in the dirt: something tantalizing you almost had, until the ants clustered all over it and consumed it.

But it *was* exciting!

The streets were shoulder to shoulder, hip to hip with people—all kinds of people—all of them waiting and milling around as if something fantastic was about to happen. He felt surrounded by sights, sounds, smells, so many that his senses became confused. There were the vivid colors of summer clothing, bright lettering on signs demanding to be read, the texture of the pavement underfoot, the feeling of being jostled and shoved, the aroma of hot dogs and booze, to say nothing of bad breath and sour sweat. And above it all, there was the frantic babble of voices.

It was like getting disoriented in a parade crowd, squinting your eyes to keep out the brightness, fighting your way through to be as close as possible to the line of march. But there was no line of march here, and certainly no distinction between those putting on the show and those merely watching. They were *all* part of it. The mass of spectators *was* the parade—the principal attraction.

There were signs everywhere screaming for attention.

> **SINATRA SINGS . . . . SMOKE CAMELS . . . . HAVE A COKE . . . . THE PAUSE THAT REFRESHES . . . . USO NEEDS YOUR SUPPORT . . . . LUCKY STRIKE, LS/MFT . . . .**

The gigantic Camel smoker on the east side of Broadway puffed his famous smoke rings of Con Edison steam, fifteen per minute, out over the heads of the throng. A great replica of the Statue of Liberty towered over everything but the electric sign on the Times Tower.

Up by Father Duffy's statue at the north end of the square loudspeakers were blaring, "You'd Be So Nice to Come Home To" and "Bell Bottom Trousers." A blind accordion player with a ragged dog tried to whip up donations near the Paramount Theater where *Incendiary Blonde* with Betty Hutton was playing, while across the square under the Camels billboard, Woody Guthrie and Leadbelly, both then playing in Greenwich Village clubs, were collaborating on an improvisation in a tiny cleared space on the sidewalk. They were engulfed by appreciative but distracted spectators, who kept looking away just long enough to check the electric sign for the first view of peace arriving. It was difficult to hear their singing over all the noise.

Bobby and Tony edged their way through the crowd, occasionally grabbing at each other's hand or shirt to keep from getting separated. Somehow, Bobby thought, it was reassuring to have a companion with you even if you had just met the guy this morning. The two of them were in this together—a kind of esprit de corps had formed between them.

It was hot and humid out there. Most of the men were in shirt-sleeves, the women in bright summer dresses. There were sailors everywhere and men in the uniforms of other American services, along with servicemen from other nations, from turbaned sikhs to French sailors with their red pompoms. There were teen-aged girls in blue jeans and flapping white dress shirts borrowed from fathers and brothers off at war. There were saddle shoes and bobby socks in evidence, even bare feet risking crushed toes. Bottles of whiskey were being passed cheerfully hand to hand. A bunch of sailors were throwing people up in the air and catching them in a blanket.

Abruptly, a microphone was thrust in Bobby's face, but he was tongue-tied and he didn't speak up quickly enough. A fat woman in thick glasses shoved him out of the way and began talking into it, responding to the questions of a short man in a gray suit with big, dark-circled eyes.

"That's Ben Grauer," Tony Ciccone shouted to Bobby. The man smiled as though he were pleased at having been recognized.

"Really?" He looked at Ben Grauer and was surprised to see that the famous radio broadcaster looked just like a normal, everyday person. "The NBC guy?"

"Yeah."

Unrecognized by the boys, there were other celebrities around. Just a few feet away, Ed Gardner, Archie of radio's "Duffy's Tavern," stood watching. Gardner, sticky and uncomfortable, wanted a drink—a tall, cool one—but like most everybody standing around him, he didn't want to leave for fear that he'd miss the big announcement on the giant electric sign.

.... LA GUARDIA BACKS CANDIDACY OF NEWBOLD MORRIS FOR MAYOR .... NO DEAL PARTY IS THE NAME CHOSEN FOR NEW LA GUARDIA COALITION .... QUEENS BUTCHER FACES EIGHTEEN MONTHS AND $75,000 IN FINES ON OPA VIOLATIONS ....

Other eyes watched the electric sign; nearly half a million pairs of them. Chief Inspector John O'Donnell, expecting a crowd that would eventually top the million mark, was estimating five hundred thousand in Times Square between Eighth and Sixth Avenues, from Fifty-fourth Street down to Forty-second, right now. Some of his fellow officers thought O'Donnell was being conservative. All police leaves had been canceled. All available men were on duty status throughout the city.

Virtually everywhere in the square were soldiers, sailors, marines, and coast guardsmen, wearing the vivid colored ribbons on their breasts that showed the wearer nearly died somewhere for the rest of us; far-off places whose names only lately had become household words—Tarawa, Saipan, Bastogne, Anzio, Bizerte, El Alamein, Truk, Midway, Okinawa.

The two boys, Bobby Noel and Tony Ciccone, having thoroughly lost the other pair of newsboys, were amazed and even a little jealous of all the hugging and embracing that was going on. It seemed to be an incredible day for kissing people. It seemed as though the whole city had skipped work and walked out on their normal everyday lives to be in the street.

Dozens of times one boy wanted to say something to the other, to share observations, but most of the time, there was simply no way to be heard. Even on the rare occasions when one of them *did* catch a glimpse of someone he considered a celebrity, by the time he'd caught the other's attention, the familiar face was lost again in the eddying, swirling mob.

Someone in the crowd pointed out Celeste Holm and Raymond Massey. The newspaper delivery boys' eyes became wider. Unknown to them, there was a gaggle of chorus girls from *Oklahoma!* posing like pretty pigeons nearby. They saw the pretty girls but had no idea who they were.

They saw a police horse named Reuben, front hooves on the sidewalk, rear hooves in the gutter, thrusting his long neck into a Nedick's stand, where a counterman fed him stale hamburger buns and sugar cubes.

Marlene Dietrich, passing through, stirred up a ripple of wolf calls and whistles. By the time Bobby Noel discovered who she was, she was gone. Sugar Ray Robinson stood in the crowd for a while and the Incomparable Hildegarde waved one of her long white satin gloves at her admirers. But even the famous, the extraordinary were upstaged by the day itself, the occasion, the heady feeling of expectancy, the ecstatic solidarity!

The newsboys, part of the great multitude, watched the signboard flashing on the New York Times Tower.

.... STUDY OF BASEBALL COLOR LINE TO BE MADE TODAY BY THE MAYOR'S GROUP .... LARRY MACPHAIL OF YANKEES AND BRANCH RICKEY OF DODGERS TO LEAD BLUE RIBBON PANEL .... ALLIES TO LET HIROHITO REMAIN EMPEROR SUBJECT TO OCCUPATION CHIEF .... MACARTHUR SLATED FOR THE POST ....

Times Square was only forty-one years old and yet it had already been recognized as an official gathering place for the nation. The huge crowd waited, watched, acted as silly and lighthearted and irresponsible as it pleased. This was to be their day. There was no way they'd be denied their fling.

CHAPTER FOURTEEN

The Sixteenth Precinct station house on West Forty-seventh Street was quiet inside, considering the bedlam in the streets. There were few uniformed officers in evidence. Every available man was out on the street.

"Can I help you, Mac?" a tall, cadaverous desk officer asked.

"I want to talk to somebody about an assault I saw committed this morning on Forty-fourth Street."

"Try tellin' me," the tall cop said, getting up slowly and sauntering over to the counter with the patient, slightly bored attitude of someone who has heard everything under the sun.

"Five merchant seamen assaulted a soldier. He was rushed to Roosevelt Hospital, badly injured."

"You say you were a witness to this . . . assault?"

"That's right."

"Well, you know they'll contact you if there's gonna be a prosecution. You'll very likely be asked to appear in court."

"I know that."

"Did you speak to an officer at the scene?"

"I'm a photographer for Time-Life Incorporated. I got a shot that shows the faces of four of the five assailants. I'd like to leave it for whoever's going to investigate the incident."

"No kiddin'? You work for *Life?*"

"That's right."

"You got a picture, huh?" The desk officer seemed very impressed by what the photographer had told him. He asked for identification and the photographer placed his press card on the counter. The policeman wrote down his name and office address. Then he asked, "Mind if I see the picture?"

"No. Not at all. Here it is." The photographer removed the 8½-by-11 glossy from its kraft envelope and slid it over the counter.

"Jesus, ain't that a hell of a shot? Real action!" Then he looked startled. "Hey, that's a Jap, ain't it?"

"American soldier."

"I mean the eyes. He looks like a Jap or some other kind of oriental."

"Nisei. American Japanese. 442nd Combat Team. Served in France and Italy."

"They ours?"

"That's right."

"What was he doin'?"

"Walking down the street minding his own business."

The tall cop shook his head. The photographer felt a subtle change of attitude with the discovery that the victim of the assault was Japanese, a pronounced cooling of interest in the plight of the attacked citizen.

"Kind of a natural, understandable thing happening today, wouldn't you say?" the cop asked with an enigmatic smile, cagy now, not anxious to say too much till he figured out just where the photographer stood.

"Why?" the photographer came back. "An assault's an assault—against the law no matter what day it is. At least that's what I was taught."

"Today's gonna be a big day. Today, everybody's got the Japs and the war on their minds." He paused for a moment and glanced down at the picture again. "In a way it don't surprise me none."

"I guess very few things *do* surprise you when you're working in a police station."

"You can say that again," the big cop allowed. "But you know, Mac, I can't personally get too riled up about a couple sailors gettin' a little rough with one of these monkeys, especially today. That don't surprise me at all you know. Human nature bein' what it is, if you get my meanin'."

"There were five sailors. Not a couple."

"I count only four."

"I got only four in the picture. The other guy was pickin' himself out of the gutter."

"Jap start it?"

"No."

The policeman pushed the photograph back into its brown envelope. "Look, Mac. I'll leave it for one of the detectives when some of 'em gets in."

"Nobody I can talk to now?"

"We're shorthanded today. You know how it is."

"Well, I hope somebody's going to follow up on it. This American soldier got pretty shitty treatment from five of his fellow citizens. I'd hate to think they're going to go unpunished. The sergeant, when I went up to the hospital to see him, told me he didn't think you people would take the time or effort to do anything about it."

"Sounds like a smart cookie, that Jap."

"*I* disagreed with him. I told him this is the United States where everybody's got rights . . . no matter who . . ."

At that point, the photographer simply stopped talking. He actually interrupted himself. It didn't make much sense, as far as he was concerned, to deliver a civics lesson to this cop. He wasn't paying attention to anything he said. It looked as though Nakamura's notion was going to prove correct. "You're not *really* going to drop this, are you?"

"It'll be investigated like every other situation where a subject is allegedly injured by another party. That's routine."

"I guess that's all I can ask for."

"Yeah," the desk officer said. And now his eyes seemed to hold a hint of mockery. "That's really all you can ask."

The interview was over.

Stait hadn't been forced to drag them up to his suite at the Astor. Both of them were primed to discuss the alarming turn of events. They had their data all collected. Both had already seen the threatening piece in the newspaper concerning Commer's forthcoming press conference, and subsequent phone calls had confirmed for them that J. Walter Stait was in a mess of trouble. Now they sat in front of him like two well-dressed Charlie McCarthy dummies waiting for him to pull the string.

"What the hell do you think I'm paying you guys for?" he shouted at them, seated across the coffee table from him. Neither seemed eager to respond. They were slender, gray men, typical of the faceless, well-clad, and barbered legal and fiscal specialists that the warlords of industry and commerce keep as court wizards. Only their eyes tipped one off to the kind of men they really were, hard eyes that seemed to move constantly from side to side as if always studying the odds, gauging the possibilities.

"You're supposed to keep me out of trouble. And I pay you a goddamn fortune in retainers to do it."

"Have you listened to us?" one of the gray men asked flatly. The only way he could be distinguished from the other man was by the color of his tie. He wore red. The other man wore blue.

"Sometimes," Stait said. "*Sometimes* I listen to you." He jumped up and started pacing the room again, not so much a walk as a controlled charge. First he'd charge off in one direction, then another. Sometimes these short, intense sallies across the floor threatened furniture or a lamp. "But what do you say?"

"It could have been avoided," Blue Tie said.

"How?" Stait demanded, turning back to glare at the pair of them. "And don't come up with some mealymouthed, half-assed lecture on morality. Your morality doesn't interest me. I've done a good job for the country and a good job for me. I've got nothing to be ashamed of."

Blue Tie shrugged and shook his head.

"What information do the bastards have?" Stait asked Red Tie.

"Banking information: deposits, current balances on all accounts."

"My wife's accounts? My own personal accounts?"

"*All* accounts."

"How?"

"IRS. The bureau. No staff leaks as far as we can determine."

"You?"

"You know us better than that, J. W."

"What about foreign banks, my foreign accounts?"

Red Tie sat well forward and studied some figures he'd spread out on the coffee table in front of him. He peered intently at the numbers like a schoolmaster. "The numbers they seem to have are large enough so that I get the impression they got the whole thing, foreign holdings as well, unless you're a lot better off than you've let me know."

"They've got all your assets located," said Blue Tie. "I'm confident of that."

"But what good is it going to do them?"

"Tax case. The foreign accounts. Fraud. Good case from their point of view. Lousy one from yours. Intention would appear to be 'intent to defraud the government—'"

"Can they prove it?" Stait demanded. "Do they have adequate evidence?" He was tugging at his collar and becoming red in the face.

"Even *before* the investigation of influence peddling. They've got more than enough for a tax case indictment. Maybe enough even for a conviction."

"They got more, J. W.," said Red Tie. "They got more."

"What?"

"International's board—Cavanaugh especially— are singing like a chorus of mockingbirds to the feds."

"Christ," Stait said weakly, his own eyes moving back and forth from one man's face to the other's, searching for the slightest hint of encouragement. He'd had no idea the matter was this serious. He hadn't suspected they had gotten so complete a case together. "What about hard proof? Not just that slimy bastard Cavanaugh's word?"

"Lots of it. All pretty convincing."

Stait thought at that moment he knew exactly what a fighting bull felt like when he found himself trapped in the ring. At first the picks and barbs seem minor, irritations more than anything else— little to worry about. But then there's blood lost— more and more of it—and before the bull realizes what's happening, he's dying on his feet, too weak to resist some goddamn matador's thrust. He shook his head.

"What are they trying to do to me?"

"They're nailin' you down," said Red Tie. "I think they're nailin' you down for the kill."

"And they haven't dropped the biggest on you yet," Blue Tie said. "This one's what Commer refers to as his 'secret weapon.'"

"There's more?"

"The meeting four months back in New London? The meeting with Smith and Reynolds and Jasper?"

"What about it? Everybody was there."

"You remember a young fellow just come out of Tufts? Kind of a handsome, innocent-looking guy, the kind that could've just come out of a Horatio Alger story, but with alligator shoes?"

"I remember him."

"He's working for Commer."

"Oh, God," Stait said in a sickly way. "I even made a pass at his wife."

"The wife's not the problem. He is. He was taking pictures with a miniature spy camera hidden in a pack of Chesterfields."

"I said I made a pass. I didn't go to bed with her."

"Lovely pictures of checks, large-denomination bills sticking out of plain brown envelopes."

Stait knew they had him. Yet there *had* to be a way out. There was always a way out somehow, if you knew how to fight, if you had any balls at all. Unless . . .

No! He couldn't really imagine what the final solution would be. Jail? Financial ruin? Loss of influence? A public scandal? It was all too gory to think about. There had to be a way out.

"What about Perry?" he asked. Stait had bankrolled Senator Perry for years. He had the awful feeling he'd just seen a small fortune go down the drain.

"He won't play with us, J. W. You know that as well as we do. He's too dirty himself. He can't afford it. Perry is a political animal and political animals always save themselves first." Blue Tie got up then and started doing some pacing of his own. "Perry's out," he said decisively.

"Why?"

"He hates you. He hates your guts. That's just for starters, but it's a pretty good reason, isn't it?"

Suddenly, in the midst of all the painful discussion, Stait felt very old and tired. Was it worth trying to wriggle off the hook? He knew that even these hired men of his would soon run away in order to save themselves.

He had been the one to profit from the deals and all the secret understandings. It was his own companies that would stand to prosper, his accounts that would grow. It was logical that when the bottom fell out he'd have to take the punishment. But he wasn't prepared for that. He had never built any provisional windbreak for himself. He never thought the elements would turn against him.

All Stait's natural optimism that had kept him

charging forward all these years was gone. He was going to be destroyed by the icy blast of public opinion. Whether or not they actually could put him in jail, the whole story would be made public. He had always been a man for covering his own ass. How had he gotten so careless?

"What can we do?" he finally asked. If the two men noted the lack of vigor in his tone, the almost-beaten quality in his voice, they masked it well.

"How well do you know Commer personally?"

"Not well."

"Can he be bought?"

"Already tried," Stait said.

"What'd he say?"

"Laughed at me."

"So that's out?"

Stait nodded his head affirmatively.

The other man, Blue Tie, summed it up. "The only thing now is to wait and see what he does. It won't be long. A couple of hours."

"What kind of legal defense do I have?"

"That's not my specialty," said Blue Tie.

"You're a lawyer, aren't you?"

"Corporate law. Not criminal practice. And I'm certainly not a PR man. Actually, J. W., what you need to get you out of this one is not a lawyer at all. It's a goddamn Harry Houdini."

Red Tie looked up at Stait from the sofa and asked, "Remember any good prayers?"

CHAPTER FIFTEEN

Dan Baron and Diana Remington were out in the middle of it. They'd been through the Times Square madhouse once, but now they were over on Eighth Avenue where it was a little less crowded. There was still some traffic moving in the street.

Diana had never seen Dan in such a mood before. She'd seen him happy more than once, but never what she called "champagne happy," bubbling, smiling, with no signs of the frightful melancholia that Barbara's death had cast on him. Today he was like a young boy, craning his neck to see everything that was going on, trying to be part of it, soaking up sensations greedily, laughing out loud. She was so grateful to have him back, to see his joy, to hold his strong hand, to walk beside him.

"You're Dan Baron," a startled girl screamed, her eyes nearly popping from her head. "And oh my God, you're Diana Remington, aren't you?" Her companions responded with equal amazement and delight.

"I was afraid of this," Dan said, flinching as though he were going to drag her off at a dead run.

"Don't be dumb," she said. "Enjoy it."

A group had formed around them now.

"You caught us," Diana said.

"Can we touch him?" another of the young women asked.

"Just a little," Diana said.

Two of the girls took Diana's approval considerably farther than she intended.

"Can we kiss you, Mr. Baron?" one asked.

Dan looked at Diana, shrugged, and said, "You told me to enjoy it." He bussed them enthusiastically. Diana was disgusted at the jealousy that welled up inside her.

Then there were autographs to sign and a lot of smiling to do. It was all very heady and euphoric, but somehow the jealous pangs, the sudden anger she felt deep inside herself, continued to bother her. But before she had a chance to express any of what was going on inside, it was her turn to be recognized.

A baby-faced soldier struck a pose right in front of her, put his hands over his heart and called out, "It's Diana Remington as I live and breathe!"

"Hi," she answered with enthusiasm. "You've got good eyes."

"That ain't her," another soldier snorted contemptuously.

"The picture in my footlocker says it is."

"The picture is right," Diana assured him.

"Really?" the baby-faced soldier said, suddenly looking scared. "I—I—"

The soldiers nervously saluted Dan and then asked timidly for Diana's autograph. She was miffed at the fact they didn't also ask for a kiss.

"Thank you, ma'am."

Diana resented the hell out of the "ma'am."

"Nice meetin' ya, ma'am," Dan mocked after the pair of young soldiers had moved on. He had laughed out loud at her.

Diana was mad enough to spit. But she said nothing. She couldn't think of suitable words. Let him laugh! She'd make him pay for it.

But then Diana had to scold herself. There wasn't going to be any little revenge scene. Stormy as their romance could be, she knew that most of her irritations amounted to exactly nothing in the face of her joy at having him back.

She let herself think back to that strange and wonderful day on location.

It was, on the face of it, an improbable romance. There were too many strikes against them. It had been referred to then as "the Water and Oil Affair."

Baron had been so emotionally destitute after the death of his madcap, wisecracking wife that many of Dan's and Barb's friends in the film capital couldn't imagine Baron's getting involved with anyone else. On the other hand, Diana remembered, there were lots of people who believed, not without considerable justification, that Diana Remington was just as willful and hard to impress off camera as she was on. Those few men she'd gone out with in Hollywood had helped build her reputation as a girl who couldn't be snowed.

"I want you to understand something," she'd said to him on that fateful day, not long after their first meeting. It was in the log mess hall, on location in the Grand Tetons. They were filming *Avalanche,* a movie that had called on most of Baron's great physical resources. His emotions still seemed to be somewhere else.

"What is it you want me to understand?"

"I'm not bowled over."

Dan laughed out loud. All morning they'd done take after take of the film's big love scene in which the principal female character, a young woman doctor, discovers to her dismay that she's wildly in love with the heroic mountain guide, played, of course, by Baron. They still hadn't gotten it right.

"You made that quite clear."

She looked puzzled for a few seconds.

"You made it clear by the superficial way you played it. It's supposed to be a love scene, not a battle scene."

For a few minutes, Diana found herself uncharacteristically speechless. Was the big jerk presuming to criticize her acting?

He had simply picked up his tray and his cutlery and started walking through the line.

She picked up her own eating implements and followed.

"You got a hell of a nerve, mister!"

Without turning to look at her, he said, "You've been working so hard at being tough and totally underwhelmed by everyone and everything that all the warmth and personal beauty you do have have gotten pushed out of the way."

Diana sputtered back at him. "What about you, mister?" she'd demanded in a rage as he reached for a piece of pie. Somehow Dan Baron could make her feel angrier than anyone she had ever known.

"What about me?"

"You work so hard at being Mr. Tough Guy, emotions held in check, giving everything and everybody the 'hard guy' look. I've got your number: Inside, you're nothing but a big cream puff."

His face fell. It was right then that Diana Remington made the critical mistake that doomed her to a life of loving Dan Baron.

"I know that," he said. In his eyes there was deep hurt.

"I didn't mean—" Diana remembered how stupid and rotten mean she'd felt then. She had been aware of the tragic business that had happened before she'd come to Hollywood. She had been aware too of the way the press had treated him. She certainly hadn't meant to wound him about that. It was the last thing in the world she'd wanted to do. "I wasn't trying to—"

"Don't explain," he had said with a surprising gentleness.

"I've got to," she'd said. "I'm not talking about those filthy columns about you. I mean that despite your hard surface, inside you're a soft and loving man."

Baron's mood had changed in a flash. It began with the famous grin and then turned to an easy chuckle. "I'll just bet you're an amateur psychiatrist."

"No," she said, shaking her head vigorously. "I think you're like a lump of coal. It's only when you're burned that you unlock your warmth and let your light shine."

"What about you?"

"I don't know."

"I thought you knew everything."

"Not by a damn sight."

They were holding up the line.

"Truce?" she said.

"Truce," he agreed, raising his big hand like an Indian offering peace.

They moved out of the line, trays loaded, and walked over to a vacant table. Neither of them had sat down.

"I'm sorry about all that happened to you."

"Most of it happened to my wife. *She* was the one to suffer," he replied, "not me."

"I don't know about that."

"She was the one who got killed."

"It's always worse for the survivors," she said.

"I hope you're right."

"Always right."

Baron grinned at her again and the next thing she knew he'd reached out, right there in the mess shack, in front of half the company, and taken her by the hair at the nape of the neck. He'd drawn her to him and kissed her. It was a long, deep, passionate kiss.

"I want to ask you one thing," he'd said when they finished with the first kiss.

"What?"

"Why do you have seven dishes of Jell-O on your tray?"

From that moment, oil and water stories notwithstanding, Diana Remington and Dan Baron were a pair, off camera as well as on.

"Hey, wake up," Dan called to her. "You'll get trampled with that faraway look in your eyes."

"Sorry," she said, holding him closer by the arm.

They stopped for a few minutes to watch a group of young men and women preparing an effigy for lynching and burning. Someone had rigged a dummy and dressed it in old clothes—Bowery bum clothes. The head was made out of a stuffed paper bag on which someone had crudely painted the features of an oriental male. He wore a Hitlerian moustache.

A rope was thrown over a lamppost and the figure was hoisted to hang by the neck with his feet just above the level of the crowd. Had it not been for a sign pinned to the dummy's ragged jacket, identifying him as Emperor Hirohito, no one would have known which of the enemy leaders he was supposed to be. He resembled the Führer despite the slanty eyes and glasses.

A youth with a cigarette lighter set the crude figure afire. For a moment, the fabric didn't seem to want to take the flame. Finally it caught. The flames raced quickly up the figure and began to lick hungrily at the paper face.

There were cheers from the bystanders and someone began to sing. Others joined in. They were singing something called "The Führer's Face." No one seemed to be bothered by the fact that they were singing about the wrong villain. They sang with gusto, with a feeling that ran very deep in the excited crowd.

Despite the crudeness of the paper-bag head and the primitive quality of the features painted on it, it was peculiar the way Diana felt as she watched the effigy burn, watched the features melting away. It was deeply disturbing to watch something that so reminded one of a human being, even a stuffed effigy, hanging on a lamppost in flames. Shouldn't this be a day to forgive?

"Come on," Dan said in her ear, taking her elbow to propel her away from where the crowd stood happily watching.

She could see Dan was bothered by it too. She could tell by the tightness of his mouth, the look in his eyes. She was glad to see that in his face. She'd been afraid, like many other women welcoming lovers and husbands and sons back from the war, that the battle had warped their men somehow, made killers of file clerks, or at the very least, stilled the men's compassion for the sufferings of others. She saw no such threat in Dan's face. He looked very distant, but troubled.

"Sick of it," he said to her almost as though he

found it important to alibi his desire to leave the sidewalk lynching. "Tired of death—even make-believe."

"I love you," Diana said to him.

"What?"

"I love you," she called louder.

"I still can't hear you," he said. "Too much noise."

"*I said I love you!*" she shouted. "*I love you!*"

People were staring and laughing sympathetically.

Dan grinned. He had heard her the first time, but he loved hearing her yell it right out there on the street.

"*I love you!*" he yelled back.

The ghosts disappeared for a while.

Beaton arrived first and sat waiting for Peck in the small, dark-paneled restaurant-bar just off Sixth Avenue called The Little Hideaway, a perfect refuge for cheaters.

Would he show up at all?

Beaton wasn't sure. Perhaps Peck would leave town in order to go on with his work unthreatened. But he dismissed the thought. Peck would never consider him a threat. Peck was a man of great self-confidence.

Actually, Beaton had to admit to himself that Peck frightened him. It was no longer by virtue of Peck's command of Team Three. It was the moral force of the man—his personal strength. Peck was always so sure of everything. He had always reminded Beaton of a finely honed steel blade. Perhaps you could bend it temporarily, but it would always spring back into shape, as sharp and dangerous as it was before.

There was something too controlled, too harshly efficient about the man. He had always seemed to be composed more of raw will than of flesh. Most men operate on emotions, hunches, whims, intuitive motivations. Peck seemed to work without any of these. Once he perceived an objective, nothing in the world could sway him from carrying it out. He was like a bullet. Once it is fired, there is no stopping it or calling it back.

Relentless or not; Beaton had to stop him. There was no choice. One way or another he would have to stop Peck's murderous activities.

"Hello, Georg," Peck said simply as he slid into the booth opposite the startled Beaton. He hadn't even seen him enter. That aggravated him a little—sent a chill down his spine.

"How are you, Richard?" the younger man asked. His eyes searched Peck's face very carefully to discover any clues as to what Peck was up to, any possible insight into what he was thinking. "You haven't changed."

"More than you think," Peck said. "In several ways."

"Really?"

"My wife is dead," Peck said simply.

"Dead?"

"Dresden."

"God," Beaton replied. "I'm sorry to hear that."

The grim news took Beaton by surprise. He remembered Peck's wife. She had come to visit once or twice when they were in training. She had been very beautiful.

As Beaton's gaze probed the man sitting opposite from him, there was one thing that most troubled him—Peck's eyes. He had never seen eyes so devoid of light, so frighteningly bereft of feeling.

"How did you find out?" Beaton asked.

"A Bund contact."

"Again, Richard, I am sorry."

A waitress came over to them.

"What is your pleasure?" Beaton asked Peck. He felt strange and awkward with the older man and his tragic news.

"A beer," Peck said.

"Nothing to eat?"

Peck shook his head.

Beaton ordered liver and onions and a beer as well. He smiled and adjusted his position in the booth to make himself relax and to create an impression of self-confidence he didn't feel. His palms were sweaty. He was sure Peck saw right through him.

"It's good to see you, Richard," he lied as the waitress walked off with their orders.

"Is it?" Peck asked, the hint of a smile showing at the edge of his thin lips.

"We're like two Jonahs in the great whale's belly. It's good to see that we have company."

Peck smiled thinly. "I never expected so poetic

an utterance from you, Georg. But it's a good metaphor."

For an instant, Beaton felt offended by what he took to be Peck's condescension. He had long felt that Peck looked down on all the rest of them. He didn't like it at all. Peck had been so good at everything during their training back in Germany. He had been the best marksman, superior at hand-to-hand combat, most expert with explosives, a phenomenal reader of terrain maps. He spoke the best idiomatic American English. He was the smartest and strongest of them all. It had always been difficult to like him.

"I brought your beers while the liver's cooking," the waitress announced as she set the two foamy mugs down on the scarred table.

"Thank you," Beaton said.

She withdrew.

"Let's get down to business," Peck said drily. "You asked for this meeting."

Beaton unbuttoned his shirt pocket and removed a neatly folded newspaper clipping and pushed it across the table to Peck. He said nothing as the other man picked it up, deliberately unfolded it, and then read it carefully. He simply watched the reader's face.

"Well?"

"Interesting," Peck commented, pushing the clipping back toward Beaton. Beaton was irritated to notice that Peck had pushed the scrap of newsprint into a wet spot on the table. The moisture quickly saturated part of the clipping.

"That's all?"

"I read the paper too. I saw the story."

"And?"

Peck shrugged.

"That's all you can find to say?" Beaton demanded. "And then you simply shrug?"

"What do you want me to say?" Peck asked, drilling the younger man with his cold, blue-eyed stare.

"I think you are responsible for it, Richard."

"Don't be stupid."

"It sounds like you."

"Accidents happen."

"Unlikely."

"Are you unhappy that the Americans lost a factory where airplane parts were being made for war?"

"No."

"Then what is the trouble?"

"I am living a good life, Richard," Beaton said with great intensity, leaning forward, elbows on the table. "A good life and a comfortable life. I want it to stay this way. I don't want to become conspicuous, to create any kind of disturbance that will let the Americans know they haven't gotten all of—"

Peck lifted a forefinger to his lips.

"You know what I mean," Beaton said then. "I don't have to finish saying it."

Peck merely stared across the table.

"The war is over," Beaton said. "It's time we put things away."

Peck sat back in the booth. His face was deeply shadowed, his deep-set eyes all but disappearing. For what seemed like a long time, he said nothing. Then he began to speak, slowly and deliberately.

"You're perceptive, Georg. You're very clever and yet you're not an understanding man. Not nearly as sensitive as you should be."

Beaton flushed uncomfortably.

"We haven't known each other well, you and I," Peck went on. "We worked together effectively for a time. I chose you for my team. I have some idea of your capabilities and you've got some notion of mine."

"What's all this got to do with—"

"Wait till I'm finished," Peck insisted harshly. "Don't cut me off."

The waitress returned and set Beaton's meal down in front of him. He had no desire to eat now. The food was repugnant to him.

"Anything else?" the woman asked.

"Nothing," both men assured her.

"You should know," Peck said when the woman had moved out of earshot again, "that I'm not political. I think our late leader had it coming."

Even now, after the final scene had been played out in the Berlin bunker, Beaton was shocked.

"Our mission is over. Our achievements don't amount to much, but it doesn't matter. We are now free to live our own lives, do as we please."

"That's my point, Richard. We should be free to live our lives as we want to. In peace."

"That's what I'm doing," Peck said. "Finding my peace."

"Not this way," Beaton insisted, pointing to the newspaper clippings. "Not this. When you do things like this, you threaten my world."

"I'm not responsible for that," Peck said coolly, pointing at the clipping. The beer had soaked it through.

"You can't fool me."

"I don't *have* to fool you. I do as I please. If I hold a grudge and wish to do anything about it, you have no right to challenge me. If I—"

Beaton stopped him with a finger leveled in accusation.

"I understand now," Beaton said. "It's Tereska, your wife, isn't it? It's Tereska and Dresden and the fact that the Drummond plant has been making aircraft components for the Americans." He added pointedly, "Like the three others in Connecticut and New Jersey that have burned down lately. Accidents, Richard?"

For the slightest instant, Peck's eyes wavered. He looked carefully around the room to see if anyone was listening to their conversation.

"It never occurred to me until you told me she was dead." Beaton continued, "This is a grudge fight, isn't it?"

Peck looked away.

"Isn't it?"

"Yes."

"You have to stop. Don't you have your revenge

already? Haven't you got it from the forty or fifty people who died in those fires?"

Peck didn't answer.

"How do you tell when you've gotten enough? How many plants will it take? How many millions of dollars worth of damage? How many human lives? Have you fixed a limit, a concluding price?"

"Fear."

"What does that mean?" Beaton felt his stomach lurch.

"Fear is my final price," Peck said.

"I don't understand."

"They have to feel it—the blind panic—knowing there's no way out."

"Who?"

"Americans."

"Which ones?"

"All of them."

It was precisely at this moment in their conversation that Georg Boetticher—having really become George Beaton—became utterly convinced that his former leader was mad, quite literally insane.

"What are you going to do?"

Peck looked across at him with those flat, lusterless eyes. He said nothing.

"What do you have planned? If I'm put in jeopardy for it, I have a right to know."

Still nothing but the hard stare.

"Tell me what it is."

Peck stood up. Reaching into his trouser pocket,

he threw a crisp dollar bill on the table. It was very much like he was, clean, stiff.

"Come on, Richard. What are you—"

"No more meetings," Peck said.

"You can't walk out of here without telling me," Beaton said, coming half out of the seat to grab the other man firmly by the forearm. "You're involving me."

Peck took Beaton's wrist in his free hand and wrested himself free. His strength surprised Beaton. "Be quiet, you fool," Peck hissed at him. "Hide yourself well."

"For the last time . . ."

Peck whirled and walked away. Had Beaton been armed at that moment, he would have been sorely tempted to put a slug in the other man's back.

But Peck was already out the door.

CHAPTER SIXTEEN

Ken Corcoran was a hell of a good cop. He had half a dozen commendations and, as far as street money was concerned, Corcoran was a nun. He simply wasn't a taker.

Corcoran hadn't liked it either when, after taking a slug in the stomach in connection with a domestic brawl, they put him on permanent traffic duty. But as Chief Inspector John O'Donnell stood watching Corcoran from the southwest corner of Eighth Avenue and Forty-fourth Street, he saw that in typical Ken Corcoran fashion, he'd turned himself into a real traffic professional. The man handled things with a flair. O'Donnell was proud of him, as he was of most of his men.

The chief inspector crossed toward the big traffic cop.

"How's it going, Ken?"

"A little on the wild side, sir, but nothing we can't handle." Corcoran still had a trace of the old country in his speech. More than forty years in this country and he simply refused to let the brogue slip away.

"Times Square is closed down altogether," O'Donnell said.

"Got 'em counted yet, sir?"

"Not yet."

Despite the fact that many enjoyed kidding about O'Donnell's crowd estimates to the press, the chief inspector was amazingly good at the tricky business of estimating the number of people in a very large crowd. The newspaper people loved it. It always provided a good handle for a news story. Not only were the readers impressed by the size of the crowd, but it helped to justify running a given piece. If the NYPD estimated a vast number of people in attendance the story was more likely to get read.

"I'd give it about six hundred thousand at the moment."

"God preserve us," the traffic cop said ardently.

"If the big announcement comes, we'll go well over a million," O'Donnell said. "I feel it in my bones."

"We'll be standing on each other's shoulders," Corcoran commented, still working his traffic.

"Just don't let 'em holler 'fire,' Ken. Let's not let anyone holler fire or we'll have the city's worst mess on our hands."

"They don't look like they'd scare easy."

"You never know."

The time was 1:53 P.M. The crowd continued to grow.

* * *

Bobby Noel and Tony Ciccone hadn't eaten lunch. They were really excited! Too excited to sit somewhere and eat a formal meal. They'd snacked on a variety of candy bars, ice cream, soft pretzels, and the current craze, papaya juice. The heat was starting to get to them and they decided to go back to their underground exploring. It was a lot better than walking around in the oppressive heat now that the sun had burned through.

It was two minutes before 2:00 P.M.

The connecting tunnels and corridors that had earlier led them from the hotel across Seventh Avenue to the Times Tower had fired their imaginations. This time, they'd take the same route, but in the opposite direction. It had whetted their appetites—especially Bobby's—for more such forbidden fruit. The Empire State Building's observation tower could wait for a while. Besides, they'd never manage to get there, get up on top, have a chance to look around, and then make it back to the Astor on time.

"Are you glad the war's gonna be over?" Ciccone asked as they moved through a dark, deserted corridor deep below the Times Tower.

"Yeah, I suppose so. But I hope they still do those neat battle things ... dioramas they call them ... in *Life* where they put all the toy soldiers and tanks down to show what battles really look like. Some guy with a funny name, Bel Geddes I think, does it. He must have at least a million soldiers!"

"My brother's comin' home from the army," Ciccone said mournfully.

"What's so bad about that?"

"I lose my own room and he's a creep."

"Why don't you go into the army yourself as soon as you're old enough?"

"Won't be any fightin' left. What good's the army when there's no war?"

"Drills, I guess."

"That's no fun."

"Shhhh!" Bobby cautioned, suddenly alarmed. He pulled Ciccone back into a deeply shadowed doorway when he heard the sharp click of heels on the concrete floors coming toward them. The boys stood as still as they could possibly stand. They scarcely dared to breathe. The footsteps came on. Though they were concealed in the shadows of a low doorway, set back a few feet from the corridor itself, if anyone should chance to look in their direction, they would be perfectly visible.

That was the closest they'd come so far to getting caught. They had felt very safe until now. It was as if no one at all inhabited this strange and fascinating world far below the street level. It had been as though everyone was outside with the crowds in Times Square.

The footfalls continued their brisk tempo and a man passed by them in the corridor. They were close enough to hear him breathing. He didn't look their way at all, but both boys saw him clearly in profile as he passed a little more than an arm's length away. Both of them were glad that this man hadn't discovered them. He was a little . . . scary. That was it. He had a very close haircut, blond hair, and his face looked kind of . . . tough. He didn't look like the kind who'd simply laugh and tell them to get lost.

The sound of his heels finally faded away. They heard the big door that led upstairs into the Times Tower slam.

"Wow!" the kid from Philly finally said, drawing a deep breath. "That was really close."

"And did he ever look mean," Bobby Noel added. "He looked like some kind of cop."

"No uniform."

"They don't always wear 'em. Didn't you ever hear of a plainclothesman?"

"Maybe we better get out of here fast. What if he comes back?"

"We'll get out of here," Bobby agreed, "but we'll get out through the hotel. That must have been where he was comin' from. Sure seemed to know his way around. He was walkin' real fast."

"Probably works somewhere down here." Ciccone laughed.

"What's so funny?"

"I would have expected little elves or trolls workin' down here. Now that big guy in the green shirt is somethin' else altogether. He looks real rough."

"Yeah. You never know. Come on," Bobby urged the other boy, having gotten his own nervousness under control.

They continued along the low, badly lit corridor, through the conduit-lined shaft that ran alongside and then down under the subway.

"Spooky place," Ciccone commented from behind Bobby as they walked through, Indian file.

"It's neat."

"How would it be to get trapped down here?"

"By who?"

"Don't know," Ciccone admitted. "But I still wouldn't like it ."

Bobby said nothing. He was having too much trouble just navigating. Besides, he didn't want to talk all that much.

"We back in the hotel?" Ciccone asked in a nervous whisper. It seemed to take him a long time now to say anything. He was glad Bobby seemed to know where he was going, because Tony'd lost his sense of direction entirely. These hallways all looked alike to him.

"Yeah," Bobby said, then stopped short, pulling Tony to a halt and motioning for silence.

A bright rectangle of illumination spilled from an open doorway ahead of them. It was right where they had to traverse next.

Of course, Bobby thought, that might have been the office of the stranger who had passed them in the long corridor. If that were his room, perhaps nobody would be there now.

For Bobby Noel it brought up a delicious fear inside him, like when his Uncle Roger gave him rides on his newly acquired Luscombe airplane. He'd have to remember to tell Ciccone about his pilot uncle and the plane rides. It wasn't every kid his age who could get to ride in an airplane just about anytime he wanted to. It had to be talked about. That's what made things like that so neat.

"What if somebody's there?" Ciccone mouthed the words without making a sound.

"Tough," Bobby mouthed back.

The boy from New Hampshire moved steadily toward the open doorway. It was a good thing he was wearing sneakers. He could walk like an Indian in them. That's why, he was sure, they called them "sneaks." He'd come up as close as possible without making a sound, so that when he peeked around the door casing, nobody'd think to be looking for anything but a rat.

Tony Ciccone stayed well back, pressed flat as he could get against the wall, looking very frightened. What was it with this guy from Philadelphia? Didn't kids down there explore the way kids in New Hampshire did?

Bobby moved forward with great care. He could hear the thumping of his own heart. His mouth tasted very dry. At one point, his sneaker squeaked a tiny bit against the floor and he froze, terrified. He didn't even let himself breathe. But there were no answering sounds, no footsteps, no scraping of a chair being pushed back. Nothing happened at all. He went carefully down on his hands and knees to peer around the door. The little room was deserted.

It was a tiny office with little more inside than a desk, a couple of worn chairs, and a metal cabinet. It was very neat and it wasn't occupied at the moment. There was a baseball cap on the desk along with a desk lamp, an old typewriter, a telephone, and some plans or drawings.

Carefully, the boy got up and signaled back to his companion. He gave the "let's-move-out-troops" sign like John Wayne in *Cimarron Soldier* or Dan Baron in *San Juan Hill*.

The other boy moved up quickly, a look of great relief written all over his face.

"It's okay?"

"The coast is absolutely clear," Bobby said out loud.

"Then let's get goin' again," Ciccone urged. He wiped the sweat from his forehead with the back of his hand.

"Worst thing in the world," Bobby said importantly. "If you go too fast, that's when they jump you. Don't you go to the movies?"

"Sure I do."

"Then you should know that you got to stay casual."

"I don't feel very casual. And besides, I gotta take a leak."

It was then that Bobby Noel did something he asked himself about many times later.

Standing there in the doorway of the small office in the Hotel Astor's subbasement, he had seen several objects in a cardboard carton next to the door. The box looked as though it had been put there to be discarded as trash. There were lengths of brightly colored bell wire and a number of curious things that looked like large caps or some other kind of fireworks. He picked up two of them and stuck them in his pocket. He also took a small coil of bright orange wire.

He was not a dishonest boy. He didn't believe it was right to steal. But he was always interested in junk. You could find useful and fascinating objects in people's trash. After all, it wasn't stealing if someone else had thrown it away. Besides, there was no way then he could have known what would happen later on.

In Times Square, Stait was having a tough time getting through the press of people. Usually, when he descended into the street, he'd step along with such self-assurance that people just naturally moved out of his way, like Moses parting the Red Sea. That didn't work today. No one had space to step aside. But it was more than that. He didn't fully comprehend it yet, but the notion that Commer had a real sword, one that could cut and kill, hanging over his head, had reduced his personal force field. His self-confidence was slipping away. He got flustered as people inadvertently bumped and shoved him. It was as though his balance were gone. He wasn't used to such treatment and it felt like humiliation to him. It was tiring. He felt a trickle of sweat running down the small of his back.

After he'd worked his way halfway across the square, he looked up at the Times Tower. . . .

. . . . PETAIN CONVICTED . . . . SENTENCED TO DIE BY A COURT OF HIS COUNTRYMEN. . . .

"Poor old fool," he muttered under his breath. They used up the old man's younger days, and when he finally made a bad error because he was old and afraid, they were going to take him out and shoot him like an old dog. He'd been a national hero, not without cause. Then one false move and the great man is torn to shreds by jackals who seek to deify themselves as custodians of public morality.

Would he permit any such thing to happen to himself? *Could* it happen? Of course it could, but it still seemed unthinkable. It seemed the same way death had always looked to him—something that gets the other guy. He had never outgrown that feeling. And Stait was intelligent enough to know that Commer could get him.

Despite the muggy August weather a cold shiver went down his spine. Petain kept coming to mind. People were always so ready to forget the good and leap onto the bad. But then how many times had J. Walter Stait been the one commanding the firing squad?

He kept moving through the crowd. He felt sick inside.

CHAPTER SEVENTEEN

It was 2:18 P.M.

Bickford looked up to see his friend Peck at the door.

"Come on in, Richard," he called to him. Strictly speaking, the sign room was supposed to be off limits to visitors; the sign's three busy electricians had made a special exception for Peck. He had been a tremendous help to them in keeping the complex electrical hardware running. Although he claimed it was simply "to keep my hand in," they knew otherwise. Peck had helped them keep the sign repaired to be a good guy, a helpful friend. He was that kind of person.

"How's it working?" Peck asked as he entered the electric sign's nerve center on the fourth floor of the Times Tower.

"Like a fine watch," Bickford answered. Peck had put in a lot of hours helping to replace some of the more than one hundred thirty-nine thousand brushes of the smaller mechanical signboard inside that energized its bigger electrical brother on the building's exterior.

"Glad to hear it," Peck said, looking much more relaxed and human than the electrician had remembered seeing him for months. "I was concerned about one thing," he added, smiling that cool smile of his.

"What's that?"

"I think I left my wire stripper inside."

Bickford laughed. "Like the surgeon who sews his scalpel inside the patient."

"Right."

"It's good to find out that even you make mistakes once in a while." Maybe he ought to invite the guy over to the house. Who knows? Maybe he and his wife's sister Polly would hit it off.

"Would you mind if I looked around for it?"

"No. Go right ahead," Bickford said. "Hey, you know it's gonna be a big day," Bickford called over from the frame where he was setting letters. "*The* big day."

"Isn't it always a big, busy day here?" Peck asked.

"Can't argue with that, Richard. But what I mean is that sometime before today's over, I'm gonna set the big news everybody's been waiting for. Old Hirohito's gonna throw in the towel. Total surrender."

"You think so?"

"In my bones. I feel it in my bones."

Peck smiled thinly.

"And listen, Richard," Bickford continued, "if it does come through today, how'd you like to come over to dinner tomorrow or Thursday? I'll be on the early shift. Me and the wife'd like to have a little celebration dinner."

Peck looked up from the mechanism before him. The look on his face was a strange one—one Bickford simply couldn't read.

"That's very kind."

"Hell, it's nothing," Bickford insisted. "Me and my ol' lady'd be honored to have you."

Bickford didn't make friends easily. He'd always been the sort of person who surrounded himself with hardware, with technological devices that were constant and predictable. People were too unpredictable. People would hurt you. Somehow Richard Peck was different. He was an educated man. Bickford could tell that. He was a man of refinement. Never laughed at people or talked down to them.

It really would be an honor to have Richard in his house.

With the same peculiar, unreadable look in his eyes Peck answered him. "It could perhaps be arranged."

"Hey, you mean you will?"

"I will accept your kind invitation."

Bickford was truly pleased. He wasn't really a nosy person. He was always willing to let others have their secrets, but he'd done a lot of guessing about Peck. He'd come to the conclusion that there'd been a lot of sadness in the man's life. Maybe Polly would cheer the guy up.

"Ah, would you believe?" Peck said, holding them up for Bickford to see, "I have here my strippers."

"Where were they?"

"Here, next to the belt."

"Funny. I didn't see them."

It was strange, Bickford reflected, to have a guy as orderly and organized as Richard forgetting one of his tools. But then it was reassuring to know the man was human.

"Let's make it about eight o'clock," Bickford said.

For a moment, there was a look of puzzlement on the tall man's face. Then he seemed to remember. "Oh yes," he said. "Eight o'clock."

What was there about the way he responded that made Bickford so unsure the man would come? He was about to add a reassuring word about the celebration when the new copyboy, the fat kid, burst in with another batch of news bulletins to set. Bickford forgot about Richard Peck for a while and went searching through the yellow sheets hoping to find the big one he was looking for.

Peck, his hands thrust into his pockets, slipped out of the room. The wire strippers had been in his overalls all along. Unknown to Bickford, Richard Peck had just made his final connection.

Jerry Grenon, back from his boat ride to Bedloe's Island, decided to try the telephone again. He really did want to have his sister come into town to be with him. Somehow, he didn't want to go home just yet. There was simply too much going on in the city to hurry out to dull Long Island.

He had hated it when they'd moved out to the Island, though Loretta had insisted it was for his benefit. He was sure she meant it. He was sure she thought it was better for him. She never did anything for herself. But it was a lousy place. Dull. There was so much more life in the city. The suburbs were dead, especially in the summer. In the city you could find just about everybody in the whole world sitting out on their front stoops. That was the way it should be.

He found a phone booth. Sticking his finger in one ear so he could shut out some of the racket from the streets, he dialed Loretta's number, his own number. He let the phone ring eleven times. There was no way she could be at home. Loretta could never resist a ringing telephone, even if she had to jump wet and dripping from the bathtub to answer it.

Just to assure himself that he hadn't forgotten, he looked up the number again in the Nassau County directory: Grenon, Loretta E., 4242 N. 4th Street, Mineola. That was it. He hadn't forgotten. He rang another ten times. Still there was no answer.

He decided he'd still hang on in town, at least for dinner. But goddamn it, he was lonely. After all that time in the miserable war—boot camp, night watches at sea, convoy duty, in the water all those desperate days when the *Merton* went down—now suddenly, in the midst of New York City, he had never felt so desolate and alone.

Gisela greeted him in German when he arrived at the florist's shop.

"*Nein*," he said, shaking his head. "It's not a day for speaking German."

"*Aber ich will Deutsch sprechen.*"

"Please, Gisela?"

"Very well," she said, flashing a mischievous smile.

George Beaton had known that Gisela would be irritated when he told her they would not be going to the zoo this afternoon. He also knew that her displeasure when he made his announcement would be nothing compared to her blazing anger if he tried to avoid the issue by neglecting to pick her up at all.

"I'm all ready and I have a delicious lunch all made for us, *Liebchen*. Ursula has relieved me and is now in the back room making up baskets for a funeral. We can leave now."

"Something has come up," he said soberly.

She stared at him, read his face, and groaned. "The zoo?"

"That's right."

"But you promised."

"It's serious."

"So is a promise to me. Damn their silly subway system. It can run without you for one afternoon, can't it?"

"It's not the subway."

V-J DAY : : 199

"What then?"

He gave a quick little shake of the head to indicate that he didn't want to explain here, in her father's flower shop, with her younger sister arranging flowers in the next room. It was something between them—confidential.

"Something has come up," he said. "I will explain outside."

"All right," she said, frowning. Of course, it wasn't all right, but Gisela did understand. She knew there were things he could speak of only with her. Gisela knew who Georg Boetticher was and why he was in the United States living under the name George Beaton. He had had to confide in someone. Now their wedding was only two weeks away and there were no secrets from Gisela. There was a great deal of discretion and understanding behind her pretty face and under that corona of corn-yellow hair. She was from a good German-American Bundist family. She would be understanding, but not *too* understanding, for there was no question that Gisela liked getting her own way.

Once they were outside, she had something definite to say on that score.

"I thought you were all through with that silly soldier business?"

"I am."

"Well?"

"Someone else isn't willing to put it away. He's been a fool. He's blown up things. He burned a factory. Twelve people are dead."

"But why?" she asked earnestly, squinting her eyes the way she always did. She was too vain to wear glasses.

"Something personal."

"Personal?"

"His wife died. I think it's made him altogether crazy."

"What do *you* have to do?"

"Stop him."

She stood stock-still in the middle of the Yorkville sidewalk, as though she'd been planted there.

"What's the matter?" he asked.

"*No*," she said angrily. Her face was flushed.

"What do you mean?"

"George Beaton, you are a stupid boy. You will not have anything to do with this—this—former associate of yours. You will have nothing to do with him. Do you hear me?"

"I must."

"*Not.*"

"There are things a man must do."

"You are no longer a part of all that," she said, her eyes flashing with anger. "You know that's dead—all of it. And if you—" All of a sudden she ran out of invective. Abruptly, her expression changed, her face looked very soft and beautiful. There were tears in her eyes.

He took hold of her arm with great tenderness. "*Liebchen*," he said softly. He did love her so and he knew that her swift anger was motivated by her caring.

"What do you have to do? And when?"

"I have to find out what his plans are now—this very afternoon."

"Have you spoken to him?"

"Yes."

He told her of the meeting and he told her of the plan he had tentatively set up in his mind so that he could at least find out what Peck was going to do.

"I'm afraid he's going to do something today or tomorrow. Don't you see, Gisela, if he's caught, the trail will lead directly to me."

"You've got to be careful," she said, alarmed at what he'd divulged to her.

"Of course."

"Where are you going now?" she asked.

"To the house. I have to pick up some—hardware."

"Hardware?" She was apprehensive. She hoped he didn't mean a gun.

"Tools to get into his room."

"What if he finds you there?"

"He's at work."

"Let me go with you?"

"To his room? You can't be serious."

"Why not?"

"This is no business for a woman." He was adamant. He needed no further worry. Peck would be difficult enough.

"Then to your place. I'll go with you there." As if suddenly aware that pleading would not work, she paused, looking up at him with hurt blue eyes. "It will give us, at least, a chance to talk together even if our beautiful afternoon was called off."

"All right. But I have to work quickly."

They went to his house, soon to belong to both of them. He headed for the basement to make up his kit from the various pieces of equipment he'd hidden there in the old coal bin.

He could hear Gisela moving around upstairs. What was she doing? He took out the set of burglar tools he had made up and stored in a small plastic purse. It was all there, everything he needed to take out locks, to cut through glass, to silence alarm systems. As an afterthought, he took his father's old Luger from its hiding place, hefting it in his hands. As bulky as it was, there was something most reassuring about it for occasions like today's. It had pulled his father through some difficult scrapes, even won him a Knight's Cross. Grimly, he strapped on the shoulder holster, and tucked the Luger into it.

When he went back up to the kitchen, he was surprised to see that the shades were drawn.

"Gisela?"

"Yes."

She came to the doorway of the dining room. She was wearing nothing at all. The nipples of her firm young breasts were standing stiffened with passion; as she held her arms open to receive him, he could see the sheen of the tiny golden hairs on her thighs gleaming in the dimly lit room. There were tears in her eyes.

"*Liebchen*," he said softly, wonderingly. "*Was tust du?*"

"You must be careful, George. What if I never see you again?"

CHAPTER EIGHTEEN

It was 3:29 P.M.

The presentation of the war bonds to the four out-of-town newsboys was one of the hundreds and hundreds of pseudoevents that take place daily in New York City—promotional, public-relations-oriented fabrications, totally without significance as far as busy, self-obsessed New York is concerned. But to the four young route carriers participating, it was a terrific experience, quite spectacular. They would remember it and speak of it all their lives.

There was a representative present from the United States Department of the Treasury in Washington, D.C. There was an associate editor of the New York *Herald Tribune* who would make the introductions. Diana Remington was there too, as a modest peace offering to the press rep she'd sent off to the Boston police station. Actually the lady didn't mind. As she presented the war bonds to the boys, more than a half-dozen photographers, including representatives of the major wire services, would be present to fix and freeze the boys' images with her own for export to various communities across the country. She liked the notion, especially today, of being able to thank someone for getting Dan home safely to her. Wars are so damned impersonal, she reflected. It's so difficult to touch the people who have anything to do with them. Somehow, it might have been the dollars hustled by these kids selling war bonds and defense stamps that got Dan home. It was a nice idea and it pleased her to be there.

Dan liked the idea of tagging along. He liked kids and he'd get to shake their hands too. He didn't mind. He'd never let himself get into this kind of thing before. Instead, he had gotten his wish for hazardous duty. Now that he was facing discharge, it would be fun to preen a little, to bask in a little public adulation.

He'd gotten more than his share of the other side of the public after the Malibu horror.

He was not surprised that the teen-aged boys seemed to have eyes only for Diana. He couldn't blame them. None of them had ever seen a movie star in the flesh before, and Diana's flesh was distributed well enough to excite males of any age.

The Treasury man had already said his few words concerning the importance of war bonds. The bald-headed, shiny-faced man from the *Herald Tribune* was speaking now.

"We've come here today," the man from the *Trib* droned, "to pay tribute through these boys to the many thousands of newsboys all across the country who have made distinguished achievements on behalf of America's war effort through the sale of war bonds and defense stamps to customers along their routes."

"It wasn't so tough," Ciccone whispered to Bobby Noel. "Everybody was proud of the war."

"Who said that?" Bobby whispered back.

"My old man."

Bobby said nothing.

"These boys are a small part of the great American newspaper business that went to war right along with our kids in the armed forces," the man went on.

"Wish he'd hurry up and shut up," Bobby whispered.

Baron noticed the kids squirming and caught the New Hampshire boy whispering to his Philadelphia friend. He gave the kid a wink. Bobby was delighted at the acknowledgment and winked back.

"There was nothing glamorous about the contribution of these four young men. It's neither exciting nor dangerous to deliver papers, unless you want to consider the teeth of neighborhood dogs as dangers beyond the call of duty. It was just a matter of going up to the door and asking one's customers to buy a little share in America."

One of the older boys yawned.

"Despite the fact it isn't combat, and it isn't being shot at or otherwise threatened, it is important. Consider the tremendous achievement of newspaper carriers all across the United States who've been responsible for better than forty million dollars worth of war bonds and defense stamps. One cannot help but be impressed."

Ciccone was impressed right now with the exciting swell of Diana Remington's breasts under her silky blouse.

"Many great men in this nation have come up Horatio Alger-like from the ranks of the newsboys."

"Bullshit," Ciccone whispered back to Bobby.

Bobby wasn't so sure that it *was* bullshit. He did intend to be someone great, someone the world would hear about. He liked what the man was saying, although he wished he'd get around to saying it a little faster.

"So it's my pleasure to present to you, Miss Remington, these four fine, diligent young Americans who have done a great service to their country while carrying out their regular duties as route carriers." Then he named each boy and enumerated the dollar value of what they'd sold.

"It's nice to meet you, Robert," Diana Remington said to twelve-year-old Bobby Noel. She had trouble finding his hand to shake as he thrust his autograph book out for her to sign. She smiled patiently, signed her autograph, gave him the bond, and then, on sudden impulse, kissed him.

Bobby was amazed and delighted. He had never —Wow! They each got to shake hands too with Dan Baron. Baron thanked each solemnly, saying to each boy, "You can be sure you've helped to win the war."

Then the unexpected.

When Baron spoke the words to Anthony Ciccone, the champion bond seller of the group, Tony looked up at Baron and mumbled, "Did you?"

Bobby Noel could tell that it had just burst out of his new friend. It wasn't really one of those big-deal, planned-for things.

"What?" Dan Baron looked startled.

Ciccone became flustered and shook his head. "Never mind. I'm—sorry—"

"No," Baron said, "What was your question?"

"My father says—" the boy began, flushing through his olive complexion, "that you're—yellow."

It dropped like something dead in the polite, rather drab meeting room. "I'm sorry, son," Baron said softly, almost wearily. "Your dad doesn't understand." Diana Remington knew that Dan Baron had been kicked hard. There was that tightening around the mouth and that flat look in his eyes—the same damned look she had seen before he had insisted on volunteering for whatever this mysterious thing was that he had done in the war. It made her very angry.

"Are all your news carriers so goddamned impolite?" she demanded of the sweating man from the *Trib*.

"He's just—just a kid and he—he was quoting his father."

"We're leaving," Diana said firmly, taking Dan by the arm.

"No," Baron said. "We'll pose for the pictures.

Let it not be said that we ran from the pop of the flashbulb." It cost Dan a hell of a lot to stay, but he knew that running would just give others a chance to potshot him in print.

There were a hell of a lot of people who thought Dan Baron might be yellow. Not the least of these active doubters was Dan Baron himself.

They stayed for the pictures. Ciccone was embarrassed at his own thoughtlessness. Bobby Noel wondered if the guy Tony was a little strange in the head. And Diana Remington knew that there were still battles to be fought before she and Dan could really be together.

Stait didn't recognize the man who opened the door of Senator Marc Commer's hotel suite at the Algonquin, but there was no doubt the man recognized him. He looked startled. There was an awkward pause.

"I want to see Commer!"

"I'm sorry but—"

"Don't give me that double-talk," Stait said angrily as he shouldered his way into the room. "I'm not going to be put off by that."

There were two other men in the room. Neither was the senator. One was the smart-ass college boy with the alligator shoes, the one who had brought his hidden camera to the meeting.

"He's not in," said the elder of the men. Stait recognized him as a major Commer aide.

"Horseshit!"

The door to one of the adjoining rooms opened

abruptly. Commer stood there barefoot, in a dark blue bathrobe, looking tanned and fit. His white hair was wet as though he'd just stepped out of the shower.

"What in God's name do you want?"

"To talk with you," said Stait flatly as he walked over to stand face to face with Commer, who was dripping all over the green carpet.

"We've talked," the senator said. "We've said everything there is to be said between us. There's no point in saying anything else."

"You've *got* to talk with me," Stait said with a terrible intensity. His voice wasn't steady. "You've got to."

There was desperation in Stait's voice—in his whole manner—but Commer didn't hear it. He heard intimidation. That was all he was ready or willing to hear.

"Always blustering," he said to Stait, his voice rising. "Always trying to bulldoze people, aren't you? Think you can ride roughshot over the whole world, don't you, Stait?"

"Please?"

"Please?" Commer grinned as though he'd perceived a rich, unsuspected joke. "Have you ever used that word before in your whole life? I'd be curious as hell to know."

"Can we talk alone? Please?"

"We'll go," said the young man with the alligator shoes.

"No," the senator commanded, extending a long, aristocratic hand and arm as if to prevent any one

of his three colleagues from leaving. "These are
key members of my staff. They know everything
there is to know about you. There's nothing you
can say to me or that I'll say to you, that isn't perfectly all right for them to hear."

"I beg you, senator," Stait began, having extraordinary difficulty in getting the unfamiliar plea
out of his mouth.

"Are you begging?"

"Yes."

The politician's eyes gleamed like agates. "I
used to tell my children what I'm going to tell you
now and I used to tell it to the accused before
my bench when I was a judge. Now I'm saying
it to you, Stait. The time to think about punishment is before you commit the offense—not after."

"I used pressure on people, Commer," Stait said,
sweat beginning to bead on his forehead. "I'll admit it. I used it to get the job done. And I got the
job done. That's what we're all celebrating these
days, the job I helped do. A hell of a lot of the
parts we used to get this war fought were from
the factories and the owners I put the screws to."

"That's a very convenient story you tell," Commer said. "It may even have a measure of truth to
it. But it's only a small part of the wide-open game
you played. What about the payoffs? What about
the bribes and the gifts and the retainers you accepted?"

"Friendship tokens, expenses." Stait was white-faced now.

"What? Friendship tokens? Twenty thousand

dollars? One thousand shares of preferred stock? Thirty-six hundred dollars a month for nearly eighteen months? Come on. You're not talking to a fool!"

"But look at the size of the contracts we were dealing with."

"Next thing, you'll be telling me it was chicken feed."

"Expenses, Commer. I was working full time for my country and I had expenses."

"You're talking to the wrong man. I'm not on the bench any more. Save it for the judge."

"But you are making yourself my judge." Somehow, Stait had—at least for a few seconds—managed a bit of control over his voice and emotions, had salvaged a little dignity. "You're sitting in judgment on me right now with this press conference."

For the first time, Commer wavered. He felt a touch of grudging respect for his longtime adversary, the victim he'd so carefully selected. The man was still an arrogant thief and a scoundrel, but there was something deep down in Stait that he envied. The old boy was tough. He must have been a savage scrapper in his day, he was so much like an old, cornered lion now. He had a kind of nobility, scaled somewhat larger than life.

Commer pushed his involuntary thoughts out of the way. The man wasn't a lion. He was a hyena, a jackal. This was no time to be getting buck fever. He had the bastard lined up in his sights. No time now for faltering.

"Get the hell out of here, Stait."

"Please give me a break—a little time."

"I said get out. Or I'll get a couple of cops up here to throw you out."

Two of the aides came alongside Stait. One of them tried to take him by the arm. Stait pulled free with a violent wrench that knocked the aide's glasses off.

"Keep your goddamn paws off me," he snarled.

"Go!" the senator ordered.

For a second or two, Stait was disoriented. It was almost as though he didn't know where he was or what he was doing.

One of the aides went over and opened the door to the gloomy corridor.

"Now get out," the senator repeated.

With a shambling awkwardness that was no more than a sad travesty of the way J. Walter Stait normally moved, he left the room. It was as though he could hear laughter all around him, cruel, mocking laughter.

If only Tim weren't coming home today.

The door closed firmly behind him.

CHAPTER :::::::::::::::::::
::::::::::::::::: NINETEEN

Peck sat in front of a typewriter. He rubbed his fingertips lightly against his poplin trousers and stared off into space. It was time to compose the text. He had a message he wanted to communicate to the assembled multitude.

For some of them, it would be the last message they would ever read. That was an important consideration for him. For those unfortunates, it would be eminently suitable to have the word DRESDEN the last message they received, the last concept to flash across the screen of the conscious mind before the lights went out forever. Somehow that would make much of it come out right. He had decided on the word DRESDEN as a trigger months ago, when he had first started making the connections in the brush mechanism of the electric sign.

Of course there had been no actual necessity for doing it that way. He could easily press a simple button or flick a toggle switch to accomplish the same thing. It would be simple that

V-J DAY : : 215

way. There would be less risk. There would be less work. It would be just as lethal. There would be as much blood and fire. But merely pressing a button, throwing a switch, didn't seem nearly enough.

The problem that now faced him was how to make the message, the bulletin, every part of it before the climactic word DRESDEN credible enough so that the electrician wouldn't question it; so he would simply pick out the metal letters, set them in the required order and run them on the sign.

The idea was to have it set without arousing suspicion. It would be easy enough to talk one of the copyboys into letting him bring up a handful of news bulletins himself. Most of these American youths were shamefully lazy in the first place. The copyboys he knew were phenomenal in that respect, even among their shiftless contemporaries. The message, typed on the same yellow paper they used in the newsroom on Forty-second Street, needed only to be slipped into the pile, well down, to afford him time to get to the roof where he could witness and be part of the final sacrifice.

AMERICANS CELEBRATE THE END OF THE WAR. How would that be? He typed in the uppercase characters and then stared at them critically. AMERICANS CELEBRATE THE END OF THE WAR.

Somehow it lacked color.

Perhaps it was too terse, too disciplined, too German. Eagerly? What about that for a color word? AMERICANS EAGERLY CELEBRATE THE END OF THE WAR. He looked at it again. Something wrong there.

Then he knew what it was. The electric sign rarely used the article. AMERICANS EAGERLY CELEBRATE THE END OF WAR.

Better!

He cranked in a new sheet of yellow paper and typed it.

AMERICANS EAGERLY CELEBRATE THE END OF WAR.

The next line came quickly.

VICTORY WON AT TERRIBLE COST.

There would be little question about that line. Everyone could agree with that one—Russians, Japanese, Germans, all of them. The Americans had little real idea of what had happened at Dresden. Perhaps that was the most deplorable thing about them, the thing one could find so disheartening living among them. They had so little understanding of what a fearful thing it is to be bombed in your own city, to be tracked down by violence and terror in the streets and buildings most familiar to you, places to which the normal human being runs for refuge.

They had little grasp of what the bombings meant. They could not imagine what it was like in Cologne or Breslau or Frankfurt. These smug, self-satisfied people had been isolated from it all. They had lived their lives in relative peace behind their broad ocean barriers. They had sent out their sons and some of them had come back broken and some hadn't come back at all. But they were always sending them away from home to fight, and there was always a place of peace, untouched, unbloodied, to which they might eventually return. A soldier can fight far more effectively if he doesn't have to think about his home being gutted and leveled, his wife and children burning in familiar neighborhood streets.

Peck had his initial two lines. He threw away the used sheet of canary-yellow paper and cranked another into the machine. He retyped the first two lines of the message.

AMERICANS EAGERLY CELEBRATE THE END OF WAR. VICTORY WON AT TERRIBLE COST.

Surely that looked, in the light of what had been happening in the world today, like a routine news bulletin. There was nothing artificial about it. There was nothing particularly ominous about it.

What of their attitudes? Could he find a way of chastising them with words? A way to make them feel, just before the sky fell in on them, that they had something coming for what they had visited upon others?

They had rejoiced at Germany's destruction. They danced in their streets at the demise of Japan and the incineration of Hiroshima and Nagasaki. It was not their reaction to Hitler's demise that angered him, goaded his act of revenge. It was what their bombs had done. It was what they had impersonally done to cultures and people far older —richer—than their own.

That was it. AMERICANS REJOICE AT THE . . . What would be best, the most accurate way to describe it? Destruction? Immolation? Demolition?

Yes. That would do nicely. Demolition. DEMOLITION. A cold, mechanical American word. Part of the jargon of engineers. AMERICANS REJOICE AT THE DEMOLITION OF CULTURES OLDER THAN THEIR OWN.

More distinguished too. God, but he despised the way Americans surrounded their lives with the cheap advertisements of hucksters. Their music, their food, the books they popularized. Add DISTINGUISHED to the line.

Again, he tore the paper out of the machine. He would start again from the beginning.

AMERICANS EAGERLY CELEBRATE THE END OF WAR. VICTORY WON AT A TERRIBLE PRICE. AMERICANS REJOICE AT THE DESTRUCTION OF CULTURES OLDER AND MORE DISTINGUISHED THAN THEIR OWN.

Would it prove too subtle for them? They are so like sleek, well-cared-for dogs. He despised dogs. After his parents, a middle-class college professor and his ambitious wife, had produced Richard and his twin sister, something they neither wanted nor expected to happen, they took to raising show dogs. In the Planck home, the dogs were always favored.

Back to the chore at hand. He still needed a final line to end with the word DRESDEN. Perhaps a litany of some of the cities murdered by American airmen.

CROWDS GATHER IN NEW YORK AND WASHINGTON,

he thought to himself in capital letters. ONLY THE DEAD OCCUPY HIROSHIMA, NAGASAKI, DRESDEN.

No!

He was displeased with it. Although it was close to the truth, it was too blatant. Bickford would likely smell a rat and call the newsroom for confirmation. That would be dangerous.

He typed another line. JUBILANT CROWDS GATHER IN WASHINGTON, LONDON, NEW YORK, AND ELSEWHERE. OTHERS MOURN IN HIROSHIMA, NAGASAKI, AND DRESDEN.

That would do it.

He cranked the completed message out of the typewriter and looked at it. It seemed good. He pushed the typewriter back out of the way and placed the copy on the desk in front of him. He looked it over with a critical eye.

AMERICANS EAGERLY CELEBRATE THE END OF WAR. VICTORY WON AT TERRIBLE PRICE. AMERICANS REJOICE AT THE DESTRUCTION OF CULTURES OLDER AND MORE DISTINGUISHED THAN THEIR OWN. JUBILANT CROWDS GATHER IN WASHINGTON, LONDON, NEW YORK. OTHERS MOURN IN HIROSHIMA, NAGASAKI, DRESDEN.

Almost unconsciously, he doodled in red pencil on the word DRESDEN. He drew radiating lines from it which suggested, comic strip fashion, a great explosion. He smiled grimly. It was as though the very word DRESDEN was exploding on the page.

Then he realized he could not leave the bulletin in that form, so decorated.

He took the typewriter again and laboriously copied the final bulletin text over. Once finished, he threw the doodled copy into the wastebasket. There. He was almost ready. He had only to wait until the announcement of victory and for the inevitable crowd to build in Times Square in front of the hotel.

There was, however, one more thing to attend to right now. He took out his wallet and found in it a photograph of a young woman with blonde hair and pale eyes that seemed to show blue, even in the black-and-white snapshot. He had to dispose of this. He needed no picture now. In a few hours, he would either be with her in some new state out of the world or he'd be in never-ending darkness. He did not want this treasured picture taken from him and profaned.

He held the picture by one corner. He took some book matches from his desk drawer. He struck one and carefully held it to the corner of the picture.

It took time to ignite, but finally it took the flame. He managed to get the fire to totally consume it even though he singed his fingers in the process. He let the last tiny wisps of photographic paper burn out on the concrete floor. Then he was ready.

CHAPTER TWENTY

Beaton patted the bulk of his father's old navy Luger in its shoulder holster. He did it for reassurance. It was still there, ready for use. He liked guns and they made him feel in control of situations. He was an excellent marksman.

Nearly two years ago, he had committed Peck's address to memory and then flushed the slip of paper on which it had been written down the toilet. Both he and Peck calculated it would be useful for them to know precisely how to reach the other in case a threat should materialize. Memorizing addresses and phone numbers would make it feasible, should the need arise, to make contact with each other. Beaton prayed Peck had not changed his place of residence since then.

Now he stood staring up at the venerable brownstone where his former leader had lived as a boarder since 1942. The house was neat and in good repair but was singularly undistinguished, too much like thousands of others all over the city.

Beaton walked quietly up the front steps and

pressed the button. He clearly heard chimes sound inside the house. They echoed loudly and he knew instinctively that there was no one inside. Something about the way the chimes caught his ear told him. He kept his finger on the button for an extra second or two anyway, listening carefully for any telltale indication of movement inside. There was nothing at all.

After a fairly long wait, during which nothing happened, he rang again.

Still there was no response. He was anxious, however, to be very careful. He'd have to ring enough times to make absolutely sure no one was in. It wouldn't do to get picked up for breaking and entering. The FBI would eventually get involved and the next thing he'd know they'd be strapping him into an electric chair like the unfortunates on the two other teams. The thought of it made him lightheaded, almost dizzy.

After ringing a total of eight times, Beaton decided to enter the house. He looked around quickly and carefully to be sure he wasn't being observed. There was no one in sight. He forced the lock. It was easy.

Beaton had been adept at break-in training. Actually, he got a great deal of satisfaction from forced entries. It was one of the few skills taught them by their Abwehr cadre at which he excelled. He had been outstanding at picking locks, at taping and breaking out glass, at silencing various types of burglar alarms. Despite the nervous tension that was making the sweat stream from him now, Beaton was a skilled housebreaker.

Once inside the front hall, he picked up a metal umbrella stand and dropped it hard on the dark wood floor. It made a terrible racket. He listened intently for a reaction. There was nothing. He chained the door behind himself. That would purchase a few extra minutes in case someone should come home while he was still inside. He went quickly through to the rear of the ground floor to see if he could find an alternate exit. There was a door in the kitchen but it looked as if there was no way out of the yard except over a high fence. Again he patted the Luger holstered under his windbreaker jacket.

He was surprised and a little pleased to see that Peck's American domicile seemed no more comfortable and attractive than his own. The brownstone was cheaply furnished and not, as Beaton saw things, in the best of taste. Beaton prided himself on his good taste. He liked living well.

The first thing was to find Richard's room and to go through it carefully, alert for any clues as to what he was planning and when it was going to take place. He went upstairs, ears straining for any sound that would hint of someone returning to the house.

He threw open the door of the large bedroom nearest the head of the stairs. Bright, gauzy curtains. Flowered wallpaper. It was obviously a lady's room. There was a garish reproduction of the Sacred Heart of Jesus over the brass bedstead, several other pieces of "devotional art," the framed photographs of two young boys and that of a proud-looking man with a high-bridged nose and a luxuriant moustache. His picture was edged in black.

He stepped into the adjoining room. Somehow, this bedroom sent a chill down his spine. It had been turned into a kind of museum or a chapel. There were all the marks that this had once been the headquarters of an adolescent male. There were planes and ship models, baseball equipment, pulp novels, and photographs of several young girls. There was a scrapbook left open on a bureau. Sneakers and shoes were lined neatly under the edge of the bed. Most bizarre, however, and what gave the room its morbid singularity, was one corner where an altarlike shelf had been erected. On it had been placed the photograph of a young soldier, resembling the younger of the two boys depicted in the next room. In front of the picture, five red votive candles flickered and spattered. Plastic flowers were banked on either side. The boy looked like an altogether normal, cheerful young man by the standards of anyone's army. He looked like someone who'd be terribly embarrassed by all this devotional clutter had he been there to see it.

Someone had kept the room just as it had been, like some small chapel designed for the veneration of a saint. It took no careful inspection of the telegram framed and hung on the wall of the shrine to know the room's original owner was not coming back. There was also a blue banner carrying a single gold star. This confirmed it.

Beaton found himself back in the present. He left the stifling atmosphere of the dead soldier's room. He liked nothing that reminded him of death.

As he reentered the hall he heard a stirring from the stairway. The door to the third-floor stairway was standing ajar just the slightest bit. He heard a board creak.

"Come out with your hands up," he said gruffly, drawing his Luger. His own hands were sweating and he was gripping the handle of the pistol so hard that it hurt.

No one stirred.

"I know you're there."

He heard the padding of feet and a large cat peered through the crack in the door.

Beaton was disgusted with himself. His hands were still trembling. The cat ignored him and moved toward the lower flight of stairs. He was tempted to shoot the wretched creature just for scaring him so badly. He resisted the temptation. He had no silencer for the pistol. Besides, he didn't want to let anyone know he'd been in the house.

Up front, he found a room he concluded to be Peck's. The door was unlocked. The room was uncluttered and clean. It looked almost as though no one lived in it at all. But there were clothes in the closets—clothes that would fit Peck. He saw no garments he recognized. All the clothes hangers were neatly spaced on the pole with the hooks all turned in one direction. Beaton shook his head. Richard was so precise.

Beaton opened the bureau drawers and rifled quickly through them. He did likewise in a chest-on-chest. He did find pictures of several women, one of which was inscribed, "To Richard with all my love, the first man to make me feel beautiful. Loretta." The woman was not much to look at.

He could still not be sure that this was the room of his former comrade-in-arms. Richard was a common enough American first name.

There was something else however.

On the neatly made bed there was an envelope. It was sealed and on it was written "Mrs. Grasso." He decided to open it.

> Dear Mrs. Grasso:
>
> I am most grateful for all the kindness you have extended to me over the past two years. My wife would have been most appreciative of your solicitude. This is a small token of my thanks. Pray for me.
>
> Richard Peck

There were eight one-hundred-dollar bills and two keys in the envelope. One had a white pasteboard tag attached. The tag said "barbershop."

"Barbershop?" he said aloud in the empty house. Where had he just seen a barbershop?

He remembered. There was a closed-up barbershop on the corner just next door. That was encouraging. Perhaps this was where he had stored and hidden his—equipment.

But the note! The money! He wasn't planning to come back. Something was going to happen—*today*.

Beaton left the note and the money on the bed. He stuffed the torn envelope in his pocket, and took the steps two at a time. He paused only to lock the front door carefully behind him.

The key fit the door of the closed barbershop. It was musty inside and, from the layer of dust covering almost everything, he concluded it had been some time since Grasso's Barbershop had seen clients.

He found what he was looking for almost immediately. Just outside the toilet in the back room was a pile of cardboard cartons and two wooden crates. They were the same containers they had wrestled ashore from the U-boat more than three years ago. He checked the boxes over carefully. Every single one of the boxes was empty. Peck had kept custody of the whole supply and now he had moved all of it out of the building. He had enough explosives to blow up a small town or the liner *Normandie*.

The bills on the bed. The thank-you note. The missing explosives. It all added up. Something was going to blow up today—tonight. Beaton's hand went again to his father's weapon. He would have to use the old Luger. There was no other way.

CHAPTER TWENTY-ONE

Ensign Duncan P. Carter, USCG, hated his goddamned duty assignment with all the pent-up feelings of his young and ardent nature. What a way to waste a great potential fighting man by shackling him to a beach patrol. He had been denied sea duty because of a recently developed visual defect. It was cruel enough to be burdened with duty ashore, without being sent out here to the edge of the world with as useless a complement of broken-down horses and men imaginable. Those misguided bastards at the Commandant's office must have had some sort of grudge against him. There was no other way he could look at it.

"I know the stinkin' war is all but over," he almost yelled over the telephone, "but I have to report finding this mess of stuff to somebody, don't I?"

Carter had been on the phone half the morning and now, at nearly 1500 hours, he hadn't yet found anyone officially willing to assume responsibility for what this man Libby had turned up on the beach at dawn.

"I've called the District, the New York Port Captain, the Commandant's friggin' office, and those blundering shits at the Federal Bureau of Investigation. My girl friend's brother is one of their people. Even he was playing coy."

"Then you've done what you were supposed to do, Dunc. Don't sweat it any more. *Your* tit's outa the wringer. It's up to them."

"It's as though no one wants to hear about it."

"Nobody does."

"Could be something . . . still," Carter insisted. "War criminals or the like."

"Not a chance. Give it up, Dunc. Forget the whole goddamn thing."

Carter stared bleakly at the pile of gear littering the floor of his office. Four sets of German navy fatigues complete with name tags. A rubber boat with two sets of oars. A spotlight with a broken lens and badly corroded batteries. Two years ago, there would've been half-a-dozen intelligence types around kissing his ass in the sweet ecstasy of discovery. There'd have been some on-the-make two-striper arguing with one of Hoover's pompous gumshoes about who was gonna get the credit. Now at the eleventh hour, he couldn't get a soul to raise a friggin' whisper about the whole damn thing.

"What if I called the newspaper guys in?" he asked his old friend and classmate who was stationed at Point Judith, up in Rhode Island.

"Watch your ass, if you try that."

"Maybe even they wouldn't be interested."

Carter was distracted by his yeoman, who was standing in the doorway signaling for his attention.

"What the hell do you want, Mal?" Carter barked.

"District's on the other line."

Forcing himself to breathe slower and to calm down, Carter sat forward in his chair. "Look, Pete. I got District on the other line. Call you back later, okay?"

"Okay."

Carter switched over to the other line. "Carter here."

"Mr. Carter?" It was a woman's voice. Probably a SPAR. "I have orders from Commander Syvinski."

Who the hell was Syvinski? He'd never run into him before.

"Mr. Carter? Are you there?"

"I'm here."

"You're to delegate someone to bring all the materials down to Washington before the end of the week."

"Transport?" Carter asked her. "What about transport?"

"The commander suggested the train."

Carter put the telephone on the desk and buried his face in his palms.

"Mr. Carter! Mr. Carter? *Mister Carter!*"

Carter heard the plaintive voice of the SPAR spilling from the telephone receiver. He made no effort to pick it up.

* * *

The subbasement office gave George Beaton a severe case of the jitters. It was not the darkness of the corridor and stairway outside, nor was it the fact that he was in a limited, self-contained world deep beneath the streets of the great city. Beaton too spent his workdays like a mole underground. It was curious, significant maybe, that both he and Peck had burrowed deep beneath the ground in the fabrication of new lives and careers for themselves.

There was something else that contributed to his unease. It was his mission, what he had, in the last hour or so, concluded he must carry out. He was here to kill a man he once considered a friend. There was no longer a war between Germany and the United States and this man was not the enemy as defined by lawful superiors. He, George Beaton, was no longer a military person. There was but a single justification and that could be said to be a shaky one. It was self-defense. He *had* to kill in order to protect his own security. He knew he could do it and yet? . . .

There was little evidence of Peck here either. As with his bedroom uptown in the brownstone, there was nothing to speak of the man himself. Only the familiar pasteboard box, now containing two detonator caps and some scraps of wire, told him this was the correct place. There were no pictures, no personal items that would identify it as Peck's office. There was no name painted on the metal door. Nothing occupied the wooden desk top but a set of architect's drawings bound together on a clipboard. Otherwise there was only a typewriter, wastebasket, and a desk lamp along with desk, chair, and steel locker. There were no explosives in the locker, a fact that led Beaton to wonder if perhaps the charges were already placed somewhere. There were a few ashes on the concrete floor. The only sound was the faint hissing of a steam pipe.

Beaton felt there was little evidence of human habitation here because there was very little humanity left in Richard Peck. Certainly there was nothing to remind him of the Richard Planck he had known and followed. He felt it necessary to keep telling himself that. He had liked Richard Planck, admired him.

Beaton tried to visualize Planck in his mind's eye. The two characters, Planck and Peck, had become separate in his mind during the last two days, since he'd seen the distressing story of the Long Island factory fire.

Like most of the others chosen for "Operation Pastorius," Planck had come originally from the United States. He had been born in this country. Once he had told Beaton, Boetticher then, that his parents were a German faculty couple teaching at Virginia Polytechnic Institute in Blacksburg, Virginia, and that he had been born in a small town nearby. It was a town with an army arsenal; Radford, it was called. There was a farm with dogs and horses and a twin sister. Planck had always mentioned them in that order.

He had spoken with a strange kind of objectivity—contempt even—when he discussed those early years. Obviously, they had been anything but happy years for him.

Planck told him he had graduated from the Polytechnic Institute in Virginia and had returned to Germany with his mother and sister after his father's death. That was all Beaton knew of Planck's early life.

It was neither the youthful American Planck nor the current American Peck that troubled Beaton, as he stood in the subbasement room with the loaded Luger in its holster. It was the German Richard Planck that trouble him. He had been a much-admired friend, a man of compassion and great moral strength. A number of times, Beaton had met Planck's wife Tereska, a beautiful girl of Polish descent who worked in a library in Dresden. She was a true lady and she and her husband had been deeply in love. Beaton had seen this and he had envied it.

He took out his handkerchief and mopped his brow.

Could he truly kill such a man?

For a time, Planck had taught electrical engineering in Dresden. He was an expert in that special field. It was said that Planck had been approached by Admiral Canaris himself about joining Operation Pastorius. The Abwehr's commander had known Planck's father. For reasons known only to himself, and perhaps his wife, Planck had agreed to join the teams which had as their objectives infiltration, industrial and military sabotage, and terrorism in the continental United States. They had trained together, spoken about love and life and their true meanings. They had given each other the mutual support of a band of true brothers.

Beaton's companions in the Abwehr program were important to him, especially Planck, his leader. Beaton had been a dreamy, romantic child. He had been raised in a cramped city apartment in Philadelphia. His father had come as an immigrant to the United States almost literally looking for gold in the streets. He had been a submarine officer in the First World War, but nothing had worked out right for him after that. Moving to the United States was a dismal disappointment. He had worked as a watch repairman and saved every penny he could scrape together to return to Germany. His wife and son merely existed in the shabby apartment in order to make the dream come true sooner. The boy, Boetticher as he was known then, had no friends. He was the subject of much school-yard humiliation for his patched clothes, his meager lunches, his quiet, dreamy ways. He often tried to imagine then what it would be like to live in a home of his own and not a cramped apartment, to have a father who would talk with him, guide him. The first true friendships he had ever found, he had found in Operation Pastorius.

Beaton forced himself to stop permitting his thoughts to wander this way. He couldn't afford to be a sentimental fool. He couldn't afford to

V-J DAY : : 235

waver. He realized that the contemplation of a now-faded friendship could weaken his resolve, sap him of the strength to act.

The facts of the matter were still there in a great, unswallowable chunk before him, like a gravestone. Peck would have to be destroyed. There could be no question in Beaton's mind about that. The man had gone mad, lost control of his judgement. He would have to be dealt with.

Do I shoot him in the back the minute he steps into the room? Beaton asked himself. That certainly would be the safest and surest procedure. It would give him no opportunity to strike back. It would give the executioner himself no chance to falter.

Would he come back at all? Perhaps he was on his way to whatever operation he may have planned. Perhaps while I lurk here in the shadows waiting to kill him, he told himself, he is already putting his dangerous, lethal mischief into motion somewhere else. It was a sobering thought and an all-too-likely one.

But the lights are on, Beaton reminded himself, the drawings are left out on the desk and the door is left open. The tin lunch pail is on top of the locker. It would be wholly out of character for Peck to leave his office like this if he were not returning. The cardboard box with the detonators was still here on the floor. Whatever might have happened to the man's mind and personality, he would not be guilty of leaving his office in such condition to go somewhere for a long period of time. He would be nearby, having stepped out for just a few minutes.

Beaton reached into the side pocket of his light windbreaker and drew out a pair of cotton gloves. These would keep him from leaving fingerprints for the police should he touch something. He could not afford to be implicated. He put on the gloves.

The notion of shooting the man in the back, in cold blood, had no appeal for Beaton. Especially with this man. One ought not to do so despicable a thing to an old comrade-in-arms. One must explain somehow, and give him the privilege of dying like a soldier. Surely, it is not more than he deserves.

Before Beaton had an opportunity to proceed further with his painful speculations, Peck walked quickly into the room. For an instant, he missed Beaton altogether as he stared down into the carton by the door. He looked troubled. He saw several fewer detonator caps than he had seen earlier. He could not possibly have miscounted. Someone had been there.

"Hello, Richard," Beaton said softly, Luger in his hand, cocked and ready to fire.

Peck stiffened and his jaw tightened. He slowly raised his head to stare at the Luger and then at Beaton himself. Beaton envied the man his coolness. He had seen evidence of it before. Peck showed no signs of fear, little evidence even of being startled.

"Put the gun away," Peck said softly.

"I can't, Richard. You have become a terrible

threat to me with this madness of yours. The war is over. It's time we forget it all."

"Put the gun away."

"I'm sorry I have to do this to you, Richard. I hope you'll understand and somehow find it in yourself to forgive me."

"Why?" Peck asked. "Why do you want to kill me, Georg?"

Curiously, the question unnerved the young man. He didn't really know why. Perhaps it was the note of—disinterest in Peck's tone. Peck, facing a revolver, actually sounded bored. Beaton, on the other hand, could feel the sweat rolling down his back. Who was the victim here?

"I know why," he said finally to Peck.

"Because you are afraid?"

Beaton couldn't bring himself to answer to that —to admit it was true. His mind started sending almost involuntary impulses to the nerves in his hands and fingers. He almost squeezed the trigger at that moment. Instead, he made himself let up slightly on the trigger.

"Can you give me a moment?" Peck asked. He wasn't pleading. There was a curious note in his voice that could nearly convince one that he didn't care.

"A moment?"

"To compose myself. To say a prayer."

Beaton recalled that Planck had been a churchgoer. Kohler had derided him for it. Beaton had found it a little curious, but then perhaps it had been his wife's doing. Poles were notoriously religious.

"All right. A few seconds."

"May I kneel?"

"I don't care," Beaton said, a note of irritation creeping into his voice. It had been bad enough that the man had put him into the vulnerable and uncomfortable position of having to kill him. Now he was adding difficulties. "You can do anything you like for the next twenty seconds."

"Then you'll murder me?"

"Execute."

Beaton didn't really mean to relax his finger on the trigger of the Luger and to let the barrel waver a few centimeters. Simultaneously, as Peck knelt, the small automatic appeared in his left hand as if by magic and it spat fire in a single movement. Beaton felt a sharp pain in his head and a stunning force that knocked him over backward, his own shot lodging into the ceiling as he fell. He went over wildly, like an ungainly marionette precipitously dropped by the puppet master.

Peck's knee came down on the middle of Beaton's chest while one hand pinned Beaton's right wrist and weapon to the floor. The pale blue eyes looked down on Beaton as he gasped for breath.

Beaton felt the strength quickly draining out of him. He couldn't summon any response in his arms or legs. He had blood in his mouth and that horrible stunned feeling, as when you take a crippling smash in the nose. He spat weakly to get some of the blood out of his mouth. It dribbled down his cheek.

"Planck," he said weakly. "Give it up."

"You shouldn't have gotten in my way." There was neither regret nor compassion in the voice. Only ice.

"Don't—kill any more."

Peck said nothing. Beaton watched, immobilized, as Peck took up his automatic again and, putting it to Beaton's sweaty temple, fired another shot. The younger man's eyes went out . . . no light, no life.

With no wasted effort, Peck dragged the corpse, still holding the Luger in its lifeless hand, to the metal locker and with great difficulty pushed it into a semi-upright position. At first, when he tried to close the locker door, he caught the elbow of the man he had just killed.

Laboriously, he thrust the stubborn limb inside and pushed the door until it caught. With his handkerchief, he mopped most of the blood off the floor. There wasn't very much of it.

He noticed there was blood spattered on the message still in his typewriter. With a sigh of impatience he ripped it from the machine and sat down to type it up another time. The bloodstained copy went into the wastebasket.

CHAPTER TWENTY-TWO

"Sure it hurts," Tim Stait said. But he was grinning.

Lil, the beautiful WAC lieutenant, was still with him. She had stood by and supported him bravely. He had created a considerable ruckus at the hospital, but finally, with much remonstration and shaking of heads, they had equipped him with a walking cast and crutches and discharged him.

They were climbing out of a taxi now in front of Sardi's.

"We're gonna have the best dinner our rich Uncle Sam's green money can buy," Tim said to Lil as he'd paid off the cabby. "I've had damned little chance to spend it."

"But it's not dinnertime."

"My biological clock is so fouled up from all this traveling that I eat when I'm hungry. I drink when I'm dry. And by the way," he said, reaching for her and turning her to face him, "I have other needs." His crutches clattered to the sidewalk. He took her in his arms and gave her a long, passionate kiss.

"Captain," she said with a half-hearted note of rebuke when they both had to stop long enough to breathe, "there are people staring."

"Tell them to go away."

"Don't you care?"

"It'll make them feel good to know that even the wounded are enjoying themselves today."

She giggled.

It was a very nice giggle, warm and pleasant to listen to. It wasn't that silly braying some women do. He had concluded some time ago that Lil was no featherhead. Despite her dramatic good looks, she seemed to have a head on her shoulders.

Still standing there on the sidewalk, his arms around her, he asked, "Are you in love with anyone right now, Lil?"

"No."

"Engaged?"

"No."

"Then how about pretending—just for a few days if you insist—that you're madly in love with me?"

"Should I be in love with you?"

"You could do worse."

It was her turn for a question. "Are *you* in love with anyone right now?" She took his hand and looked down at the lighter area where the wedding ring had been.

Tim paused for a fairly long time. He held up Kathleen's image before him. He thought about all the anguish he'd gone through after getting the letter. He asked himself whether he could forgive and forget, and glue some of the pieces back together.

"I don't think so," he finally said. "I really don't."

"When will you know for sure?" Lil asked. She looked at him very carefully. He was a good-looking man, boyish but intense. A strong jaw—something she always saw as having a great deal to do with character. She noted clear eyes—eyes that weren't afraid to look at you. He was an honest guy. She felt sure of that. A little nuts perhaps. She liked the fact that he laughed easily and made little jokes about himself.

"I know now," he said.

"How?"

"Because getting kicked is a sure way to get all the love out of you. I make a lousy martyr. I've always been a guy who knew when he wasn't welcome. I guess I trained myself to believe that if I'm not wanted, then I don't want to be included."

As the young WAC listened to Tim Stait, she had this deep-down feeling that she had just met a man who was on the level. I like him, she admitted to herself. I like him a lot.

"Captain," she said, with a ghost of a smile playing around the corners of her mouth, a slight tremor in her voice, "I'd love to make believe I love you." She didn't say it at that time, but she was a believer in self-fulfilling prophecies. She didn't want to say it for fear that the words might keep it from coming true.

They kissed again there, in front of Sardi's.

"Damn," said Tim enthusiastically, "but this is a spectacular day!"

Peck had plenty of time. There was no chase. He was no longer threatened. Beaton had been taken care of. It was regrettable, but it would ensure that the plan would not be jeopardized. No one would go down there to find the corpse in his cupboard. It was quite dead. It would go nowhere on its own.

Peck was somewhat more concerned with the missing detonators. He hadn't thought to search Beaton's pockets. But if Beaton didn't have them, where could they be? Why would someone have taken them? Who?

The elevator stopped on the tenth floor. The doors opened.

"Good afternoon, Mr. Peck," said a buxom chambermaid as he stepped off the elevator. She was a blonde Brünhilde with a voracious appetite for flirtation.

"Good afternoon," he said pleasantly, trying to be impersonal. The woman was a fool who was always throwing her wretched self at him. It was nauseating to see a young woman allow herself to get too fat. Had he recalled that she worked on the tenth floor, he would have gone to the roof to make his observation. He had never been impressed with Rubens' nudes.

244 : : V-J DAY

"You gonna celebrate?"

"I beg your pardon?" he asked, somewhat distractedly.

"This is gonna be the big day."

"Oh yes," he said quickly, discerning her meaning. "I have a celebration planned." He knew the irony would be wasted on her even if she survived.

"With anyone special?" she asked.

Peck pretended not to hear her. He kept on walking down the long hallway.

He wanted to view the crowd again, to see how big it had grown. So far, to his knowledge, there had been no announcement of the war's end. But there was the question of being greedy. How large would the crowd become after the announcement from Washington? How long should he wait? How many additional people would pack their way into the square?

He put his passkey into the lock and opened the door of a corner suite, high above the corner of Seventh Avenue and Forty-fourth Street. He had checked to see that it was vacant. He closed the door firmly behind him and strode over to the window.

The crowds were remarkable. They were packed in so densely, one could literally have walked on their heads from one side of the square to the other, from the north end to the south. They milled about in the streets. There were no vehicles down there, just people swarming like a host of insects.

He smiled bitterly as he stared down on them and dried his sweaty palms on his trousers.

Give it more time, he said to himself, holding his impatience in check. Wait until movement is impossible. Make them stand there with their white faces turned helplessly upward as their retribution crashed down on them from above. He was reminded of the phrase from the Gospel according to Matthew, "His blood be on us and our children!"

He would wait.

CHAPTER TWENTY-THREE

Stait had come and gone nearly an hour ago. Senate Commer had made a date with his eldest daughter and her newest husband. He'd meet them for a quick drink and an abbreviated conversation at the Yale Club at 3:45 P.M. They were heading back to their own place in Chicago and he wanted to bid them a fond good-bye. Commer not only loved his kids, but he would always make room for them, no matter how crowded his schedule. He was never too busy to talk with them. He felt a twinge of self-satisfaction as he thought about that.

There was also a practical angle to the drink date. He was enjoying the idea of entering his 5:00 P.M. press conference just a couple of minutes late, rushing in breathless from "an important meeting somewhere else in town." Yes, let them wait for him—not too long—but just long enough to build a little suspense and demonstrate even more dramatically than usual how important this press conference was to him. See how important you gentlemen and ladies of the press are to me? See how anxious I am to be fully accountable to you and the public you represent?

Commer was accustomed to playing out dramatic scenes like that. He had a feel for drama in politics. He called it "the rubrics of victory." He was convinced it had been just this knack for the right gesture at the right time that had kept him in the United States Senate for nearly twenty years.

"Gentlemen," the senator said to his aides as he put on his Panama hat, carefully adjusting it to just the right jaunty angle. "I leave it to you to guard the citadel till I return."

Commer gave himself a final inspection in the mirror. He was dressed in a navy blue summer-weight Palm Beach suit, white shirt, plain navy-blue necktie. His shoes were polished to a high shine. He saw the image of a highly responsible, honest politician staring back at him with a marvelous degree of calm and self-possession.

"When I get back," he said to Flanagan, his newest assistant, "I want you to hand me the folder with all the material in it just as soon as I'm seated at the head of the table. I think that'll be the most impressive way to handle it." Commer could see himself taking the file from his lieutenant, opening it slowly, looking up to face his expectant audience, heightening the moment.

"Right, senator."

He gave the aide his sternest look. "And don't

be afraid to stuff plenty of papers in the folder. I want to give the impression of the heaviest possible documentation."

"Right, sir."

Commer turned and opened the door to the hallway only to leap back startled. Someone was standing just outside the door. It was Stait. There were conspicuous tears running down the man's flushed face.

"What did you come back here for?" Commer demanded. It had taken him several seconds to get hold of himself.

At first Stait said nothing, but simply stood there facing Commer's cold, accusing glare. He was actually weeping. Commer had never been able to entertain the notion that a fully grown man weeps.

"I never left," Stait said brokenly.

"Get hold of yourself, man. We've been over it twice now," Commer said impatiently. "Can't you get it through your head that there's nothing left to do but to take your punishment like a man?"

"Please," Stait pleaded thickly. "Please, Marc. By all that's holy."

"I can't. I won't."

For a moment, the politician was actually afraid of the big man standing in front of him, the dark bulk looming there in the dim hallway. It was the feeling that Stait was going to do something physical, something drastic. If the man were carrying a gun, this would be the time and place to use it.

"My son's coming home and I—I—I can't and I—won't—"

"I said pull yourself together, man."

"Please?"

"Get out of my way," Commer snapped contemptuously. He had little respect for a man who couldn't control his emotions. He had mastered his own brief moment of apprehension. Goddamn coward wasn't going to do anything. "You've taken up altogether too much of my valuable time already."

For a long span of seconds it was an impasse. Commer recalled, much later, how amazed he had been at Stait's behavior. The man looked as though he were falling apart, as though his face were melting like candle wax.

"You—you—mustn't—" Stait seemed incapable of speaking coherently. Then, with a look in his eyes that Marc Commer would never be able to forget as long as he lived, Stait put his head down and, like a bull, he charged. He pushed past Commer, shoving him back roughly against the door frame. He blasted through the doorway of Commer's suite with a great, wordless shout and then, without breaking stride, he propelled his bulk across the room and hurled himself through the window.

For a fraction of a second Commer saw the burly man as if frozen in a camera's lens in midmotion, surrounded by fragments of shattered glass and splintered wood, suspended in the great void beyond the Algonquin's facade like some grotesque parody of a crucifix. And then, abruptly, Stait disappeared.

"Oh, my God!" Commer shouted and then held his breath, a look of disgust and horror on his face.

Outside, as he plummeted toward the pavement, Stait felt suddenly exultant. He'd shown these bastards who were out to get him. He'd fixed them good! They'd have him on their consciences.

Then, abruptly, he realized what his moral victory would cost him. He realized where he was and what he'd done. There was no way to take it back, adjust it, make it right. He was going to . . .

There was a great blinding flash! *Tim, forgive me!* his spirit cried out.

In his suite, Commer heard the sound and winced. It reminded him of a great melon splattering open.

"Oh, you son of a bitch," Commer cried. "You malicious son of a bitch."

"Hello?" came a man's voice from the telephone.

For a moment, Jerry Grenon was confused. Too confused to say anything at all. He certainly didn't expect to hear a male voice answer the phone at home—his and Loretta's apartment. Could this be the boy friend his sister had mentioned?

"Hello?" the strange voice repeated insistently. "Hello!"

"I'm trying to reach Loretta—Loretta Grenon."

"Who is this?" asked the unfamiliar man's voice.

"Who are you?" Jerry demanded. This guy didn't seem to know what was happening. What had he done? Called a wrong number?

"I'm a neighbor—and a friend."

"I'm her brother Jerry. I just got back to the States and I want to talk with her. I got a leave before going to discharge processing. Put her on the line, will you?"

"Wait a minute, will you?" the voice said. Then it sounded as if the unknown man had cupped his hand over the telephone.

"It's him," Jerry heard the man say to someone else in the apartment.

"Tell him, for God's sake," a muffled woman's voice replied. It wasn't Loretta's voice. He could tell that over the phone. Loretta had a beautiful voice. This one was high and scratchy. Could it be Agnes, the lady who lived downstairs and collected the rent?

"You tell him."

"No."

"Listen," the male voice came back on the line loudly again. "Would you do me a big favor and call the Nassau County Police and tell 'em who you are?"

"Police?" Jerry asked dumbfounded. "What the hell's going on? I want to speak with my sister. What do I want with the cops?"

"No," the woman's voice was loud in the background. "Give me the phone, coward!"

"My wife wants to talk with you," the man said awkwardly.

"I want to talk with my sister, not your wife."

"Hello, Jerry," the woman said. "Is that you?"

"This is Jerry Grenon. What the hell's going on there?"

"This is Agnes—from downstairs?"

"Where's Loretta?"

"Jerry, I hate to be the one to tell you, but—but—listen, Jerry, can you get out here?"

"Anytime. I wanted Loretta to come in and meet me in the city. But why all this? What's going on? Where is she?"

"She's dead, Jerry." Agnes started to cry.

"Dead?" He was too stunned to know what else to say.

"Yeah, Jerry," she sobbed. "The plant burned down. She's—she died—a day later—this morning." She was weeping, terribly upset. "Are you home, Jerry? We knew you was comin', but not when."

"She died?" He couldn't believe it.

"She was burned something awful, Jerry. She couldn't have lived the way she was burned. It was a blessing. Really."

"Is this Agnes from downstairs?"

"Yeah."

"Look. I don't believe you."

"It ain't no joke, Jerry. Believe me. I wouldn't kid nobody with something like this. You know I wouldn't do that."

"I know."

"She died this morning at the hospital. The nuns called us."

"Are they sure it was . . ." He didn't know what

to say, what to ask her. He had no idea how to react. He was so young when their folks died.

"You comin' home, Jerry?"

"Home?"

"You comin' out here? Fred'll help you make the arrangements. He's already been over to the priest's house and he—"

Jerry replaced the telephone receiver on the hook. He couldn't listen any more. How could Loretta have gotten killed? This was home, where it was safe. People didn't get killed here. They get killed in the war. You see it happen all the time. All those guys who died hitting the beach in Normandy. His shipmates who were scalded or burned or drowned when the *Merton* took a fish and went down mid-Atlantic. They were all living on borrowed time there—at war. But home's safe and—and stuff like that . . .

It was then Jerry Grenon started to cry. The tears came quickly and copiously and he sobbed out loud. Poor Loretta. He'd loved her. She meant home. What the hell was he going to do without her? She was the only mother or father he'd ever known.

Jerry put his head to one side and leaned against the glass of the phone booth. The glass was so hot from the afternoon sun that it burned his cheek. It hurt like hell, but he wouldn't take it away.

The goddamn war! Why did it have to take him away? Why couldn't he have been around home just to look out for her, to see to what was his?

Someone knocked on the glass, startling him.

"You all right?" asked a female voice.

Grenon looked out through the dirty glass. It was a girl in a nurse's uniform. She was pretty with dark hair and brown eyes.

"Yeah," he said. "I'm okay."

What the hell was a nurse doing there?

"You finished with the phone?"

"Yes," he said, trying vainly to wipe his tears with the back of his hand. He opened the door to come out.

"I don't want to hurry you," she said. "It looked like you were going to be sick or something." She looked more closely at him. "You crying?"

"I'm sorry."

She looked at him strangely. "Listen," she said. "There's something wrong. Something big. Can I help you?"

"My sister's dead."

"I'm sorry," she said. "It doesn't help much, does it? Someone else being sorry, I mean."

"A little."

"My boy friend is dead too."

"I'm sorry," he said.

"Thanks."

"The war?"

"Yes."

He shook his head. "Look, I'm finished with the phone." She was beautiful, really beautiful.

"I don't want to use it any more," she admitted. Then impulsively, "I want to help you. You can talk to me about it. Sometimes it's important to talk to somebody who's had the same kind of thing happen."

"She died this morning."

"This morning?" She wondered if she'd ever get used to death, even working in a hospital, facing it altogether too many times. Death's a sneak. You'd think she would have gotten somehow hardened to it. Some of those with whom she worked seemed to toughen up so they took it in their stride, joking about it even.

"That's what they told me."

The poor sailor was really lost. He looked shaky.

"Would you talk to me for a while?" he asked her. He was so young looking. In a certain way he was like Vince.

"I said I would." She would have said no if she had felt this was anything like a pickup. That simply wasn't her style. This was altogether different. This wasn't a pickup at all. This was a nice young guy in a tough situation. She was feeling blue also.

"Want to buy me a glass of iced tea?"

"Sure," he said and then he looked at her curiously, as though he were wondering why he was saying the words even as they were issuing from his mouth. "You wouldn't have supper with me, would you? I was trying to get her—my sister—to come down and eat with me, a sort of welcome home meal."

If this was a line, it was the most effective one she'd ever heard.

"Look," he added, "I'm just so damn lonely!"

"Sure I will," she said. "But don't you have to go home?"

"Not sure I have one any more."

She looked at him, startled.

"I mean it. She's dead. My folks died a long—"

"Come on," Anna Sangillo said. "Let's go somewhere where you can tell me all about it, somewhere you can sit down." She wanted to keep him from falling apart. She'd seen too many people crack wide open at times like this.

"We live on the Island, near Mineola. These people, Agnes and Fred, fixed up a little place up over them and we rent it."

"Are you hungry?" she asked.

"Not really. But I promised to buy you iced tea."

He took hold of her arm. It was a solid, manly grasp and it felt good. She smiled to think that she didn't even know his name.

But then it was that kind of a day.

CHAPTER :::::::::::::::::
::::::::::::::: **TWENTY-FOUR**

The fat copyboy was puffing with exertion. Making his way from the newsroom on Forty-second Street over to the Times Tower at the southern apex of Times Square on a muggy, hot day like this one was a grim chore. The streets were choked with people, and he was having trouble pushing his way through. Why didn't they simply telephone the news bulletins over to the sign room on the fourth floor of the Tower? It was a mystery to him. As the bastard editor always said, however, his was not to reason why.

The whole world, as the copyboy currently saw it, was divided neatly into two categories of people. There were the "go-fers," fated to spend their days shagging coffee and bagels, and there were the "blessed" who sat back sipping the coffee and noshing on the bagels. Unfortunately, he currently found himself mired in the first of these categories. A degree from CCNY just to be a lousy go-fer! With his luck, had he chosen to go to medical school like his mother wanted, they would have changed the rules somehow, and just as soon as he'd gotten his M.D., doctors would be fetching coffee for the nurses.

The streets were a battle zone. Peace was turning into a riot. People seemed crazy as hell. Some sailors were tossing a woman in the air on a blanket. She'd yell shrilly each time she went up. People were trying to be friendly, a revolutionary idea for New York City. They wanted to kiss, to shake hands, to pat on the back, to hug. Personal physical contact in weather like this reminded him of Uncle Remus stories with the tar babies. In this humidity, the whole world became a collection of tar babies.

Just as the copyboy got to the corner by the Times Tower, he met the tall, blond engineer from the Astor who was buddies with the electricians upstairs.

"They got you too?" he asked, greeting the man from the Astor, who also carried the trademark brown bag. He held it out in front of him, well away from the body, in that characteristic way of the experienced go-fer.

"What's that?" the man asked.

"You're a go-fer too," the copyboy said triumphantly. "Welcome to the club."

"Go-fer?"

"You know. You 'go fer' coffee, you 'go fer' hero sandwiches, you 'go fer' coffee or a coney. You bring stuff here and there." The tall guy was slow, not all that quick on the uptake.

"Oh," he finally smiled, indicating the brown

bag he carried. "I'm bringing back iced tea for Bickford."

"Like I said," the copyboy continued, "you just joined the brotherhood of those who securely hold the shitty end of society's stick."

The man smiled tolerantly.

"The brotherhood of go-fers," the fat young man concluded.

That's the trouble, the copyboy reflected. The blue-collar types in our society lack the subtlety to savor real irony. They've all got their noses too close to their own individual grindstones. What the hell! He was used to casting his pearls before swine.

"I'll be happy to carry those papers up to Bickford for you," the tall man said.

"Thanks a lot." The young man made it a policy never to turn down a favor.

Peck took the handful of bulletin copy from the fat youth. He wouldn't add the bulletin he'd composed yet, but he would have the advantage of a trial run. He'd break Bickford in to the notion of accepting copy from him.

"Careful not to get 'em out of order," the copyboy warned. "That's a red-hot one on top of the pile."

Peck scanned it quickly. It was the *Japanese* announcement of surrender. Without the presidential announcement, it still wouldn't draw more of a crowd, the supercelebration he was waiting for.

"Thanks again."

260 : : *V-J DAY*

"It's nothing," Peck replied.

He went up to the fourth floor.

"Hey, what'd you leave up here this time?" asked Bickford good-naturedly from where he was pulling and setting the metal letters for a labor story out of Detroit.

"Thought you might like something cold to drink," said Peck.

Bickford finished setting the message for the sign as Peck took a couple of iced-tea containers out of the brown bag.

"Hey, that was thoughtful of you, Richard."

"There's little to occupy me right now at the hotel so I thought you might like something to cool off."

Bickford noted the stack of copy.

"What's this?"

"I relieved the young man on the way up. He seemed close to expiring in the heat."

"The fat guy?"

"That's the one."

"He's a lazy bastard. And snotty as hell. Thinks he's gonna be an editor some day."

Peck didn't respond.

"Hey," Bickford said excitedly, happening to read over the top piece of copy after taking his first swig of tea. "Here's the first one."

"First one?"

"The Japanese announcement that they're gonna surrender."

"That's not the one the crowd is waiting for, is it?"

"Hell, no. The big one'll be the official announcement from the White House. You wait. That'll be the one that blows the lid off things. That false start Sunday will look like nothing compared to when they get the word out there."

"You think it'll come today?"

"Sure," Bickford said knowingly. He had a sense for these things. Some people—his wife for example—would call it superstition, but after a while you got to be kind of psychic about what was going to happen, the rhythm of public events. It was funny. There were times when Red Bickford believed he could feel catastrophes coming on. There were actually times when he grabbed a handful of copy from the newsroom and he could tell by the feel of it, or the heft of it, or some damned way he simply couldn't understand, that there was a calamity hiding in the pile. Like the other day when they'd announced the cruiser *Indianapolis* had gone down with most of the boys on it.

It wasn't just the bad things. There were lots of times when the good news came the same way: like D-Day in Normandy or when Hitler killed himself. In both cases, he'd sensed it before reading the actual words.

"I hope you get the one you're waiting for today," Peck said, "the announcement from your President."

Bickford looked at his friend curiously. "*My* President? Not mine any more than yours, Richard. FDR was terrific as far as I'm concerned. I'm not so sure how I feel about Kansas City Harry."

Peck managed to mask the genuine discomfort he felt at his own carelessness. He should never have said "your President." There was no excuse at all for such a mistake.

"How late you working?" Bickford wanted to know as he went over to the letter frame and started picking out the letters for the Japanese surrender announcement.

"Late," Peck responded. "When most of the celebrating is over."

"Brown-bagging it?"

"I have my lunch pail."

"Good. Why don't you bring it back over here?" the electrician suggested. "By then we ought to be putting up the big one. I can feel it in my bones. Should be a hell of a performance down there in the square. We can eat and watch it all from up here."

"You seem confident."

"I am."

Peck was confident too. Suddenly, he knew his plan was going to work.

Bickford ran the metal letters announcing the Japanese statement of capitulation on the mechanical signboard that energized the gigantic electric one outside.

. . . . TOKYO ANNOUNCES JAPANESE GOVERNMENT HAS ACCEPTED ALLIED SURRENDER ULTIMATUM . . . .

It was 4:45 P.M. The crowd went wild in a frenzy of cheering and self-congratulation. For all the tumult, however, it was just a modest harbinger of the delicious madness yet to be savored.

Baron stood tensely in the middle of the suite, in his military trousers and his tailored uniform shirt with the cuffs turned back. His necktie was draped across a lampshade and his uniform jacket was a balled-up mess on the sofa. His hat with the American eagle brass lay upside down on the floor where he'd hurled it.

Though he'd discarded most of his uniform, Baron was not relaxed. He looked harassed and tired and distracted. There was that awful, tormented look across his eyes—a look that hadn't been there a couple of hours before.

Diana sat slumped in a chair looking up at him.

"It's only the thoughtless remark of a dumb kid."

"That's not it."

"You're upset."

"No, I'm not. I'm just ready to get out of this uniform once and for all."

"Don't try to fool me. Your phantoms are back."

He shook his head emphatically. "Look, it did startle me. But I don't give a damn what people think. They can say anything they want to say about me. I've been flayed by real professionals, the best hatchet-job columnists in the business. People still come to see my films. The fact that somebody's old man in Philadelphia thinks I'm yellow is of absolutely no consequence to me. To hell with him."

"Tell it to someone else. I don't believe you."

Diana talked straight to Dan. She was not the girl to adopt a different mode of speaking, a special manner for everyone she conversed with. Diana let whatever was on her mind come out of her mouth. Almost never could one find what others might call prudence or circumspection about her. Diana would refer to either quality as "bullshit."

"That's up to you, whether or not you want to believe me," Dan said irritably.

"But it does bother you, Dan. You're still mired down in that business at the beach house, that poor dead girl. There are still ghosts between us."

"Ridiculous."

"Then why have you been doing the raging lion routine up here ever since we got back? You're going to wear a path in that rug, marching back and forth. And that scowl is going to cause a rainstorm."

"We could use it to break this goddamned heat," he said. And he grinned. But there was not much mirth there.

"It hasn't worked, has it?"

"Diana, get off it," he warned.

"I can tell you precisely what's bothering you."

"Don't."

"I'm going to explain something to you, about you."

"What makes you an expert?" he challenged.

"Love," she said, challenging him back with her look as well as her words.

"All right," he said, not meeting her gaze. "We'll let you tell me exactly what's bothering me."

"You think exactly what that boy's father thinks. You think Dan Baron's yellow too."

"What?" He was startled.

"You heard me." She got up and walked over to the windows. She picked up his tie from the lamp. She took his hat from the floor and brushed it off. "None of this is new, Dan. It's the same crap we went through before. It's the same damn-fool notion that took you off to war."

Dan knew she was right, even if he didn't want to admit it.

When Dan had gotten the chance, through Admiral John Ford, to go with General William Donovan's newly formed OSS, he had visions of being sent deep behind enemy lines to organize and carry out clandestine military activities, to hunt and destroy the enemy man to man. The training, lethal and intensive, was dedicated to the development of such skills: unarmed combat, the use of explosives (even enemy explosives), the employment of a variety of vicious weapons.

"I want to be put into one-on-one situations," he had told his mentors. "It's about time the man lives up to the movie image." Dan knew he was in good physical shape. He never used a stunt man.

"In good time," his instructors had told him. "We'll make good use of you. Don't worry."

"That's all I want," he'd said.

Actually, he felt they knew what he needed.

They surely had a full psychological profile on all the men they drew from civilian pursuits. But he wanted to make sure they fully understood that he wanted to be cast in the role of hunter-killer. He had something to prove to himself.

The final training exercise for Baron had been a break-in at a plant in southern Connecticut where bombsights were built and the theft of highly classified documents. Baron had been equipped with a phone number to get him out of trouble as a last resort if he were apprehended by plant security or local police. He was not armed. He got into the plant, cracked a safe, and turned the blueprints over to General Donovan. The OSS chief genuinely relished the discomfiture of the industrialists as his graduating operatives proved how inadequate their security measures were.

The graduation problem gave him the notion that they would truly use him in a manner that would take advantage of his movie experience and his athleticism, the fact he was a hunter and a mountain climber, the further fact that he was in top-notch physical condition.

But instead of the kill-or-be-killed manhood test he'd set his heart on, they cast him in a role that required more acting than fighting. Sly bastards!

"You're all the man I'll ever need," Diana said, calling him back to reality. "Don't you know that?"

"Yeah," he said with a brand of assent that meant almost nothing.

"But it's not enough for you, is it?"

Baron's face was a mask of inner torment. "No," he said.

The phone rang. Ensign Carter was tempted to let it ring, to ignore it. The yeoman had already left and Carter himself was just getting set to walk out the door. What the hell, he said to himself. He picked it up.

"Mr. Carter here."

"Dunc, this is Andy." It was his future brother-in-law, the G-man. He'd been speaking to Andy only a few hours back asking advice on the materials Libby had turned up on the beach.

"I was just leaving," Carter said. Actually, he had a date with a hot little number over in Riverhead and he didn't want to be late. He didn't want Andy to know about it either. He'd be sure to tell Cecile about it.

"Did you ever get anyone to take that junk you were talking to me about?"

"Junk?"

"The stuff buried on the beach."

"They want me to bring it to headquarters."

"Thought they were cool about the whole thing."

"Some commander named Syvinski called back. He wants me to bring it in personally."

"Forget it," said the FBI agent.

"Look," Carter came back, "I don't know how you run things in the bureau, but around here when some commander in the commandant's office says squat, I squat."

"We're taking over."

"Thought you didn't want it."

"We squat too when the director's office speaks. I let 'em know about your problem."

Delay or no delay, Carter felt pretty good. First they make him feel like a jerk for bothering them with evidence concerning the beaten enemy and now here they are on the phone asking questions. Another day or two and they'd be battling about who was going to grab the credit.

"I want the names," Andy said. "You said there were name tags on the fatigue suits."

"Right."

"We'll have our people out there tomorrow to examine the evidence, but I want the names now."

"You think they're real names?"

"Sure. They probably took good old American names once they landed, but if they follow true to the other teams of saboteurs—and that's what it sounds like—they were probably all residents here under the original names much earlier. We want to check and see if we can get a positive identification that way."

"Okay," Carter said. "Got 'em written down right here. The names are G. Boetticher, B-o-e-t-t-i-c-h-e-r. F. Kohler, W. Braun, and R. Planck."

"How do you spell that last one?"

"P-l-a-n-c-k."

"Right, Dunc. That's good work you guys did turning all this up. We'll see you tomorrow."

"Think it'll keep, this intriguing case?"

"Hell, they're probably all settled down brewing lager beer in Milwaukee or Pittsburgh. It'll keep."

"So long, Andy. Glad somebody's interested."

"Take care."

Carter felt a sense of relief as he left. It was nice to know somebody was looking out for the national security while everybody else was going out getting drunk. He pushed his white officer's cap back at a jaunty angle and locked up the evidence for the night.

It'd keep.

CHAPTER TWENTY-FIVE

"You know," Bobby Noel marveled again to Ciccone, "you really have to be some kind of a jerk."

"I said I was sorry. It was dumb to say it."

"Did you see *Fort Defiance*?"

"Huh?"

"The movie."

"Yeah."

"You remember the way Baron ran out into the middle of the stockade after the Indians busted in the main gate and attacked?"

"Sure I remember."

"You call that yellow?"

"Naw, but that was just a movie," Ciccone insisted. "It wasn't real."

"But the way those horses were galloping right at him. And the flaming arrows. Tell me that wasn't real."

The two boys were standing near the elevators on the seventh floor.

"Why do I have to say I'm sorry again? One time was plenty." Ciccone had been standing there for a full ten minutes, shifting his weight from one leg to another, stubbornly trying to resist the idea of knocking on Dan Baron's door to apologize.

"You want Diana Remington to think we're all jerks?"

"I was the one who said it, Bobby. Why should she think about you guys?"

Bobby Noel was definitely in love. It was something a lot deeper than the peculiar feelings and sensations he experienced when he looked at Miss Rouillard, who sat on the desk in Room 204 at Manchester Junior High and showed the naked flesh of her legs over her stocking tops. Miss Rouillard was really sexy. Diana Remington was sexy too but in a way that was altogether different. To Bobby she was pure looking, like some kind of princess.

"What if she comes out of her room and sees us standing here like a couple of geeks?" Ciccone asked.

"Then she'll see a jerk who's too dumb to make a personal apology."

"Hey look," Ciccone protested. "I'm getting sick of getting called names."

"Then act like a grown-up and go knock on that door and tell Mr. Baron you're sorry for saying something so dopey."

"Maybe they'll come out and I can do it then."

"Fat chance!"

While Bobby Noel stood there vainly trying to convince the other kid to do the right thing, feeling very stupid and conspicuous hanging around the elevator landing with its elaborate gilt chairs, his hand was in his pocket, finding the peculiar-looking caps he'd hooked in the subbasement. He felt them experimentally and then took them out to look at them closer.

"What's that?" Ciccone asked.

"Some little souvenirs," Bobby said. "From that room way down in the basements."

"What are they?"

"Looks like some kind of cap—like a cherry bomb or something like that."

"Let's see."

"You can have one if you want." Bobby put one of the caps down on the small lamp table between the elevators.

"They make a big bang?"

"Dunno," Bobby said. "I haven't set one off yet."

"Let's try one out." He hoped Noel didn't see just what he was up to. If they set off a bang in the corridor, they'd have to run like hell so as not to get in trouble, and then he wouldn't have to make a fool out of himself by going up to Mr. Baron's door.

"We'd need a hammer or a cap pistol or something. That's the only way you could set it off."

"Look," Ciccone said. He had just bought an inexpensive metal replica of the Empire State Building, about ten inches high, to go with the Statue of Liberty Bobby had given him that morning.

"You think we oughta do it?" Bobby asked doubtfully.

"Now who's being chicken?" Ciccone was tired of being belittled by his younger colleague just for having some simple common sense.

He took the metal statuette and tried to bang the lower corner of the base against the caplike device. He missed twice.

"You're beating hell out of that table," Bobby Noel said.

"So what?"

"Want me to do it?"

"Naw," Ciccone said, trying a third time.

There was a sudden, terrible flash followed by a terrific bang, and Bobby found himself on the seat of his pants on the floor, ears ringing, eyes stinging from the acrid smoke. To his horror, he saw Ciccone leaning up against the wall with a dumbfounded expression on his face. He was staring wide-eyed at his right hand. It was covered with blood. There was blood everywhere.

"My God," Bobby Noel cried out.

Ciccone began to scream.

Diana Remington was still standing by the windows talking with Dan when the report went off in the corridor.

Then they both heard what sounded like a child sobbing in pain and terror. Neither she nor Dan hesitated a moment as they ran out into the hall.

They saw the two boys near the elevator. One of them was the kid whose father had considered Dan yellow. Both youngsters were frozen there, staring in utter horror at the taller boy's hand. It no longer looked as much like a human hand as a bloody rag. The boy was still screaming, a high-pitched, harrowing wail.

"Jesus," Dan said, moving fast down the hall, putting strong arms around the boy. "Bring a sheet, Di, so we can put something on the wound. He's lost fingers and he's bleeding bad." The boy's injuries required instant attention. "I think we'll need a tourniquet."

Diana did exactly what she was told. Dashing back into the suite, she yanked the top sheet off their bed and was already ripping it into strips as she returned. She also grabbed Dan's army necktie and brought that along.

"What's this?" he asked as she gave him the tie.

"Tourniquet."

"What happened?" Dan asked the boys as he took the youngster's wrist to apply pressure. The blood was dripping thickly from the shattered hand. Baron fought back a wave of sickness. The last time he had seen an injury like this one had been when he helped a youthful partisan who had been shot up by the Germans. The boy's leg had been mutilated, and he had died from loss of blood as they were trying to amputate.

"A cap thing," said the other boy. He appeared uninjured. "Like this." He held out another in his hand.

Diana took it.

"This is no cap like on the Fourth of July," she

said. "I'm a coal miner's daughter and I know a blasting cap when I see one."

"Let's see," Dan said as he continued to apply pressure to the kid's wound. She showed it to him. "Turn it over," he told her.

She did so.

"Look," he said. "Those letters. That detonator was made in Germany." Then to the boy: "Where'd you get it?"

"Just—just on the floor."

"Tell him, Bobby," the injured boy insisted. He was gasping with pain.

"The truth!" Baron's eyes went right through Bobby Noel.

"In the subbasement of the hotel. We were exploring."

"Exploring?"

The boy looked down at his shoes.

"Can you show me the place?"

"Yessir."

By this time, Baron had the bleeding under control. He began bandaging the wound carefully. He was no expert, but again his OSS training stood him in good stead. Diana watched, admiring his coolness and his gentle way with the terrified boy. She had moved behind Tony, her arms around his shoulders. She could feel him trembling with pain and fear.

"I'm sorry about what I said, sir."

"Forget it. As long as one of us is brave." Then he looked up at Diana. "What the hell are German detonators doing in the Hotel Astor?"

"War souvenirs?"

"Maybe." He didn't seem to think that notion was plausible.

"I want you to see that this kid gets to the hospital as quickly as possible. Won't be easy with the mob out there."

"What are you going to do?" She was hugging Tony tightly to her.

"Find out who had this."

"The police'll have to check it out," Diana said.

"Police hell. I'll do it."

"No."

"I'm gonna find out where the hell this came from." He turned his attention back to Bobby Noel, the uninjured youngster. "Can you show me where you found this?"

He nodded affirmatively.

"The war's over, Dan," Diana insisted.

"This is real blood, lady."

"I know. I don't want yours added to it."

"Don't sound so much like a wife. Now get this brave kid to a doctor."

He was already stabbing at the elevator button.

CHAPTER TWENTY-SIX

Dan Baron and Bobby Noel left the elevator at the main floor where Diana and the injured boy got off. From there it would be a matter of going into back corridors, moving down obscurely located stairwells.

"There must be a more direct route," Dan complained.

"This is the way we found it. I don't know any other way to go."

There was no arguing with the boy on that score.

"You didn't see anyone there?"

"Nosir. The lights were on, but there wasn't anyone there."

"And you're sure you can find it again?"

"Yessir."

For a moment, Baron wondered whether he was doing the right thing. Maybe he should just let the hotel management know. It was their job to see what was going on.

"You don't happen to know where the house detective's office is?"

"Nosir. I didn't even know they had one."

Dan was glad in a way the kid didn't know where the house dick was located. That'd give him an excuse to follow up on this himself. He was angry. Angrier then hell at the damn fool that had left detonators around. Along with anger, there was something else. He was troubled, and at the same time intrigued, by the fact that these were German military detonators. How dumb would someone have to be to save that kind of lethal hardware as a war souvenir?

"I thought with this 'exploring' of yours, you'd know every inch of this place."

"Nosir."

"Look, kid," Dan said gruffly. "You're not in the army. You don't have to call me sir."

"Nosir?"

"Can the yessir, nosir crap, will you?"

"Okay—okay, Dan." The boy grinned widely.

Baron grinned back. He didn't want the boy to think he was angry with him. Picking up the detonator was pretty foolish, but it was a natural thing for a kid to do. Dan had done worse in his own childhood years.

"Didn't mean to bite your head off."

"That's okay—Dan. My pa gets crabby too every once in a while."

As they emerged into the long, dark, tunnel-like corridor in which the little office was located, Dan asked again. "You sure where you found 'em?"

"Yessir," the boy said.

"What in hell made you come way down here?"

Bobby shrugged. "Curiosity," he said as if to indicate that was the most natural reason in the world.

"Curiosity can get you into a hell of a lot of trouble."

"It's right here," Bobby said, ignoring the warning.

"There's no one here."

"We did see a guy passing by just a few minutes before."

"Did he see you?"

"Nope."

"Must be somebody around." Dan stepped into the brightly lit office.

At just that moment, Baron spotted something that shook him up considerably. From the bottom of the large-steel locker against the wall there came a long trickle of something that looked like human blood. It filled the expansion joint along the concrete floor. It was flowing, still being supplied by something, some*one* in the locker.

The boy saw it too, eyes widening.

Baron moved quickly over and tore open the locker door. He had to leap back out of the way as the body of a man half slid, half toppled out onto the floor.

There was a terrible hole in his head. He was youngish with blond hair. He wore khaki pants and shirt with a green windbreaker jacket. His eyes were open, and what remained of his face wore that strange, perplexed expression one finds often on the faces of those who die violent deaths. He still clutched a pistol in his hand.

"He's—he's—" The kid looked as though he were going to heave.

"Dead."

Baron reached over and grabbed the kid's arm. He squeezed the arm as hard as he could. "Pull yourself together."

"Owwww!"

That was one way to take his mind off what his eyes were telling him.

"You're alive, kid," Dan said, squeezing again. "See. You can still feel pain."

The boy seemed to pull himself together.

Now Baron forgot the kid altogether.

He had really gotten himself into something— something altogether different from the careless misappropriation of a war souvenir.

The man appeared to have been shot in the chest and in the temple. It was recent, as far as Dan could tell. He had been armed and still held his own weapon, a Luger. That meant there had been another gun.

Baron looked around the room. There was little of significance. On an impulse he took a couple of pieces of paper out of the wastebasket which was next to him. He pressed them out flat on his thigh. Both were typed in capital letters. It was almost the same message.

AMERICANS EAGERLY CELEBRATE THE END OF WAR. VICTORY WON AT TERRIBLE PRICE. AMERICANS RE-

JOICE AT THE DESTRUCTION OF CULTURES OLDER AND MORE DISTINGUISHED THAN THEIR OWN. JUBILANT CROWDS GATHER IN WASHINGTON, LONDON, NEW YORK. OTHERS MOURN IN HIROSHIMA, NAGASAKI, DRESDEN.

On one of the copies, someone had drawn in red pencil. There was an irregular circle drawn around DRESDEN with lines radiating from it the way a child might draw the sun. The other copy had a blood smear on it. It had to have been either on the desk or in the typewriter when the man was shot.

What the hell did all this mean?

"Is this the man you saw down here before?" Dan asked Bobby.

"Nosir."

Dan looked quickly around the room again. The boy went over to the door and picked up the cardboard carton. "Here's the box with the caps and the wire," he said.

"I see 'em." Then Baron looked at the top of the desk. There was a sheaf of architect's drawings on the desk top. They were labeled *Astor Hotel*.

What the hell are you getting yourself into, Baron? he demanded of himself. But he didn't have time for self-doubt. There were other questions—urgent ones—to be figured out.

As if by reflex, his mind started racing ahead, patching in the scraps of information he had now. First: Explosives! Explosives in a midtown hotel. You don't have a box of detonators if you don't have a charge to blow with them. This box was pretty near empty. That suggested there were a hell of a lot of detonators rigged. Someone was working with explosives in large quantity. What was there to blow up here?

Second: There was a corpse, a fresh one. It took no forensic training to see that the man hadn't taken his own life. Someone had shot the man on the floor at least twice. One seemed to be a coup de grâce. And it wasn't a neat job. Desperation! Someone was in a hurry to cover his tracks, buy some time. But it was too messy. Nothing planned. There hadn't been a fight. But he felt that someone was being pushed.

Third: Whatever the hell was going on, it had something to do with the building. The Hotel Astor was involved. He picked up the sheaf of drawings. Again the red pencil marks. There were red Maltese crosses all over the building drawings. He turned to some of the other drawings. Floor plans. And more crosses.

Why in these particular spots?

He flipped through the drawings, floor after floor. Finally, there was a large Maltese cross drawn in at a point at the front of the Astor Roof. What did the crosses represent?

Why were all the crosses drawn on the front edge of the building? Most of them seemed to be actually on the front wall or next to it.

It all reminded him of something. What the hell was it?

The training program. He thought back. Demolitions training. A guy who wrecked buildings for a living had been brought in to train them. Pepper Hungerford, Hannaford, Hannigan? Handred. That was it. Pepper Handred. He had diagramed for them the best way to take down a building. Then they'd gone to Atlantic City with him on a job, and watched him blow an old hotel to make way for something else.

"Blow the supports, boys," Handred had said to them. "Find the supports and blowing it'll be duck soup. Get those main supports and the biggest one'll come down like a deck of cards."

But there was something wrong here. The crosses were all on the front of the building. Only the front would come off and tumble.

Then Dan caught the drift of it. Someone was going to drop the building's front into Times Square on the heads of the crowd.

For a moment, Baron felt like getting out of there, running up and out of there to warn them, to scream at all those people out there, to get them away! But he forced himself to stay put. He had to keep thinking it out. He had to get the whole thing worked out.

Maltese crosses. Why not swastikas? If the guy was a German, a fool who thought the war was still on, why so fancy? Just doodling?

Maltese cross. World War I. Fokkers. The Red Baron. Albatross. Very German. The guy on the floor looks German. Luger pistol. Demolition devices with German words on the boxes.

Okay, he said to himself. You've got some idea of what you're up against, what's going to happen.

"But why me?" he said out loud.

"What?" He had startled the kid.

"Why me?"

Bobby Noel's expression said he was scared. Here was a dead body with a chunk of his skull blown away. Here was the great screen idol in the uniform of the U.S. Army, an army just proven to be invincible, muttering to himself. Bobby had no idea what was going on in Baron's mind.

"Don't be scared kid, it's just that—"

"What are we gonna do, Mr. Baron?"

We? Had the kid actually said we?

"You don't think *we're* going to do anything about this, do you?"

"Why not, sir?"

"Because—because you're just a kid and I'm just an—an actor."

"Who else is gonna do it?"

"Cops. FBI, anybody." Dan knew he was wrong even as he said it.

Bobby Noel stared at the screen hero. His eyes were asking questions, hard questions, questions that could only be answered with actions, not words. He had heard his friend Ciccone challenge Baron at the awards ceremony, quoting his father to the effect that Dan Baron was yellow. He had argued that Baron was really a brave man on the basis of slim proof from an old movie. More than anything, Bobby had defended Baron because he had *wanted* him to be brave. And now it was time that the actor face his big test, to make the mask the face. Baron could see it all in Bobby's questioning gaze.

The kid had a point. Who else? What's the timing on this mad scheme of the unknown man? What if the guy's charges are planted now? The box that had held the caps was nearly empty. There were thousands of people vulnerable. There was no time for getting the cops. No time for getting some lard-assed government agency crackling. He, Dan Baron, had to figure it out. Where would Diana be if the charges went off? There was no choice.

"We gotta move fast," Dan said to the kid.

"Okay," the boy said, relaxing in a strange sort of way. His would-be hero had risen to the challenge.

"How does it get set off?" Dan asked, talking out loud.

"What?"

"The charges. I think this hotel is rigged as a bomb."

"Wow!" The kid was scared—trembling—but he was also excited.

"Too many points," Dan said, staring at the drawings of the building. "There's got to be a location he'll fire the charges from."

"How come we're just standing here?"

"Can't move without thinking, Bobby. I got to figure out where he is and how he plans to do this."

Again, the boy looked at him searchingly. He was looking now to see if what Dan was saying was only so much grown-up evasion—twisting away from responsibility by pleading that it takes time. Dan knew; he remembered when he was a kid.

"What about the yellow paper?" Bobby asked.

"Let me see it again."

The boy handed it to him, smoothing it out over his knee.

"This guy really stinks," the newsboy said, gesturing toward the corpse sprawled on the floor between them.

"They do when they die sudden like that," Baron said absently, staring down at the crumpled yellow paper. His mind kept turning.

Yellow paper. Canary yellow. Newspaper copy paper. All typed in capital letters. Why? Innocuous message. Few articles used. All very telegraphic. Like a wire. Like a wire? He kept repeating the phrase over and over in his mind. Like a wire. What else did it make him think of? WAR PLANT FIRE AT SMITHTOWN . . . . TWELVE DEAD.

Wait a minute! Wait a goddamn minute! He yelled inside his head. The electric sign. The goddamn thing across the street. Could that be the tip-off? Could it be?

"They didn't waste their money at all, Bobby," he said out loud, jumping to his feet. There was blood on the knee of his trousers. "You know that?"

"Don't get you."

"All that special training they gave me. You gotta think the way they do. Only some crazy bastard that went through OSS training would ever think of something so nutty."

"OSS?"

"I'll tell you about it some time. He's got it hooked into the sign. I feel it in my bones. You say you know a way to that tower through the underground?"

"The Times Tower?"

"Right. The wires have got to be underground. Can you lead me?"

"Sure I can."

Baron pried the Luger out of the dead man's hand and stuck it in his belt.

"Then let's go."

"To the Times Tower?"

"Right. And we gotta make it fast!"

Baron grabbed a piece of bell wire from the box containing the detonators. It was a peculiar color, an orange with a decided gray tone to it. It'd be easy to recognize.

They left the room temporarily to the corpse.

Diana Remington nearly panicked at the side entrance of the Astor on Forty-fourth Street. The crowds in the street were simply too heavy. She'd never be able to get through. No vehicles were moving and there wasn't a chance of getting an ambulance through. Even making their way on foot seemed hopeless. Tony was stumbling and lurching as he tried to walk. Shock was settling in. He looked pathetic with blood-soaked strips of sheeting wrapped around his mangled hand; his face was a yellowish white. He'd surely collapse before making Eighth Avenue.

"Can I help you, ma'am?" came a gruff voice. Its owner was the tallest, ugliest United States marine Diana had ever seen. He looked beautiful to her.

"He's badly injured," she said. "Lost fingers. I have to get him to a hospital."

"There one near?"

"Not really," she said, trying to remember what might be the nearest one. She looked around desperately, trying to figure out the best thing to do. "If I can get him to Eighth Avenue maybe I can get a cab or a police car."

"Maybe we can do it," the marine said.

Tony looked like he was ready to crumple. With a single move, the big marine picked the boy up like a rag doll.

"You lead, ma'am."

"Eighth Avenue," Diana said, relieved at the unexpected support.

"Okay. We're with you."

The big serviceman had a voice like a foghorn. He was not afraid to use it. "Out of the way. Kid's wounded. Move out!"

Progress was slow and once, when Diana caught sight of the pair of them just behind her, she was alarmed at the way the blood was soaking through the improvised bandages and the hand towel she'd added at the last minute.

"Hey, you jarheads," the marine yelled to three of his fellow members of the corps. "Break us out! We need somebody to run a little interference over here. Got a hurt kid to get through." The knot of leathernecks formed a human wedge and began moving fast through the crowd. The pace picked up considerably. Once the big bearer stopped to rewind the towel in order to better soak up the blood.

There seemed to be traffic moving on Eighth Avenue despite the fact there were only two lanes left open. Pedestrians flooded off the curbs on both sides of the broad street.

"Can we find a cop?" Diana asked.

"Flag something," the marine asked his companions.

"Right," a burly lance corporal said. He stepped out and started trying to wave a vehicle down.

The sound of a siren startled them. But it wasn't an ambulance. The car that pulled up next to them was a black limousine. The back door opened.

"What's wrong with the boy?" a high-pitched voice inquired from the backseat.

"Hurt," said the marine.

"Get in quickly then."

"We need to get him to a hospital," said Diana.

"I know. Get in here."

The marine climbed in, still cradling Tony in his arms.

"You too, mother," the man in the backseat insisted.

Diana scrambled into the back seat.

"I'm not the mother. I'm just a friend."

"Good thing there were friends around," said the small man in the dark suit. "Aren't you Diana Remington?" he asked.

"And aren't you the mayor?"

"Right." He leaned forward to speak to the driver. "Swing by Roosevelt Hospital. And don't spare the horses!"

"Will we have time, sir?"

"We'll make time."

The big limousine took off quickly, siren blasting. At each intersection the policemen waved them through. Several saluted.

"What happened?" the mayor demanded.

"Fingers mangled."

"Fireworks?" the mayor asked reproachfully.

"Nosir," the boy answered himself.

"That's good," La Guardia said. "Too many people are getting hurt today. When there's celebrating to be done, people seem to forget prudence and caution."

Diana hoped the mayor wouldn't preach a sermon to the boy. Things were tough enough for the youngster. But La Guardia surprised her.

"What's your name?" he asked instead.

"Tony Ciccone, sir."

"*Paisan*, huh?"

"Yessir."

"Brave too."

"Don't feel brave."

"You're doin' fine," La Guardia said with a big grin.

"Thank you, sir."

Somehow the attention seemed to be taking Ciccone's mind off his fear and pain.

"They'll have you patched up in no time."

"This is good of you," Diana said.

"It's nothing. I saw a boy hurt. It's the least I could do. I work for the people, you know."

"Thank you."

They pulled into the emergency entry of Roosevelt Hospital.

"Good luck, Tony," the mayor called as the marine quickly carried the boy inside.

"Was that really the mayor of New York?"

"That's right," said Diana.

"He's something."

She nodded.

CHAPTER TWENTY-SEVEN

Mary Grasso walked all the way home. It was humid, the streets were crowded, and she was exhausted by the time she reached the front stoop.

The police had given her no assurances. Her bag was gone and with it her wallet. There was little chance she'd see any of it again. She would have borrowed money from her niece who worked in Gimbels, but the girl had the day off.

She reached up, found the key hidden on a ledge and went inside. As she entered the front door, she was puzzled to find the umbrella stand on its side, halfway across the front hall. It was too heavy for the cat to have knocked over. She certainly hadn't left it like that and Mr. Peck was at work. No one else had a key.

For a moment, her heart leaped. Could it be that Greg had gotten home?

"Gregory?" she called, her voice trembling with excitement. "Gregory?"

There was no answer except the cat padding down to greet her, meowing hungrily.

Then a little alarm bell rang in her head. Had she been robbed here? Could it be that she was getting victimized twice in the same day? Would God allow such a thing to happen? She winced, knowing all too well that He could.

With her heart in her mouth, she took down the sugar bowl from the corner china closet in the dining room. This was her principal hiding place for "house money," the little cache she kept of funds for everyday expenses.

It was all there as far as she could tell. That was some relief.

Then she went upstairs and checked her jewelry box, the top bureau drawer, and under her mattress. Nothing had been taken from any of those places either.

She was puzzled. Could someone still be in the house? With dread this time, she called out, "Hello?"

Still there was no answer.

"Hello! Is there anyone here?"

What about Mr. Peck's room? Could someone have robbed him? Quickly she went to his quarters and entered. Everything seemed all right and—

Suddenly, she froze inside the doorway. What was on the bed? It looked like money and some kind of a note. She picked up the piece of paper and read it. It was addressed to her.

She had to read it twice. Then she sank down weakly on what had been Mr. Peck's bed. He was leaving and he'd left her all that money. She counted the eight one-hundred-dollar bills. She didn't understand.

And why did he knock over the umbrella stand?

She got up and went over to the closet. It was still filled with his clothes. He had left all his clothes!

She checked the bureau. It was also filled with his things.

Mary Grasso was deeply upset. What was going on? Had she done something terrible to offend him? Had the poor man lost his mind? Was he in some kind of trouble? Mary didn't like mysteries unless she was in on them. What in heaven's name was happening? When a good, steady man like Mr. Peck just runs off this way, what was this world coming to?

The time was nearly 6:00 P.M. The police had concluded the first round of questions and had made their initial investigation. With their permission, management had allowed Commer to make a quick switch to another suite. There was no sense in being too obvious concerning whose suite Stait had jumped from. While the scheduled press conference went on downstairs, Commer, who was to have been its star, sat with Flanagan, his youngest aide, upstairs in the hotel.

"Do you think the police will want anything else?" Flanagan asked.

"I don't know." The senator sounded very distracted. He was staring into his glass of scotch.

Commer was letting his man Henderson conduct

the meeting with the press. Following a hastily improvised plan, Henderson would do a routine exposure of the general evidence they had gathered, to the effect that there were abuses in the operations of the War Production Board. No names would be used, however. All evidence that would readily be recognized as relating specifically to Stait would be soft-pedaled or left out altogether.

"I wonder how it's going?" Flanagan asked. Then he answered his own question. "Probably going smooth as silk. Henderson's quite a guy!"

The senator merely nodded and took another swallow of his Chivas Regal.

Commer knew all too well that the gentlemen of the press wouldn't like his sending in a last-minute pinch hitter, even if it was Len Henderson. They would resent being denied names and specific data after having been promised a major revelation. He knew that his "something critical has come up concerning Senate business" wasn't going to wash either, but there was no way he was going to face their questions after what had just happened. He was shocked. He couldn't go out there in front of any public body right now, despite all his self-discipline. He could still visualize Stait's big, meaty face as he charged past, eyes fixed on something Commer couldn't see, features set in an intense expression that reminded him of a beast in pain.

Marc Commer wasn't squeamish. Normally, he could handle the kind of emotional heavy-going that disclosures like this can lead to. He had had a lot of practice in administering punishment. During his career as a judge, he'd handed out more than his share of stiff sentences. Tears, defiance, speeches of deep remorse, tales of ailing parents, dying wives, hungry children never really got to him. When prisoners were brought before his bench, Commer knew how to deal with them.

Only one nightmare got to him. That was the one that had an innocent man being sentenced by his court.

"He deserved it," he said abruptly out loud.

"Did he?" asked Flanagan.

"Of course." The question irritated him.

"I don't know," the youthful aide said. "It's hard to believe that any man deserves to die—like he did."

"The cost of corruption," Commer said weightily.

"I think we all have our areas of corruption," Flanagan said thoughtfully. "Both guilt and innocence seem to be handed around with great impartiality."

Commer jumped to his feet again.

"Anything wrong?"

"Nothing."

Flanagan looked back down at the *Life* magazine he had been paging through.

"Why don't we stop kidding ourselves?" Commer said.

"Sir?"

"Things aren't good at all. The plan has been spoiled. This would have been a big political windfall. Now the bottom's dropped out of it. And that son of a bitch did it. He turned *me* into the villain of the piece. He managed to turn the whole thing around."

Basically, what Commer claimed was true. By killing himself in so public a way just before Commer was about to expose him, Stait had gained a degree of sympathy that could only make a public bogeyman out of the senator if he went through with discrediting him as he had planned. It was a drastic way of striking back.

"He certainly did that," Flanagan agreed aloud. "Any messing around with the name and reputation isn't going to set too well with the public."

A shiver went down Commer's spine. The aide had mentioned Mr. John Q. Public. That was the magic word; in Commer's religion, the public was the deity before whose shrine he rendered all sacrificial offerings.

"What time is it, Richard?" Bickford asked.

"A few minutes after six," Peck replied, carefully refolding the waxed paper from his sandwiches and putting them back in his lunch pail. It was habit alone that led him to do so. There would be no sandwiches tomorrow.

"Within the hour," Bickford said. "That's my guess."

"Perhaps I'll come back yet another time to visit with you," Peck said. It would be necessary for him to return with the right message. He would bury it in a pile so he could get to the Astor

Roof. He had promised himself his *Götterdämmerung* on the upper floor of the hotel. He would ride the juggernaut down even as he loosed it.

"Hell, I hope you do come back. Can't think of anybody I'd rather share the celebration with."

"I'll be back," Peck promised, picking up his lunch pail. "I wouldn't miss this party for any price."

There was nothing devious in Peck's words. It was altogether true. He had lived in expectation of this particular moment for the last nine months. It was as though his whole being had been refocused to execute this one plan.

It was going to be an even bigger event than he had anticipated. Actually, there'd been no way to guess in advance the number of Americans who would be packed into the Times Square area below the big hotel's facade. And there had been no way to gauge the number of others who would effectively pen them in the killing zone. He had not really understood at the inception of his grand program of personal revenge, how enthusiastic Americans were about this war of theirs.

Despite the fact the war had been waged, except for the U-boat phase of it, far from American shores, there was an overwhelming unity among Americans about it. It was, incredibly, a popular war. Even in the Third Reich, there had been considerable opposition to the war—well hidden, but there nonetheless. This was not the case in America. Peck could see that clearly.

"I have a few things to check at the hotel and

then I have a couple of letters to write," Peck said at the door. "But I will come back, even if for but a few moments."

"Good. I'll count on that."

Peck did plan to write a letter, consigning the remainder of the funds he had taken from the original currency supply the Abwehr had given them to the International Red Cross, his contribution to the victims of American bombing. Despite the lethal course he had embarked upon, Richard Peck remained an altruist.

He debated whether to walk back through the square. He had no fear of second thoughts. There was no possibility now that he would wish to reconsider. There was no possibility that he would see something in the faces of all those people out there which would tempt him to relent.

Never.

CHAPTER TWENTY-EIGHT

The kid was unbelievable. He had the sense of direction of an Indian scout. He gave Dan Baron the impression he'd been running around the cellars of the Astor Hotel all his life.

"Be careful," Dan cautioned him. "We don't want to run smack into him."

"Don't worry," Bobby said. "We'll hear him long before we see him. He really walks heavy."

It was unsettling in the honeycomb of corridors and passageways deep beneath the streets. Baron felt for the nine-millimeter Luger stuck under his belt. It was still there. He had checked it; there were seven rounds in the magazine.

At one point they found themselves next to a subway track. The sheer volume of noise and vibration made for tension as a train went roaring past. Twice, Dan caught his skull a hell of a whack, ducking under overhead pipes. The second time it happened, he chanced to look up at the asbestos-swathed conduit he hit. He broke into a grin.

"Hey," he exclaimed excitedly. "Pay dirt!"

Bobby Noel scurried back quickly to see what Baron had discovered.

"Here's some of the wire."

"You really think you found it?"

"Look," Baron said, holding the grayish orange, insulated wire from the box alongside a length of wire supported overhead. They matched perfectly.

"Matches all right," agreed the boy. "Gonna cut it?"

"No."

"Why not?"

"Don't know how it's set up," Dan said. "I have no idea whether closing or breaking the circuit will trigger it. Also, unless we know where he is, he'll realize the circuit's been cut and he'll get away."

"What's he trying to do?" the boy asked. "You never really told me, but you must have some kind of an idea."

"He's going to try to blow up a major piece of real estate in Times Square. He's gonna try to destroy everybody up there above us. The whole crazy mob of them."

Bobby was stunned by the enormity of it. "You got to be kiddin'!"

"No kidding. Now let's get moving. We don't know when."

"But how do you know?"

"Just believe me. I know."

They resumed their underground odyssey, following the strange and ominous wire.

302 : : V-J DAY

* * *

The time was 7:14 P.M.
Suddenly, the electric signboard on the Times Building read:

. . . . TRUMAN ANNOUNCES JAPANESE SURRENDER . . . . TRUMAN ANNOUNCES JAPANESE SURRENDER . . . .

The noise was terrific. The great crowd screamed itself hoarse for a full twenty minutes. It was as though the whole area had been infiltrated by a host of madmen, totally deranged, doing a crazy, uninhibited dance. Even though there had been several false starts over the past few days, now it was the real thing and people were going even higher than before. The noise was a great physical force—a thousand thundering Niagaras all at once.

General Elliott Roosevelt, sitting in Times Square next to a police booth with his wife, Faye Emerson Roosevelt, saw the announcement. His eyes blurred momentarily. He wiped them.

Jerry Grenon, standing with his arm around Anna Sangillo, recognized the officer. As the sound began to let up a little, Grenon overcame his natural reticence and spoke to the general, FDR's son.

"I wish your father could have been here to see this, sir."

"So do I. So do I!"

In the middle of the great multitude, Richard Peck, knowing himself again as Richard Planck, sought to insulate himself from the jubilation, to keep himself from sharing in the crowd's great emotional triumph. Almost as soon as he had gotten out there among them, he wished he had chosen to return to the Astor underground. It troubled him deeply that they were not monsters. It troubled him that they seemed normal, happy people giving full vent to relief at the end of a long conflict.

A tall, blonde girl reached out for Peck, trying to kiss him. He uncoiled like a steel spring and pushed her roughly away. The girl nearly fell. A sailor shouted at him.

"What the hell'd ya do that for? She was only tryin' to kiss ya, for Crisssakes!"

Peck didn't reply. He just put his head down and continued edging his way through. The sailor made a move toward him, then, with a shrug, turned back to the blonde.

At another point in his progress across Seventh Avenue, he was grabbed by a couple of whisky-smelling men who caught his arms and tried to draw him into their dance. Peck tried to get away, but they wouldn't let him. Finally, he punched one of them hard to the midsection. The hapless man doubled over, gasping for breath.

It had become a nightmare for Peck, seeking to pass through them and yet trying desperately to ignore them all. His mind was smudged with images, the calm gray eyes of an elderly woman, the fresh faces of a pair of young girls, the noble profile of a tall man with an American flag in his lapel.

Hands seemed to keep grabbing for him, bottles were thrust in his face. In front of the hotel, he stumbled over an overturned trashcan and fell to his knees on the curb. A teen-aged boy reached out to help him up. Peck snarled and pulled away violently.

But all over the square people continued to laugh and to cry. They danced. They drank. They kissed passionately. And most of all, they looked forward to a new world, a bright, peaceful future.

Baron reached out and grabbed Bobby by the back of the shirt.

"Hold it," he hissed in a loud whisper.

Both the man and the boy froze in the damp corridor. Baron tried to figure out where the loud reports were coming from.

Several more rounds were fired. There was no doubt it was gunfire. The sound came from the stairwell ahead of them. Baron had the Luger in his hand. He switched off the safety and moved cautiously forward. The boy followed silently, trying to stay as close as he possibly could.

Again there were shots. They sounded no closer. The twosome moved cautiously to the open stairwell.

POLICE PISTOL RANGE—SUBBASEMENT FIVE said a sign at the stairwell. An arrow pointed down the stairs.

Both Dan and Bobby let out a sigh of relief.

"We're in the Times Tower now," the boy said. "Right up these stairs."

Dan concealed the big Parabellum Luger again as best he could. Then he and the boy moved up to the street level.

"Now, you get back to the hotel. Go across the street. I don't want you meeting him in the basements if we missed him."

"I'd rather wait here for you," said Bobby.

"Okay. But you're to stay right here. You be my lookout. I'm going to find the room with the controls for the electric sign."

"I don't know where it is," Bobby admitted.

"I'll find it," Baron assured him. "Look," he said, indicating the same strangely colored wire insulation. "It goes up here."

Sure enough, there was a length of the characteristically colored wire taped to a pipe in the stairwell.

"What's he look like—the man you saw down there?"

"Just a little shorter than you. His hair's blond and cut real short. He had on a baseball cap—dark green—and a green shirt and pants."

"That's a good, complete description," Baron said. "But of course we don't really know whether that's our man."

"He looked mean enough."

Baron smiled. The kid judged so much on what his eyes told him.

"Hey!" Red Bickford shouted as Baron barged in. "No one's allowed in here."

"I need to ask you a question," Baron said. "It's an emergency."

Bickford saw the Luger stuck under the big man's belt. It alarmed him.

"Okay. What do you want?"

"I'm Major Dan Baron. There's something very dangerous going on around here."

"You mean out there in the square?"

"No. I'm talking about explosives."

"A bomb?"

"Something like that."

"Maybe you better identify yourself, mister."

"Here," Baron said. He showed the electrician his identification: Baron, Daniel, Major, U.S.A. It bore a serial number, a thumbprint, and a picture.

"Okay, major. What do you want?"

"Do you know you're hooked up with light-gauge wire to the Astor Hotel?"

"What?"

"I want to know why you should be wired into the Astor's subbasements with this." He held up a piece of the wire he'd taken from the box by the door of the small office underground.

Bickford took the wire and studied it. "We shouldn't be. I've never seen this stuff before."

"Do you know a man—tall, blond, short haircut, green shirt, green pants?"

"Sure I do. He just left here."

"Who is he?"

"He works for the Astor. Name's Peck. Richard Peck. Why do you ask?"

"What's he do there?"

"One of the building staff. Takes care of the refrigeration, water, electricity, that sort of thing. He's got an office in the subbasement." Bickford was carefully eyeing the big man with the gun. "What the hell's goin' on?"

"Don't have all the details yet," Dan said. "But there's a dead guy in that basement office—not your friend Peck—and I have reason to think there are a lot of explosives planted somewhere around here."

"Jesus Christ!"

"Now I want to find him."

"If he comes back, I can tell him—but—he said he wasn't coming back," Bickford lied.

"Did he say where he was going?"

"No."

"Thanks," said Baron. He left, leaving Bickford troubled as hell. This was a freaky day. Bombs? Guns? Dead guy in Peck's office? This big guy, with the army shirt and pants, with the gun stuck in his belt, looked pretty tough. What the hell was going to happen to his friend Peck?

CHAPTER :::::::::::::::::
::::::::::::::: TWENTY-NINE

Diana was disgusted with herself for turning down the big horse-faced marine's offer to escort her back to the hotel. She should have foreseen at least some of the difficulties. She'd been on the street trying to hail a cab just as the long-awaited announcement from Washington was made. She heard it blaring from a radio in a corner newsstand. Drivers leaned on their horns, setting up a continuous, nerve-straining wail, people yelled and threw hats and newspapers into the air, and she could hear bells and whistles sounding all over New York. People were leaning out of windows beating madly on pots and pans.

Finally she got a cab. It was a Checker with a grinning maniac of a driver, but there wasn't much choice.

The spontaneous demonstrations of affection, the delicious excitement, and the cheering, dancing, laughing wonder of earlier today seemed nothing compared to the bedlam that grew block by block as she drew closer to her destination. It seemed as though everyone in the whole immediate world was heading toward the point where Broadway crosses Seventh Avenue—Times Square.

"This is it, sister," the hack driver said as he pulled over to the corner of Ninth Avenue and Fifty-fourth Street. They had only gone three blocks.

"But I'm going to the Astor."

"You want I should carry you on my back?"

There was no way a vehicle could get much closer. She paid him, got out, and started to walk.

It was impossible to hurry and nearly as much of a problem to stop. One was simply borne along by the great mass of humanity. It was like marching in a parade. It reminded her of when she was three and her father and big brother used to walk holding her hands in a crowd. She liked to lift her feet off the ground and let them carry her over curbs and catch-basin covers. She was amused to think she could do the same thing here and let the mob carry her all the way to Times Square. She laughed. It'd be just her luck to fall over on her head and get trampled.

"Have a drink, kid," a woman said, thrusting a bottle of gin in her face. "Bottoms up!"

"Thank you, no," she called to the face on the other end of the arm proffering the booze.

"Come on, for Crissakes. It won't hurtcha!"

"No."

Before the intoxicated woman could cuss her out for refusing the bottle, Diana was swept away again as the crowd surged forward.

Actually, the whole thing had become a little

terrifying. Now you could take a step or two, catch your breath, but then things closed up again and you were being crushed once more between walls of flesh.

Diana's clothes were badly mussed, her hair a mess, and her lipstick smeared when she finally fought her way into the hotel lobby. She leaned against one of its ornate columns to catch her breath, feeling cool marble against her cheek.

First she'd call the suite. By now Dan should have returned from wherever he'd gone to check out the story about the blasting caps.

She rang again and again, but no one picked up. Damn, she said to herself. Where can he be?

The police shifts were totally messed up. Normal work loads meant nothing. Corcoran was getting tired as hell at the intersection of Forty-fourth and Eighth. A little more time on and he'd have a couple of collisions going without meaning to.

"Corky," called a voice from the curb.

"Where you been?" Kelly had been supposed to relieve him half an hour ago.

"Goin' nuts like everybody else," said Tom Kelly.

Kelly strode out into the intersection.

"They want you to take a statement from a guy who works at the Astor on your way back."

"What guy?"

"Name's Peck. Works there," said Kelly. "He saw some guys beat up a Jap soldier down the block near the hotel this morning."

"A Jap soldier?" Corcoran asked, suspecting a joke. Kelly was a clown.

"American soldier, Jap descent. It's Granahan's squawk, but they asked if you'd take it on your way back."

"Okay," Corcoran agreed. Normally he liked doing extra bits like this for the other guys in the precinct. Made him feel more like a real cop again and not a goddamn ballet dancer. But after a day like this one, he hoped the guy Peck wouldn't be around. He trudged up Forty-fourth Street. His feet were killing him.

Why don't I just wait till tomorrow, he asked himself. It was tempting. But what the hell, he might as well go in now and see if he could find the man. What with peace at last, tomorrow could be even worse.

The clock on the wall said 7:28.

The crowd was still in full voice outside, and growing by the minute.

Red Bickford's stomach was giving him hell. He was disturbed about his friend Richard Peck and the big guy with a gun who'd just been in looking for him. Majors in the U.S. Army don't go around hunting people with a German Luger. There was something about the soldier that looked dangerous as hell. He couldn't put his finger on it.

What was going on? Somebody murdered? Wires connecting the hotel with this room? Was Peck coming back up here like he said he would?

Did he dare to confront Richard? To ask for an explanation? So goddamn many questions!

While Bickford stood there pulling out letters, trying to make some sense out of what the big stranger had said, the door opened again. It was Peck.

"So you got your wish!" Peck called out cheerily as he came in, a handful of copy held out in front of him. "I intercepted Lard Ass again, your copyboy."

"I told you it'd come through today, didn't I?" Bickford asked, knowing that his tone of voice, the expression on his face, would tip the man off to the fact he was upset.

"I didn't know you were a prophet along with all your other accomplishments."

"More than you think," Bickford came back.

Peck looked strangely at him. He'd caught the message. It was almost a challenge.

"What's the matter?" Peck asked sharply.

"I've been getting feelings again."

"From the news bulletins?" Peck asked, thinking back to what the man had told him once about his clairvoyance.

"Something like that," Bickford allowed.

"Tell me about it."

"Seems like I get this strong image of a murdered man in the basement of the hotel."

Peck's strong face underwent a terrible change. Just the sight of it made Bickford sweat. Should he dare to go on with this?

"A joke?" Peck asked hoarsely.

"Not a funny one," he answered, wondering if he wasn't pressing his luck. Peck was a big man himself and Bickford always suspected he might have a terrible temper.

Peck worked to keep himself calm. Bickford was on single duty here, no opportunity to leave. How could he have gotten to the basement to find Boetticher's corpse? Did he have a confederate or was this just a lucky guess?

"Is the victim me?" Peck asked.

"I—I don't think so."

Peck decided to brazen it out. "One has to be careful with dreams. They leave something to be desired in terms of precision."

Bickford took a deep breath and went on. "And then I had a vision of this—this—great web of wire in orange, a peculiar shade of orange."

Who was Bickford? Was he counterespionage? Or was he just a blundering fool who'd stumbled across something he didn't understand?

"What about the big story—the peace announcement?" Peck asked, buying time. "Did you have a peculiar feeling when you picked that one up?"

"Just happiness, Richard."

Peck carefully weighed the pros and cons of killing Bickford. A single shot could do it. Or he could do it with his hands. But then the message would stop or simply keep repeating. That would never do. There'd be a dozen cops up here in a matter of minutes and his plan would be in danger.

Then again, he could force Bickford to set up the fatal message now. But he'd be denied his carefully chosen vantage point on top of the hotel.

"Do you know a big guy named Baron?" Bickford asked him.

"Baron?"

"Think that was his name. He showed me papers."

"No. I don't know him."

"He came barging in talking about murdered men and orange wire. He's looking for you," the electrician said. Then, with an expression that spoke of his concern for a friend, he asked, "What are you involved in, Richard? He was carrying a gun."

"A gun?"

"A Luger."

"Here are more bulletins for your sign," Peck said. He put the news copy on the table and turned to go. He dried his palms against his trousers.

"Hey, I want to help you," Bickford said. "Ain't that what friends are for? If you're in some kind of a jam, maybe I . . ."

Peck looked back over his shoulder as he went out the door. It was the strangest, most confused expression Red Bickford had ever seen on a human face. It made him want to cry.

He stood there for a few seconds. Then he tried to shrug it off. He went back to work setting the new sheaf of news bulletins Peck had brought him. Had he done the right thing in warning Peck?

Of course, he reassured himself. Peck is my friend!

V-J DAY : : 315

* * *

The station was WNYC, the municipal radio station. The broadcast originated from Gracie Mansion, home of the mayor.

". . . celebrate and be happy. Do not injure anyone or destroy property. People who would destroy property or injure anyone are not happy about our victory; they're mad, they're disappointed and we must watch such people. But I know that won't happen. I know the people of my city. I know what they've gone through since December 7, 1941."

The alarm bell sounded and Fireman Luke Tarrantino headed for the truck as the mayor concluded his radio message to the people of New York. Tarrantino knew it was going to be another damned false alarm.

CHAPTER THIRTY

Dan Baron's mind was developing a plan. It was the only way to go and there was no telling how little time he had. The blueprints were the place to start. He could have kicked himself for not having homed in on them first.

No time for crying over mistakes. He had to get the drawings. He figured if they'd lead him to the charges on the lower floors, he could disarm the whole mechanism, cutting it off from wherever it was going to be fired. But there was no way he could be sure until he saw how the thing was wired, how the charges were fused.

He had tried to make the boy take off, but it was obvious that Bobby, thoroughly shaken by all that had happened to him, all he'd seen, needed to be near him. Reluctantly, he'd agreed to let the boy stay with him. If the damn thing blew, nobody'd be safe in the neighborhood, anyway.

Dan was cautious, but they had to move fast. He walked into the office with the Luger ready in his hand. He was afraid the man Peck would be there before him. Then why would he come back to the corpse? Could he feel that secure?

Dan saw nothing suspicious. Everything was as they'd left it, the dead man on the floor, everything else unchanged.

He reached out and picked up the building drawings from the desk, Bobby looking over his shoulder. He skimmed the pages, each representing a floor of the Astor, and he whistled between his teeth in appreciation of what the saboteur was trying to do. If he had figured it out correctly, the whole front of the building would collapse into the square, raining bricks, chunks of masonry, flaming debris down on the heads of thousands. What the tons of rubble didn't destroy would be swept away by panic.

"Put your hands over your heads," came a flat, unemotional voice from the doorway.

Baron and the boy did as they were told. Before dropping the drawings, Baron had seen one thing, a clue that made him think he'd gotten it, figured out what the next move would be.

The big question, however, was whether there would be another move at all.

The man almost filled the doorway. He matched the boy's description: tall, dressed in green, blond hair cropped close. And he *did* look mean. He was the man Bobby had seen earlier in the tunnel. And he was holding a gun.

Dan had made his own transition—turned back into the trained fighting man—but he was in a damned precarious situation. It might have been an easy Dan Baron scrape in a movie. Something the public would expect him to handle, but this was no movie with a director ready to yell "Cut!"

The odds were lousy. There was a gun barrel looking him square in the eye. The other man had a finger on the trigger and the weapon was at full cock. The man was a professional. There was that look in the eyes, as clear as a stamped trademark.

One look into those pale blue eyes and Baron knew, with a sickening certainty, that murder was as natural to the blond man as dispatching a fly or swatting a mosquito. It had no more moral value than that.

"Who are you?" Dan asked.

"Why do you want to know?"

"One likes to know who's gotten the best of him."

"Planck. Richard Planck, Abwehr."

"I thought we'd beaten you guys."

"And who are you?"

"Dan Baron, OSS."

The man with the gun smiled thinly.

"Leave the kid out of this."

The gunman shook his head ever so slightly.

"He won't spoil your plan."

Baron's mind was working at ten times its normal speed. He'd let himself get suckered down here. Now he had to get out of it. All sorts of choices were being tried against the situation and then rejected. They were all lousy ones. Not enough room. Not the right distance. Would he still be trying solutions out when the slug spattered his brains all over the wall? How do I get to this guy? How do I shake his nerve before he fires?

There was no fancy way. It was go for the gun fast, trying to make the shooter guess wrong. It was a crappy gamble but it beat doing nothing.

Abruptly, there was a stirring outside. Footsteps. Someone out there. The gunner's attention shifted. Dan leaped. There'd be no second chance. The gun fired, but the slug tore into the wall.

"Peck? Are you Peck?" a voice called out.

The man with the gun was gone. Dan heard a door slam across the corridor.

There was a cop in the hall. He was going for his gun. His eyes bugged when he saw the corpse on the floor.

"Nice timing," Baron said. "The bastard was going for the hat trick."

"What's going on?"

"The guy's got bombs planted. I'll explain while we go after him."

Corcoran, the cop, sized Baron and the kid up fast. Soldier half in uniform. Kid. Luger. Corpse on the floor and a man running.

"Okay," the cop said. "Let's go."

When Tim Stait finally got around to calling, there was no answer at his father's suite. He dialed the answering service his father had listed.

"You know where he is?"

"No, sir."

"This is his son."

"He thought you might call," said the young woman on the other end of the line. "He left a message. He said that if you don't get him first, he's got a table reserved at the Cotton Club in his name at nine o'clock. He'll meet you there."

"Terrific!" Tim said with enthusiasm.

"And there'll be room if you have a guest."

Captain Stait laughed. It was as if the old man had read his mind. "Just what I was about to ask," he said. "If he calls back, tell him I *will* have a guest." He reached out and took Lil's hand. It felt soft and warm in his.

"Are you sure I won't be barging in?" the WAC asked.

"Not a chance."

"What's that?" asked the telephone voice.

"Nothing."

"Do you have a message for your father, sir?"

"Tell him we'll join him later. In the meantime we'll be in the middle of Times Square. If he doesn't find me in that particular haystack, we'll see him later at the Cotton Club."

He smiled at Lil, who had squeezed into the phone booth with him. She smiled back warmly. He hung up the phone. They kissed. It was good to be home.

The big news was out everywhere. Euphoria ruled. People poured by the thousands into the area known as Times Square. They streamed endlessly from the subway entrances. Cabs disgorged them blocks away and they walked in. There was

V-J DAY : : 321

laughter and cheering and singing. People walked around with champagne glasses, beer mugs, and bottles. All the wild and enthusiastic things that had been happening all day were emphasized and intensified.

At the Hotel Astor, the lobby, the public rooms, the Astor Bar were thronged with people. It was as though the increased pressure on the street outside had forced a certain amount of seepage into the building. And the trickle became a full-fledged flood, as celebrants crowded the lobby, pushing their way in. Some, on the ground floor, were guests on their way to or from their rooms. But many had just come in off the street in search of a little elbow room for their merrymaking. At first, the hotel staff tried to limit the jubilant entry, but it didn't take long to see that it would be a losing battle.

In one of the elevators a gunnery sergeant with a fifty-mission crush in his cap, a fifth of Puerto Rican rum in one hand, and a quart bottle of Coke in the other was bellowing the air corps song at the top of his lungs, and beckoning the crowd to come for a ride.

Police officer Corcoran was being led by Bobby Noel up a back fire tower toward the Astor Roof. Dan Baron was heading for the same destination from the elevators near the Forty-fourth Street entrance. He avoided the singing sergeant and got on the next car.

"Dan," Diana called out, catching a glimpse of him as he boarded the elevator. "Dan! Over here!"

"Going on top," he called out to her. "Go to the room and wait for me there." He thanked God their suite was on the other side of the building, well back.

The elevator doors closed before he could be sure she heard him.

Actually, she had heard him before the elevator left. Up top? she asked herself. What did that mean? Could he be talking about the Astor Roof? He was obviously onto something. He had told her to go back and wait for him in the room. But Diana was sick and tired of sitting and waiting.

She squeezed onto the next up car.

"Do you know that you're beautiful?" asked a tall, skinny man getting onto the elevator behind her.

"Yes, I've been told by experts," she said devilishly.

"I love you."

"That's a nice way to feel," she said, "but I wouldn't take it too seriously. It'll pass once you sober up."

"You got me wrong."

"Good."

"What about today?" he asked.

"Beautiful. Exciting," she said.

"Why don't we share it?" He started to put his arm around her. She simply shifted her balance and ground the heel of her shoe into his instep. He grimaced and grunted and pulled his arm away. Even today, she told herself, you can't afford to drop your guard altogether. She inched away from him as the elevator stopped on the fifth floor.

"Bitch," the man muttered under his breath as he got off.

"Have a nice day," Diana said.

Other occupants of the car smiled sympathetically. Finally, only Diana remained aboard when the elevator got to the roof.

"Are you meeting a gentleman?" asked a tuxedoed maître d'.

"Yes. He's up here somewhere."

"Unescorted ladies are not to be seated," he said. It was obvious he didn't believe her.

She gave him a dazzling smile. "I'm not an unescorted lady and I promise I won't sit down," she said, and pushed past him. She caught sight of Dan near a flower-and-plant-bedecked arch on the far side of a kind of terraced stairway.

"Dan!" she called out. He didn't hear her. "Dan! Dan Baron." She moved swiftly down one of the stairways toward him.

"Don't move or look around," a man's voice said close behind her left shoulder. "I have a gun." She could feel something prodding her in the back.

She opened her mouth to speak. Nothing came out.

"You have nothing to be afraid of, if you do exactly as I tell you and do nothing else."

"What do you want?" she finally found the breath to say.

"A hostage. You are a friend of Mr. Baron's?"

"Yes," she said defiantly.

"Yes, a hostage," he repeated.

Diana was almost as embarrassed as she was frightened. She had always been something of a fatalist about danger. On the other hand, her pride didn't easily let her accept the fact that she'd been dumb, stupid, headstrong. She was such a goddamn fool, allowing herself to be set up this way.

"We are going to walk slowly along this corridor," the voice explained. It was a flat voice, totally without emotion, like a schoolteacher being very dispassionate as he instructed a singularly slow pupil. Diana felt a chill. How could he be so calm with a gun in someone's back? It was almost inhuman.

"What do you want?" she asked, her voice starting to function almost normally now.

"Cooperation."

She noticed the way he said cooperation. It sounded vaguely foreign, just a hint of somewhere else in his inflection. Slavic? Perhaps German.

"I'll cooperate," she assured him. Her voice was nowhere near as well controlled as his. But then it was her back into which the gun was pressed.

Who was this man? Was he the man who had the explosives? How did he know Dan's name? He had shifted his position slightly and she could see him now, out of the corner of her eye. He was about forty and good looking in a clean-cut, serious way.

But there was something about the eyes, an ice-blue stare that would have made him lethal look-

V-J DAY : : 325

ing even without a gun. And, oh God, she didn't want to die. Life was too full.

"What do you want me for?" she asked. "If you're demanding cooperation at the point of a gun, the least you can do is give me a reason for it."

He didn't answer her.

"Can't you tell me?"

"No conversation," he said sternly. "Walk ahead now and keep quiet."

"All right."

They came to the corner where another hallway adjoined theirs. This one was dimly lit and seemed to be connected at various points along its length to the supper club and dance floor in the middle. Through several archways Diana could glimpse a polished hardwood floor and couples dancing, could hear the beat of the Krupa band.

Taking a deep breath, she decided to take a chance. "Did you know one of your detonators blew off a young boy's fingers?" She thought this might be the man Dan had been looking for. It was, at least, a good way to find out.

"Is that where they went?"

"Is that all you've got to say?"

"You talk too much."

"Do you know about the boy?"

"No."

"Would it have made any difference?"

"No."

"Well, that's what happened." She knew now there was no effective way of shaming him. She could tell by the bleak look in his eyes when he'd admitted that knowing what happened to Tony wouldn't have made any difference. But she had to try something—anything—that would keep her focused, ready to take advantage of any opportunity.

"The war is over."

"They say so."

"It *is*. What do you think they're celebrating out there?"

"*Their* end of the war."

"But it's not the end as far as you're concerned?"

"Be quiet."

"And what about the boy?"

"Boys are injured; the innocent are injured in every war. Many die."

"You don't care, do you?"

"I do care. But not about your boy."

Diana did not pursue it. She sensed he was becoming impatient with her. Of course, he wouldn't shoot her unless she tried to get away. I'm his hostage, she reflected, trying to keep herself from panic. While he's got me, he can negotiate and threaten. He can apply leverage on other people: Dan, the police, whoever. If he shoots, he's got nothing to bargain with.

I was a damn fool to let myself get taken. Dan will be furious. I should have done exactly what he told me to do.

"Sit down. There," the gunman said, gesturing at a small bench in the corridor near a potted palm.

"Right there on the bench where I can see you."

Diana glanced nervously around. But he had been very clever at masking the gun from the view of the merrymakers who were just feet away from them. At worst someone would think they were having a lovers' quarrel.

There was a window to her right that looked out over Times Square. She had caught a glimpse of some neon sign or other. It was probably the Bond sign on the east side of Broadway.

"What are you going to do now?"

"Stop asking questions."

"I'm scared. I talk a lot when I'm scared."

"Control it," he insisted, "or you'll have a lot more to be scared of."

"Bully!"

He didn't respond. He had taken a seat on the bench next to her and was reaching behind him, poking around in the planter. He seemed to find what he was after. As he straightened, she saw that he was holding a small black box with toggle switches and lights on it. It was attached to a cable of fine wires taped together. He took the device in his hand and rose, turning to the window. The other hand still held the postol, aimed point-blank at her back.

"What happens now?"

"We wait."

"For what?"

"For a certain message on the signboard on the Times Tower."

"What message?"

He didn't respond for a while, he merely moved slightly so that he could see outside. After a while he asked a question of her.

"Have you ever been to Dresden?"

"No."

What did this mean? She had never been to Dresden. Dresden? It brought images of porcelain and fine china to her mind. It was in Germany. She knew that.

"It was a beautiful city—civilized," he said. "Very unlike this one." Now there was emotion in his voice.

"Is that where you're from?"

"Yes. I lived there once."

Again, there was silence between them. The orchestra played loudly, trumpets and drums beating a background to happy voices. There was a lot of laughter. Diana was envious. As a hostage, it was easy to resent and envy those who were free.

"Please tell me what you're going to do with me."

"I am going to do nothing whatever with you as long as your friend Baron keeps away from me."

"And what are you going to do with him?"

"Nothing. I have no real quarrel with him."

"Then why?"

"Never mind. Be quiet."

But, having warned her to be quiet, he started talking himself. There was a new note in his voice, almost tender.

"She was very beautiful. Different from you, but

very beautiful. Her hair was blonde and her eyes the most intense blue. She was gentle."

"Who?" Diana asked.

"My wife."

"Where is she?"

"She's dead. She was burned when your American bombs destroyed—"

"Dresden," she broke in. Now she was beginning to put it all together, to comprehend.

"Yes."

"I'm sorry."

She stole another look at him. Suddenly, he didn't look at all hard, emotionless. He looked very young and somehow vulnerable. It was peculiar. One minute, he was terrifying to her, a monster. The next, he reminded her of the newsboy with his fingers blown off, the shock in his eyes. But in another way, a deeper way, etched in lines of pain, he reminded her of Dan when she'd first become his woman.

"What are you going to do?" she asked once more, her voice quieter now, not angry, frightened, apprehensive as before, but like the voice of a friend, of someone who really wants to know and understand.

"Make them pay."

"Make who pay?"

"Them. Your fellow Americans." He gestured with his gun hand and his head. He was talking about the mob below in the street.

"They didn't do anything."

"They did."

He smiled a hard smile, a cynical grimace, and seemed to change back into the cold-eyed killer of moments before.

"They're innocent."

"No," he insisted. "They are not innocent."

"They didn't do it. They didn't bomb Dresden. Don't you understand? It was the war. All that madness and hate."

"They approved. And it was done. They were happy about it, proud of it. I was here to see their faces when they read the news off that sign out there. I studied their faces when the atom bomb was dropped, just days ago, when Hiroshima was annihilated. I saw them slapping each other on the back, cheering. They were ecstatic about it."

"Does it make any sense to continue the killing?"

"Be quiet."

Diana knew she was getting to him, bothering him. But where was Dan? She had caught sight of him just once before she'd been captured. Was he looking for her? How much time was left?

And what was this madman about to do? He was obviously waiting for something. A message on the sign, he had said. Then what? Once the something happened—the message or whatever—he would put his plan into operation. It would involve an explosion. That was certain. And it would involve the masses of people down there in the street. What would blow up? The Times Tower? Did he have the street mined?

"How are you going to get away?" she asked.

He just shook his head.

Suddenly she knew. He didn't intend to survive. And it meant that she was in the same boat. It was the hotel itself. She knew it.

Diana Remington perceived a very hard choice coming up. If he didn't have her as a live hostage, perhaps he'd be vulnerable. On the other hand, if she opted for living as long as possible, he'd succeed. Countless others would die in the square and she'd still die herself. Diana wasn't at all sure she'd have the courage or the opportunity to do something, but she knew she was going to try.

It was a chilling realization.

CHAPTER THIRTY-ONE

The policeman had moved cautiously up the firetower, the boy showing him the way. Baron, in the meantime, had gone directly to the roof from the main floor by elevator. Somehow, Peck had slipped out of the loose pincer movement they'd devised for him. But he was up here somewhere. Because of the way the drawings had been marked, Dan figured the charges would be set off from either one end of the setup or the other. Perhaps it was a double system of some kind. Either Peck had rigged something in the Times Tower itself to trigger the explosions, or there was something up here on the Astor Roof.

The three pursuers had now linked up and moved cautiously to the point close to where the largest Maltese cross had been penciled on the floor plans. It had been drawn directly at the front of the building near one of the small windows that broke the curve of the big copper mansard.

"That's where he'll be," Dan said grimly under his breath.

It was at that very moment he saw Diana sitting

miserably next to Peck on the low bench at the window.

"He's got Miss Remington," Bobby Noel said, horrified.

Baron shushed him.

For a few seconds, Baron felt light-headed, almost dizzy. It all came flooding back into his mind: the pool at Malibu, the three intruders, the blood, Barbara's screams, himself helplessly trussed to a pillar. It was all repeating itself grotesquely. He had been through it before. Would it be like the other time, cradling the corpse of the woman he loved in his arms, her blood drenching him?

It was the boy who brought him back to the present with a start.

"You gotta get him, Dan," Bobby whispered.

"Get back." Neither Peck nor Diana had caught sight of them yet. Bobby and Corcoran drew back through the doorway. Dan squatted slowly behind a potted fern, avoiding sudden movement for fear that Peck would pick up a sound, a flash of color.

Sweat was running down Baron's back. His shirt was soaked, plastered to his flesh. His muscles seemed to be tied into knots. He could see that Peck was holding a pistol to Diana's back. Although the man's attention was focused for the moment out the window, the distance was too great to rush him. By the time they got a third of the way across the lobbylike space, Peck would have a chance to blow Diana away and to set off his charges.

As Dan studied the situation carefully, vainly trying to moisten his lips with a tongue that felt like a wad of cotton batting, Peck looked carefully to the right, the Forty-fifth Street side, and then, seeing nothing, to the left where Dan was concealed.

Dan understood. The gunman was looking for him and the cop. He knew they'd be coming after him. He was ready and he held all the cards—the gun, the hostage, and likely, the mechanism to trigger the explosives.

Baron realized at that moment that he should have warned the man in the tower about the message. The message Dan had found in the wastebasket was the trigger, what the blond man was waiting for. Dan mentally kicked himself for being in such a hurry.

But there was no sense playing Monday morning quarterback. He had to concentrate now on what he had to work with.

There were four directions from which he could mount his attack. He could move in parallel to the front wall, taking whatever cover he could from plants, from railings, benches, and the like. But Peck was watching both directions and there was simply no way they could work in close enough to catch the saboteur unaware.

He could do a stunt man number and come in the window from overhead. But as he remembered the outside of the building, there was little chance he could get down over the copper mansard without falling off. It'd take too much time. Time was something he didn't have. There was no telling what the cue would be for the final explosion.

There was only one other way. Right out of one of his first films, *Sabres of Morocco*. It was the bar scene where the hero had devised . . . Why not? It was the best chance he had—the only chance.

Carefully Dan Baron moved under the cover of the Astor Roof's luxuriant vegetation to the alcove where the cop and the boy waited.

The burly merchant seaman looked embarrassed as he stood awkwardly in the doorway of the hospital room twisting his cap in his hands.

"Sarge?" he called out. There was only one patient in the double room. He was in traction.

The man in the hospital bed turned his head to see who was calling him. He could barely make out the visitor's face through swollen, bloodied eyes.

"I'm sorry, sarge," the man in the doorway said. "Sorry as hell I was in on it."

"Who the hell are you?" The patient tried to sit up in the bed.

"I—I'm one of the guys who busted you up, put you here this morning."

"Get the fuck out of here," Nakamura said.

"I came to tell you I'm sorry. I was drunk and mean and—"

"All right. You said you were sorry. Now get the hell out of here. Get lost! I don't need your apologies."

"I brought you somethin'."

"What you talkin' about?"

"Here," the big sailor said, advancing now into the room, holding a brown paper bag out in front of him.

"I don't want nothin' from you," the patient said.

"It's Johnny Walker Black."

"Johnny Walker Black?"

"Yeah, I couldn't think of anything else to bring you," the sailor said. "I've heard it's pretty good for cuts and bruises, internally applied."

Nakamura laughed. He had to, despite his anger.

"You son of a bitch," he said. "Think you can make up for putting me here like this with a fifth of booze?"

"It's a start, ain't it?" He just stood there looking like a guilty little kid.

"Suppose so."

"I ain't good at apologizin'. Never did it much before. But I wanted to try to square myself with you."

"If I wasn't in traction, I'd square off your goddamn head," the Nisei soldier said.

"I know."

"Suppose I just tell you to go to hell?"

"You got the right."

"Or what if I call the cops?"

"Guess you got the right to do that too."

There was a long pause.

"Sit down for Christ's sake," Nakamura said, "and let's get workin' on that bottle."

Diana was surprised at how positive she felt, how clearheaded here on the brink. She had always refused to think about dying. She had considered such thoughts morbid, unworthy of a vital, future-oriented person.

Now, however, death had become an immediate certainty. Either this man who held her hostage would succeed in his mad plan of revenge or she'd be shot trying to stop him.

The trick was to make her death effective. There'd be no point in getting shot without first destroying the killer's plan. If Dan would only show up, perhaps she could wrest the gun from him so Dan could capture or kill him. But without the threat, there was no possibility she could overcome the man.

Come on, Dan, wherever you are! Come on!

CHAPTER THIRTY-TWO

The man sprawled across the sidewalk near Jack Dempsey's place, head almost off the curb, a pool of blood, dark and ominous, spreading under him, oozing into the gutter. The handle of an army bayonet projected from the middle of his back. His left fist was filled with greenbacks of several denominations.

The old poppy seller in the preposterous overcoat was shouting to the onlookers. "They forget, damn them. When we was fightin' in France we thought the world would never forget us. Now they kick us around, steal our dough."

"What's goin' on?" a mounted cop demanded, working his horse into the circle of onlookers. Another policeman, on foot, joined him.

"Jesus," the mountie muttered under his breath, getting down off his horse. "Somebody really nailed him."

The old man in the oversized army overcoat leaned over and tried to pull out the bayonet.

"Hold it, Pop," snapped the mountie. "Leave him be."

"It's my bayonet," objected the old-timer. "That's my bayonet."

"Then what'd you stick it in his back for?" asked the patrolman. "You stuck it there, you leave it there."

"He took my money. He robbed me. I was defendin' myself." The old soldier reached down to pry the bills out of the corpse's rigid hand.

"We said, leave him be," the mountie ordered, showing irritation.

"Move back, people," the other cop pleaded with the crowd. "How 'bout givin' us a little room to operate here? It ain't some kind of a show."

It appeared as if people were really trying to back off, but the pressure of the surging mass of human bodies behind them was simply too much. They were helpless. The circle held.

"You want to frisk him for ID?" the foot patrolman asked his colleague.

"Okay, we'll see if he's carrying a wallet for identification," the horse patrolman said, carefully reaching under the man's body to see if there was a billfold in the victim's inner jacket pocket. There was. With great difficulty the policeman managed to extract it. There was another wallet there as well. He took that one out too.

"Hey," the foot patrolman said, flipping up the dead man's coattail. "Looks like he's got one in his back pocket too."

"Well, that explains it," said the trooper. "The guy's a dip. And he got greedy one time too many."

"Anybody see it happen?" asked the foot cop.

"We did," a tall, slender soldier answered. "Me and my buddies here seen the guy on the ground just grab a whole fistful of dough off the old GI's table. He started to run with it. Next thing we knew, quick like anything, the old guy shoves the pigsticker into him. Musta had it under his coat."

"Is that right, Pop?" asked one of the policemen.

"That's right."

There was a disturbance in the crowd. "Is someone hurt?" A youthful-looking priest was pushing his way through.

"He's beyond you, Father," said one of the cops. "He's probably knockin' at hell's gate right now askin' to come in."

"Don't be too sure of that," warned the priest, going down on his knees next to the victim. "You know his name?"

"Well, it ain't Mary Grasso or Carmen Sanchez," said the mounted cop, checking out the three wallets. "So it's probably Mettich."

"Mr. Mettich?" The priest was leaning over the body. "Mr. Mettich, can you hear me?"

"He ain't gonna answer, Father," one of the cops said.

The priest touched the man's forehead, then his cheek. "Still warm," he said. He took a stole out of his pocket, unrolled it and put it on. He began giving the fallen man the last rites.

"It's a big day for forgivin'," said the mounted officer who was still holding the old soldier by the arm. "You forgivin' him, Pop?"

The old man shook his head. "Not on your life."

"I thought you'd say that."

The cop's laugh had a strange, plaintive note in it.

Baron roughed his plan out for the policeman who had just saved his neck and Bobby's in the subbasement.

"It's the only way," he said. "It's the only way to get close enough to get off a good, clean shot. It's the best angle we can get without hitting Diana."

"Diana?"

"My girl, Diana Remington."

"Diana Remington?" the cop asked with a puzzled look. "Then that makes you—" The cop looked awed.

"Yeah. I'm Baron."

"I can't let you do it," Corcoran said. "You're a private citizen."

"The hell I am. I'm an intelligence officer in the U.S. Army tracking an intelligence man from another country."

"What if he gets you?"

"Then we'll both have some explainin' to do. It'll be your ball game then." Baron said curtly, "Come on, man, we're wasting time."

"Still can't let you do it," the cop insisted.

"As far as your superiors are concerned, you're still chasin' him up the back fire tower," Baron said. "You don't know anything about it—what I chose to do."

"Jesus, man. There's no way you can pull out a gun in the middle of the dance floor and take a shot. There's gonna be a panic!"

"I'll be in the archway, with my back to the dance floor. There are so many people here, most of 'em will never notice."

"I don't know," the cop said, rubbing his chin with the palm of his hand.

"I need a jacket and a dancing partner."

"Do what you have to."

Baron, the policeman, and the boy moved over to a tall couple standing fairly near them. The man was wearing a good-looking green checked jacket.

"Would you help us?" Baron asked them.

"Help you?" the man asked.

"Who are you?" asked the girl.

"We need your jacket for a couple of minutes and we need your lady."

"What are you, drunk?"

"We got an emergency situation," said the cop.

"No!" said the woman, vigorously shaking her head.

"What is this?" her escort demanded. "We're celebratin'."

"It's a very dangerous emergency," the police officer said. "Don't have time to explain it now. You'll have to trust us. It's a life-threatening emergency."

"Well, okay," the man said dubiously. "But why us?"

"You're the right jacket size," Baron said. "I'll

just put on the jacket and dance with the lady. I'll take care of the rest."

"This is the nuttiest thing I ever heard."

"You'll get back your coat and your date in five minutes or so."

"Come on," urged the woman, pulling her escort's sleeve. "Let's get outa here."

"It's for your country," Bobby Noel said, anxious to get involved.

"Is this some kind of scavenger hunt or some party gag?" demanded the young woman.

"Take off your jacket," Dan said harshly to the man. "That's an order."

There was a lot of moral authority in the way Mr. Baron gave commands. Bobby Noel shivered appreciatively. It was just like in *Scarlet Guns,* Baron's last cavalry movie, when he told the kid bugler to sound the charge even though the Indians were all around and they were all wounded. He'd seen the film three times.

"You can't give me orders," the man with the jacket said.

"He's not in the—" the girl started to say.

"Do it!" said the cop, cutting her off.

Angry and confused, the man unbuttoned his coat and started to take it off. He handed it to Baron. Baron put it on. It fit reasonably well.

"You want the tie?"

"No. Keep it."

"Come on," Dan said to the girl. "Like the kid just told you, it's for your country." Dan pulled the big Luger from under his belt and partially concealed it in the sleeve of the borrowed jacket. The man saw the weapon and his eyes widened. The couple exchanged glances. Dan saw the man signaling his date that she'd better accept.

"All right."

"I'll see you don't get hurt."

Ungracefully, she allowed Dan to take her in his arms. Gene Krupa's orchestra was playing a smooth arrangement of "Dream." Dan, a mediocre dancer at best, managed to steer them in the general direction in which he wanted to go. At one point, concentrating on Peck and Diana, he stepped clumsily on his partner's toes.

"Was that for my country?" she asked.

"Think of it that way," Dan suggested. "It won't hurt so bad."

She made a face.

Baron's plan was simple. If he could appear to be one of the merrymakers on the dance floor and not a threat, he could get close enough to wheel around and get off the killing shot. It'd have to be a good one. There was no question of that. At least, however, this plan could get him in close before alerting the saboteur. They'd pulled it off in *Sabres of Morocco*. There was no reason why it couldn't work in real life.

"Now listen," he told his unwilling partner who had started to relax somewhat. "When we get to that doorway, I'm going to let you go. When I do, I want you to get back to your guy over there as fast as you can. The big thing is to get away from me as quickly and as smoothly as you can."

"What's going on?"

"Someone's taken my girl as a hostage and he's about to kill her and God knows how many of the rest of us, if I don't get him first."

Her expression showed her disbelief. "You expect me to believe that?"

"It's true." He looked her square in the eye.

"Oh God," she said. "Who would do such a thing?"

He didn't have time to explain. He needed to concentrate only on what he was going to do. If he miscalculated, the results would be . . . He didn't even want to finish the thought. Panic. Death. The explosion raining death into Times Square.

They worked their way around among the chattering, laughing couples until they were almost to the line of arches near the plant-decorated anteroom where Peck held Diana. It was about as close as Baron could get. Now if only the band would do a fast, loud number.

As if on cue, the next piece in the set was a Krupa solo. Most of the dancers moved in toward the bandstand.

"In about ten seconds, I'm gonna let you go. Get away as fast as you can back into the room," Dan said.

"Saying good-bye to you will—"

"Go!" Baron interrupted, pushing her roughly away from him. He drew the Luger swiftly from his sleeve and held it extended, aiming with two hands. He squeezed off a round just as Krupa began his solo run. Most of the crowd was up around the stage watching Krupa's performance. The sound of the pistol report hid itself among the drummer's sharp rim shots. Baron saw a puff of dust against the plaster about ten inches to the left of Peck's head.

He had missed. He didn't panic. He simply forced a long, even breath, maintaining his concentration. Shifting his aim slightly, he raised his arm to fire again. . . .

Across Seventh Avenue, Red Bickford had just unknowingly set the fateful message.

Bickford would have loved being out there in the crowd watching it all, joining in the revelry. He would have liked kissing and squeezing some of those luscious gals who smiled and cheered there in the streets. Maybe one of those long-stemmed, soft-lipped show girls that lived with and loved him in his dreams. Hell, it was that kind of day, a day for picking up new leads, making new starts! It was a day when being an American was damned special.

"We're *all* heroes today!" Bickford said out loud as if some dream girl were there with him.

The multitudes were reading Peck's message on the outside of the building now:

. . . . AMERICANS EAGERLY CELEBRATE THE END OF THE WAR . . . . VICTORY WON AT TERRIBLE PRICE . . . . AMERICANS RE-

JOICE AT THE DESTRUCTION OF CULTURES OLDER AND MORE DISTINGUISHED THAN THEIR OWN . . . . JUBILANT CROWDS GATHER IN WASHINGTON, LONDON, NEW YORK . . . . OTHERS MOURN IN HIROSHIMA, NAGASAKI, DRESDEN . . . .

On the Astor Roof, the red light flashed on the face of the switching device in Peck's hand, and reflected demonically in the pupils of his eyes.

The signal light told him the word DRESDEN was being displayed on the electric sign. When the last of the brushes he had wired to respond to the particular sequence of characters D-R-E-S-D-E-N had done so, the power would go off in the sign mechanism and the small black box in his hands would be armed.

Only seconds left.

The sign went dark.

Now!

Richard Planck had only to press the button and his dreams of revenge would come true.

The mobs in the streets outside were snake dancing through the square. The blizzard of confetti and torn newspapers was still falling. An agile sailor had shinnied up a lamppost to place an American flag on top of it. Tim Stait had contributed a crutch to use as a flagstaff. A single crutch and Lil, his golden-haired WAC, were all the support he craved.

From high atop the Astor Hotel, the dancing

mob looked to Richard Planck like some huge snake writhing in a viper pit. He was about to kill the serpent. It was his privilege. He had earned it. He paused for an instant to savor his triumph.

It was precisely then that Diana Remington caught sight of Dan Baron. He was standing balanced on the balls of his feet no more than fifty feet from her. He was in a semicrouch, a lethal-looking pistol extended in his two hands. His face was terrible to behold.

This was the moment!

Her hand, swift as a snake, knocked the black box from Peck's hands.

He lunged desperately for the box and managed to snag it by the cable before it hit the floor. He still had the automatic pointed toward her. She heard it roar, saw the flash, but there was no pain, not even a jolt.

Her mind worked quickly. I *have* to survive, she told herself. If I don't, Dan will surely go mad. Strange that she hadn't thought of that before.

Then she heard another report, a bigger one, and her captor's head exploded before her eyes, in a burst of pink, white, and red, to splatter thickly on the wall. The man's body crashed hard against the unyielding surface. He fell awkwardly and heavily behind the bench.

"Diana," she heard Dan calling. "Don't touch that box. Don't touch it!"

Her moment of terror had passed, but she was trembling.

"He was going to—"

"I know," Dan said.

Corcoran, the police officer, kept the curious onlookers back as word spread and the guests began pouring out of the nightclub. Baron quickly disarmed the black box. It was a setup he recognized from training. Weapons of death and destruction are amazingly alike. They have no nationality.

Bobby Noel had been scared. For most of the last hour, he'd been more frightened than he could have imagined. He hadn't wanted to see Miss Remington injured. He didn't want to see Baron die. He didn't want to see more blood of any kind. Even seeing the blond man with the gun sprawled there on the floor was bad.

"I knew you were going to save her," Bobby said. His voice still sounded very scared, a whisper.

"What?"

"I knew you'd find a way."

Baron smiled and put a big hand on Bobby's shoulder.

"There's no way we could have done it without you, boy."

"Bobby," Diana corrected him. He had always experienced difficulty with names.

"Thanks, Bobby," Baron said, giving the boy a friendly punch on the shoulder. "You're quite a guy!"

It was only then that Bobby felt really shaky.

"Everything's gonna be all right," Dan said to his woman—the woman he'd rescued from the brink of death. They were the same words he'd used so many times in the movies, the words of Diana's dream just hours before.

"I love you, Dan," she said from a place secure in his arms. She was still trembling.

"Let's get out of here." Finally, Dan Baron had forgiven himself. It seemed an appropriate day.

It was 8:37 P.M.

In Times Square, far below them, the world seemed awash with sound. It was an overwhelming physical force that could numb or stagger the unwary. It showed no signs of letting up for hours.

Chief Inspector John O'Donnell made up his mind that there were, at that moment, two million people jammed into the area between Fifty-fourth and Forty-second streets, Sixth Avenue and Eighth. He had never, in all his years of experience, seen the like.

At Lewisohn Stadium, Fiorello La Guardia gave the downbeat for "Semper Fidelis," second of the four numbers he would guest-conduct tonight. He was thinking of the young boy with the mangled hand, the boy he'd transported to the hospital. There were so many boys not much older than this one who'd been maimed or killed by the war. The music, the day of celebration itself, was for them as well as for the sound and the living.

Near the statue of Father Francis Duffy on the square, Jerry Grenon, beery-breathed, gob hat askew, pulled Anna Sangillò ever closer to him and shouted in her ear, *"Marry me?"*

"Why?" She mouthed the question, smiling broadly.

"*I love you. I need you!*"

"Okay," she called into his ear. "All right. Yes!"

He looked at her dumbfounded. "You mean it?" he asked, forgetting to shout. She read his lips and nodded a happy affirmation.

Jerry swung her around to face him and he kissed her with all the ardor and enthusiasm he felt at that wonderful, sad, triumphant, overwhelming, crazy, never-to-be-forgotten moment.

Behind them, the photographer who had witnessed George Nakamura's beating that morning took up his camera to record their kiss for posterity. Many had died. Many had wept. Many had lost all there was to lose. Others had discovered more than they ever thought they had. There was a great enthusiasm for the future, some mourning for the past. Together, Americans had won a terrible, grueling war; and having brought it off, they shouted, laughed, and cried out as one, under the Times Tower signboard, at the Crossroads of America.

Dell Bestsellers

- [ ] **THE PROMISE** a novel by Danielle Steel based on a screenplay by Garry Michael White $1.95 (17079-6)
- [ ] **PUNISH THE SINNERS** by John Saul $1.95 (17084-2)
- [ ] **FLAMES OF DESIRE** by Vanessa Royall $1.95 (14637-2)
- [ ] **THE HOUSE OF CHRISTINA** by Ben Haas $2.25 (13793-4)
- [ ] **CONVOY** by B.W.L. Norton $1.95 (11298-2)
- [ ] **F.I.S.T.** by Joe Eszterhas $2.25 (12650-9)
- [ ] **HIDDEN FIRES** by Janette Radcliffe $1.95 (10657-5)
- [ ] **SARGASSO** by Edwin Corley $1.95 (17575-5)
- [ ] **CLOSE ENCOUNTERS OF THE THIRD KIND** by Steven Spielberg $1.95 (11433-0)
- [ ] **THE TURNING** by Justin Scott $1.95 (17472-4)
- [ ] **NO RIVER SO WIDE** by Pierre Danton $1.95 (10215-4)
- [ ] **ROOTS** by Alex Haley $2.75 (17464-3)
- [ ] **THE CHOIRBOYS** by Joseph Wambaugh $2.25 (11188-9)
- [ ] **CLOSING TIME** by Lacey Fosburgh $1.95 (11302-4)
- [ ] **THIN AIR** by George E. Simpson and Neal R. Burger $1.95 (18709-5)
- [ ] **PROUD BLOOD** by Joy Carroll $1.95 (11562-0)
- [ ] **NOW AND FOREVER** by Danielle Steel $1.95 (11743-7)
- [ ] **A PLACE TO COME TO** by Robert Penn Warren $2.25 (15999-7)
- [ ] **STAR FIRE** by Ingo Swann $1.95 (18219-0)

At your local bookstore or use this handy coupon for ordering:

Dell | **DELL BOOKS**
P.O. BOX 1000, PINEBROOK, N.J. 07058

Please send me the books I have checked above. I am enclosing $_____
(please add 35¢ per copy to cover postage and handling). Send check or money order—no cash or C.O.D.'s. Please allow up to 8 weeks for shipment.

Mr/Mrs/Miss_____

Address_____

City_____ State/Zip_____